Mischief in the Air

Max Afford
(Courtesy of the Australian Broadcasting Commission)

Mischief in the Air

Radio and Stage Plays

by MAX AFFORD

UNIVERSITY
OF QUEENSLAND PRESS

Set in Baskerville 11/12
Printed and bound by Peninsula Press Pty. Ltd., Hong Kong
Designed by Cyrelle

Distributed in the United Kingdom, the Middle East, Africa, and the Caribbean by Prentice-Hall International, International Book Distributors Ltd., 66 Wood Lane End, Hemel Hempstead, Herts., England

National Library of Australia
Cataloguing-in-Publication data

Afford, Max, 1906–1954.
Mischief in the air: radio and stage plays/by Max Afford. – St. Lucia, Q.: University of Queensland Press, 1974.
ISBN 0 7022 0957 0.
ISBN 0 7022 0918 X Paperback.

I. Title.

A822.2

Contents

Foreword

For most of us, Australian drama in the twentieth century has seemed to develop in a series of waves, with decidedly flat periods in between. First came the Louis Esson and Pioneer Players wave, in the twenties; then a long pause before the realism of *Summer of the Seventeenth Doll* and its followers in the fifties; now, after another lengthy silence, the free and experimental Buzo-Hewett-Hibberd-Williamson (and of course many others) wave. In between, one has the impression that native drama almost ceased to exist, as effectively as when Cromwell closed the theatres of England. One myth says that the reason why the Australian drama waves have to date always ebbed away into disappointing nothingness is that Australian audiences are basically hostile or at best indifferent to the local product. Max Afford's plays are a healthy reminder that even in the apparent troughs, plays were being written by Australian playwrights and, sometimes at least, attended enthusiastically by Australian audiences. Until the spectacular advent of David Williamson, Max Afford was probably the most successful, in terms of commercial production, of our playwrights, with plays produced in Sydney, for instance, at the Theatre Royal, the Minerva Theatre, and the Independent Theatre – not to mention a production on Broadway and another in England.

If it is true that audiences in the forties were somewhat more sensitive than they are now about seeing themselves analyzed and scourged on the stage, perhaps one of the reasons for Max Afford's wide appeal was the particular form of the "Australianness" of his plays. In his later radio plays, such as *Lazy in the Sun* and "Out of this Nettle", he set out, sincerely and conscientiously to examine some peculiarly Australian social problems; but not in the earlier stage plays. In his stage plays, Max Afford was not aiming primarily at realism, or to probe the Australian psyche; he was out to provide good theatre entertainment. This was, after all, the era of Agatha Christie and Terence Rattigan, of urbane and polished dramas providing temporary escape from the real world. The models for most of Max Afford's stage plays were unmistakably West End, the setting too was occasionally London, but the characters remain subtly Australian: not of course in the way of Alan Seymour's Alf, "I'm a bloody Australian and I'll always stand up for bloody Australia", but rather with the Australianness of those who speak in neutral accents and do not specially think of themselves as Australians, bloody or otherwise. These characters were familiar to the audience, but did not challenge it.

The great secret of the success of Max Afford's plays was however his ability to tell a good story, to maintain suspense, his sheer technical ability and control of his material. These are skills that have not been specially evident in many of our stage playwrights. Max Afford learnt his profession in a particularly tough school. He wrote primarily for radio, in an era when a limited number of writers poured out an enormous number of radio serials, an unending stream of words for which there is no real equivalent in today's age of television. Each episode had to be shaped to its climax, the invisible characters clearly identified solely through the dialogue, the interest of the audience caught in the first few sentences. When Max Afford turned to the theatre, he had already learned to make every word functional, and how to write for a very wide audience.

Although in his early stage plays Max Afford was in no way aiming to hold the mirror up to Australian society, one of the fringe interests of reading them is to realize, mostly from the unconscious attitudes and casual phrases of his characters, just how much water has thundered under the bridges of the world since the plays were written. In *Lady in Danger* (1942), Bill Sefton loses his job as reporter on a newspaper, and his wife Monica decides to write a play, to pay the rent. Bill admits that he hates owing money but, when Monica suggests "Perhaps I could get a job somewhere . . .", he thunders "I'll earn the salary in this family! You stick to playwriting." It is a joke, of course; but a subtly pre-women's liberation one. *Consulting Room* (c. 1946) is a gentle play about a young couple who attempt to commit suicide because the wife has cancer, and find themselves in some kind of limbo between life and death, a "waiting room", presided over by the "specialist", Sir Arthur Brown. He tries to show them that despair is often based on ignorance, and gives as an example the story of a young man, horribly injured in the American civil war, fighting under General Lee. "Young . . . idealistic . . . sensitive, even as you two, this boy saw nothing but his whole world crashing and crumbling about him. He tried to take his own life. Like you, he was convinced that there was no future nor hope for the future . . . Now he knows that from that cruel welter of pain and agony and violence was born that great and shining force that men call . . . freedom!"

Max Afford's plays are very pleasant to read, they grip the interest and they can be very funny. *Lazy in the Sun* shows him as a thoughtful and socially enquiring playwright. *Awake My Love* has probably been underestimated among Australian dramas; though it takes the liberty of inventing a heroine for romantic interest, it also escapes the dullness that seems to descend on so many historical dramas, however entertaining their authors may normally be. The plays of Max Afford represent a kind of play that has never completely disappeared, though we find it more frequently now on television. Hopefully, the 1970s may indeed prove our highest wave yet in Australian drama; but we ought not to close our eyes to the possibility that we could learn a great deal from the skill and conscientious craftsmanship of playwrights like Max Afford.

Alrene Sykes
University of Queensland, 1973

Introduction: Max Afford, Playwright

Max Afford, who became one of Australia's outstanding and most popular radio and stage dramatists, began writing for radio when it was in its infancy. But it was not until 1938 that I met him.

In that year the Australian Broadcasting Commission was taking active steps to appoint a central staff that would help lay the foundations of the nationally-based broadcasting edifice of the next twenty or more years. Afford, a young Adelaide writer, was among those invited to come to Sydney. I remember when he arrived. Only a month or two previously I had myself been appointed to the A.B.C. Max Afford, Edmund Barclay, and I were to work from our different standpoints to build up the supply of radio plays for A.B.C. programmes – I by encouraging freelance scribes to take the radio drama form seriously, Barclay and Afford by providing plays and serials of their own and by adapting others' plays.

It seemed that we were at the beginning of a phase. There was little professional theatre in Australia, certainly none that encouraged Australian writers; the film industry was as unpredictably periodical in its activities as it had always been in this country; television was not even on the horizon. So that, more so than in some other countries, the radio play bade fair to be a major people's entertainment and perhaps a medium for serious literary expression as well.

The Max Afford of those days was an athletically built, tall, spry, handsome fellow of thirty years. He had a well-formed face, with strong bones, perhaps a bit too much lower jaw and chin, grey alert eyes, and prematurely silver-grey hair. The contours and structure of that head had already attracted a young Adelaide portrait artist, Ivor Hele (since then an Archibald prize winner on several occasions), who had made a striking study of Max in pen and ink.

Max was, from the beginning, a spirited talker, with a quick wit and a high sense of humour based on his appreciation of ridiculous situations or quirks of character. He had in some things a likable naivete, a readiness for expressing opinions and a humorous explosive indignation that seldom had any rancour in it. Under it all, his was the most equable of temperaments, and artistic "moodiness" was unknown to him. He and I, of similar ages, immediately became friends in the office and out of the office. We talked plays, playwrights, play techniques, radio acting, stage acting, and radio production (then in the hands of a separated unit of the A.B.C. under Lawrence H. Cecil).

Max Afford had been born in Adelaide in 1906. When his father died, he went out into the world equipped with only a year or two of secondary education. For a time he worked at odd jobs around Adelaide. Then, a feeling for words manifesting itself, he began to write articles for the Adelaide *News* – the city's evening paper. In due course he joined the staff of the *News* as a reporter and then became a "special" article writer. He had five years of journalism, and did not care for it. Soon he was sniffing around the purlieus of the newly established broadcasting studios in Adelaide's Hindmarsh Square. The gleam of a chromium microphone interested him far more than the whiff of printer's ink, with the result that he became one of the true pioneers of the broadcast play in Australia. He began to write short, simple plays with rather sensational plots, and the local management of the A.B.C., and later a commerical station, encouraged him and produced his work or allowed him to produce it. Those were 'prentice efforts – but radio drama generally was in swaddling clothes.

As early as 1932 Max Afford was writing articles for Adelaide magazines to ventilate the difficulties and excitements of this new kind of home entertainment. In one article he perceptively pointed out the part that radio listeners themselves could take in securing the success of a play, for instance by putting themselves in a ready and fully sensitive condition of mind when the play began.

By 1934 he was his own regular producer.

Soon after that, Max Afford found himself on the crest of a wave – and not merely a radio wave. He had set himself up as a freelance writer in his mother's home, quite determined to produce works of fiction. He wrote a couple of detection novels, a stage play, a musical comedy, a radio operetta, an hour-length radio play. The novels were sent off to England. The stage play, "Colonel Light the Founder" (afterwards renamed *Awake My Love*), was entered in a newspaper competition associated with the South Australian centenary celebrations and won first prize of a hundred pounds. The musical comedy was successfully staged (produced by Max) in Adelaide. The radio operetta and the radio play were entered in A.B.C. competitions and both of them won first prize. Amid all this thronging success, two letters came on the same day from London, from Hutchinson's and from the American Appleton Century's agents, each accepting one of the novels.

No wonder that Charles Moses, the general manager of the A.B.C., decided to pluck Max Afford out of Hindmarsh Square – where he had been associated with people like the young Robert Helpmann – and transport him to 264 Pitt Street, Sydney, the headquarters of national broadcasting. In this new surrounding, Max quickly made his mark with a series of lively and diverting mystery plays.

This was the Max Afford of the late 1930s when radio drama had a real sense of emergence about it. Edmund Barclay was writing his marathon serial of Australian life through the generations – "As Ye Sow"; young writers like Richard Lane, Alexander Turner, Catherine Shepherd, Charles Porter, Gwen Meredith, Catherine Duncan, and Maxwell Dunn were sending in their first play scripts; Cecil Fraser sat in an adjoining room-with-a-piano, notating mellifluous tunes for musical comedy scripts by Mark Makeham; and Max Afford at his portable typewriter was tapping out highly ingenious, spine-chilling murder themes such as "Five White Fingers", "The Queer Affair at Kettering", "Whistle While You're Happy, Little Man", or the half-hour serial episodes of "Fly by Night", "The Mysterious Mr. Lynch", or "Greyface". All of these were for immediate studio representation by such talented players as the young Peter Finch and Neva Carr-Glyn.

At his flat, meanwhile, Max's fingertips were tapping-in the preliminary dialogue for the three-act plays with which he hoped to make a signal success in the theatre.

Each Max Afford plot, however imaginative, was worked out with the most conscientious calculation: in fact, Max had become a serious student of this lighter form of literary expression, the crime story. And he not only delighted in his own inventions of Borgian devilry but was *au fait* with the homicidal methods employed by every other detective or thriller writer (he made a clear distinction between the two), whether in novels or in plays. I remember with some affectionate amusement the tone of near reverence with which Max would unfold to me some new ingenious and imaginative lethal device or situation or clue, thought up by one of the noted overseas writers in this field. So it was not surprising that he should devise the play, "The Fantastic Case of the Four Specialists", in which the police fail to unravel a murder-knot, and the problem is actively taken over by Sherlock Holmes, Philo Vance, Hercule Poirot, and Father Brown, who argue out the issues in the precise idiom and tone required by their creators, Conan Doyle, S. S. van Dine, Agatha Christie, and G. K. Chesterton. Max's own sleuth-hero, moving from novel to play to serial and back again, year by year, was the Max-like Jeffery Blackburn, an engaging amateur, constantly helping the police out of their bogs of muddle and ignorance. Perhaps it was no coincidence that Blackburn should have acquired a charming and useful wife not long after his author, on the plane of pleasant actuality, married the similarly endowed Thelma Thomas. Thelma too was from Adelaide, where she had laid the foundations of a successful career as a stage costume designer, including vivid costumes for Max's early plays.

Thereafter Elizabeth and Jeffery Blackburn collaborated in solving every crime problem just as Max and Thelma became partners and co-workers in half a dozen professional and social fields within the busy and ever-broadening life of Sydney.

The zest for the macabre, for the death-dealing instrument

or potion, for the blood-refrigerating act of human eradication, naturally enough had no counterpart in Max Afford's private thought or habit. And yet sometimes he had to explain himself. "Because I write detective plays or thrillers for the stage and for the air," he said in an interview, "People think I should be tough. They think my wife should be afraid of me. Or, alternatively, they say to me: What nightmares you must have!" Max expounded his own experience of catharsis: "They are wrong. Putting those murderous doings into a play makes a writer free of them himself. He gets all the mad criminal urges out of his system."

One of his publishers described him as a master of suspense – "the keystone of all mystery stories worthy of the name" and compared him with Edgar Allan Poe. Not only his novels but some of his radio plays were readily taken up in other countries. The B.B.C., the South African Broadcasting Corporation, the New Zealand National Service and, less likely, the Egyptian and Polish radio organizations broadcast his plays.

Leaving the A.B.C. after some years, Max Afford set up as a freelance writer of serials, while working as well on more novels and stage plays. Notwithstanding initial struggles, his mounting successes in this next phase were remarkable. It was a period of hard, unrelenting work and prolific output. Some statistics of the radio serials written for Sydney commercial stations indicate clearly both the degree of his typewriter activity and his great popularity as a creator of characters in an endless variety of dramatic or humorous situations. He wrote no fewer than 624 quarter-hour episodes of "First Light Frazer"; his "Digger Hale's Daughters" had 416 episodes; "Danger Unlimited", another Jeffery Blackburn adventure, had over 600 episodes; "Hagen's Circus" ran to the momentous figure of 800 episodes, spread over four years, and since then has been repeated twice in its entirety. Max never dictated either to a machine or to a stenographer. Sitting in an airy room of the Afford duplex flats at Balmoral, he picked out every word himself on a neat, evenly margined script that allowed him to see at a glance exactly how many minutes the episode would run on the air.

In this period Max also wrote a scenario and "treatment" for the well-known film *Smithy,* the story of Sir Charles Kingsford Smith, which was being made by Ken Hall for Columbia films. He published another novel or two with Angus and Robertson while the English firm, William Collins, reprinted his Blackburn novels into their White Circle crime club editions.

He also wrote four full-length stage plays. These plays were produced professionally in Sydney, one reached Broadway, and one toured the English provinces.

The play *Lady in Danger,* a comedy thriller, was tried out at Sydney's Independent Theatre and, through the efforts of Sydney Tomholt, himself a dramatist and then a critic on the *Sydney Morning Herald,* was presented at the Theatre Royal. It was a success. Sent by Harald Bowden of J. C. Williamson Ltd. to the firm's New York agents, the play was taken up by the Lee Sherbert management, toured several big American cities, and finally appeared at the Broadhurst Theatre, Broadway – one of the first Australian plays, and one of the few, to do so. A little later, Max's comedy *Mischief in the Air* was also successfully produced at the Theatre Royal, Sydney. This meant that two plays by the one Australian author had been staged at the same Australian professional theatre within a few months of each other – an unprecedented happening. *Awake My Love,* a serious drama, was produced by Doris Fitton at the Independent Theatre and rated by major Sydney drama critics as "a significant milestone for Australian drama". Max's "Dark Enchantment", a suspense drama, was bought by Whitehall Theatre management and ran during lightless post-war nights at the Minerva Theatre, Sydney. By the time Ralph Lynn's management was ready to tour it in England, the Affords had transferred themselves to London, the better to foster the play's fortunes.

To dwell a little on the qualities of these plays for the theatre. One of the attractive things about *Lady in Danger* (as

I wrote in my volume *Towards an Australian Drama*) was that the author succeeded in making you like his two young people as well as believe in them; and when the sticky web closes round Monica and her husband, you share their shock, amazement, and fear. In other words, the play was not merely a piece of pattern making, ingenious, logical, unexpected, and knit into current events and dangers, but it also had human quality. The mechanics were concealed beneath backchat and a variety of character-imprints, each figure seeming to be there in his own right of contributing entertainer. For instance, the keen-witted Monica herself; Andy Meade, the crime-reporter friend, mentally flat on a diet of grated carrot and orange juice but rising to heights of deductive brilliance on whisky; or the two detectives with their private worries.

Mischief in the Air, when we first saw it at the Theatre Royal, revealed a pattern of comedy and intrigue in which the world of commercial radio which Max knew so well was held up to good-humoured fun. Once again the author's exuberant delight in ways of killing had full scope. There was character writing – the Jewish sponsor for instance. There were quick-answering lines. "In his chosen sphere," wrote Lindsey Browne of the *Sydney Morning Herald,* "Afford is an able and admirable craftsman."

"Dark Enchantment" grew (as indeed did *Lady in Danger*) out of an Afford radio script, a useful example of how the two mediums may both serve the interests of their author and be served by him. It exploited the sinister idea of a continuing relationship between a dead ventriloquist and his doll. But as an unashamedly theatrical piece it offered much more in a rich brew of gipsy incantations, theatrical boarding-house vignettes of the gaslight nineties, circus oddities, and cold chills down the spine caused by the repetition of a mysterious whistled tune offstage. "Suspense", "Macabre inventiveness", "Ingenious twists", ran the notices.

Different entirely, *Awake My Love* was Max Afford's venture in the field of the historical play. The original version of "Colonel Light the Founder" was rewritten in the light of greater experience of drama techniques. The play mainly told of Light's bitter struggle against Governor Hindmarsh to preserve his own choice of the site of Adelaide. The two scenes showing clashes between these men, Light aloofly determined and Hindmarsh hotheaded and autocratic, were lively drama when *Awake My Love* was produced – with stylish costumes by Thelma Afford – at the Independent Theatre. But Afford did not rely entirely on an official conflict; admittedly without much historical justification, he gave Light a love story. It was a hopeless love, doomed by the prim conventions of the 1830s as well as by Light's failing health. Although seen in his more negative phases, this character exemplified the forward spirit of a visionary. Sydney Tomholt, a champion of Afford's work, wrote that the author was closer to the poet's vision than to the cold analysis of a scientific and documented statement, but he had succeeded in highlighting the actual facts of his subject's public life and in estimating the magnitude of his services.

Back on Australian soil, Max Afford moved slowly but unerringly towards his fourth phase of play writing. His short visit abroad had produced changes in him, as in many other travelling Australians. He was excited by some things he saw abroad and critical of some things he saw back at home. Nevertheless, he now felt that his destiny was as a specifically Australian writer, and local places and story subjects seemed to acquire a new bloom. But he was also seriously concerned about the fate of humanity at large in a world just emerging from the turmoil of one war and already overshadowed by the bruise-coloured clouds of an impending atomic death struggle. It seemed to Max that his true place was with the A.B.C., where he would have a more varied opportunity for expressing ideas that were yeasting in his imagination and brain. It was characteristic of Max Afford that he was continually outgrowing himself, like a crayfish from its shell or a schoolboy from his suit. His amusing vocal contempt for the immature outpourings of pretentious or careless rough-writers extended to many things he himself had turned out five years or so previously. It was a disposition of mind that sometimes went too far.

Reaching his middle forties, Max no longer wished to be known as a crime writer, or at least as a mere crime writer. His experience of life and affairs had broadened and deepened, his mind wrestled with serious themes in the postwar world and asked for an opportunity to exemplify them in play scenes. He was becoming ever more observant of local people's ways and of the spoken idioms around him, and was anxious to place the characters minted from that observation in patterns not dependent on merely sensational "who-dunnit" endings.

Accordingly he came back to his old department at the A.B.C. and threw himself into the writing of a marathon serial on the subject of postwar immigration to Australia, with all its domestic stresses and heartbreak, and new adventure and promise for those pulling up roots in England or escaping from old tyrannies in Europe. This was "Stranger Come In" which ran a course of 400 episodes (four a week) before its main characters were safely assimilated into Australian life.

Where in his early plays Max had made the most of picturesque or legend-impregnated English settings (such as the Abbey Darkmere with its hollow, horrible passages of nerve-prickling menace and its silent spectres carrying nooses of hemp), now he preferred easily recognizable backgrounds in Sydney or the bush. Following "Stranger Come In", he brought his characters Jeffery Blackburn and wife Elizabeth to the Atherton Tableland in northern Queensland for the intriguing serial "Double Demon". He adapted Jon Cleary's novel *The Sundowners* into half-hour episodes, then wrote his own mining town serial, "Silver Ridge", also in half-hour episodes. The elusive, still crystallizing facets of Australian real-life characters were a challenge to him. He wrote such hour-long radio plays as *Lazy in the Sun,* expressing the concern he felt, following his return from Europe, about our national easy-goingness and lack of realism in outlook; and "Out of This Nettle", with its themes of latter-day pioneering against the north Queensland scrub-jungle, of family conflict and new-old loyalties to the land. *Consulting Room* is another hour-long play which dates from about 1946. This little drama, with its haunting sense of human perplexity, the aching losses but also the compensatory balances of life, contained (if only we could have seen it as such) a strange and poignant half-forecast of the author's own personal future – but that is by the way. Or is it, entirely? Whatever the answer, *Consulting Room* is one of the most moving things Max Afford ever wrote, perhaps because of its loving regard for two people wholly dedicated to each other and because of the restraint and delicacy with which the play's semi-spiritual atmosphere is evoked. Although he wrote this originally for radio, he liked it well enough to re-shape it into a long-short stage play.

At the age of forty-eight, the end came suddenly and unexpectedly for Max Afford. I was only one in a legion who felt the almost unbearable loss of a gay and unique personality, as well as a valuable writer at the height of his productivity. I can recall no man in whose company I could spend so many hours without ever for a moment tiring of his good humour, conversational gusto, warm variety of interests, and reformist zeal in things that touched him. Truly Max Afford was a man much loved. Between him and his wife there was the deepest and most tender affinity in all matters and on all levels.

During his last years, his versatility manifested itself in further ways. With the encouragement and approval of the A.B.C. Director of Drama, Mr. Neil Hutchinson, Max had entered anew the production field, this time on a highly responsible national basis. He proved himself a first-rate producer of his own and other people's plays and serials, bringing to the task that keen-edged, zestful approach to characterization, a fractional sense of timing, and an ear for nuances that make all the difference between "average" production, heard in so many routine soap-operas, and truly compelling radio.

In 1954, when I left Australia for a nine-months' tour of other countries, it was Max who was appointed to sit in the drama editor's chair. However early in November, as my wife and I stepped on board the liner *Queen Elizabeth,* leaving Southampton for New York, we received the tragic news of his death.

Always a planner, a dreamer of new dawns, Max had envisioned the opportunity of working in the television medium that was already on the threshold in Australia. It is certain that had he lived he would have contributed substantially to the forms of television drama that are now so popular. His was a spring of ever-fresh talent which had never ceased to fountain inventively, and it is one of the fearsome and baffling mystery-dramas of life that his final curtain should have fallen so prematurely.

He believed in radio drama as an art form and as a popular entertainment that could live side by side with the stage, the cinema, and television. He was himself vividly interested in the techniques of all four, but the conditions of the drama field dictated that he spend most of his time writing for radio. Perhaps this was for the best. Looking back over the thirty years history of radio drama in Australia, I sometimes think that here is a medium that has allowed Australia writers, actors, and producers opportunity for success of a kind only half-realized in the other mediums. And the opportunity has been richly taken. For years we have had our own radio writers working on equal terms and receiving equal billing with overseas writers. Our standard of radio acting and production has long been acknowledged as equal to the English or American. Because radio plays are relatively inexpensive to present, and because the A.B.C., at least, is in a position to cater for minority tastes, we have been able to risk experiments, both technical and literary, which would have been virtually impossible in the commercially controlled stage or cinema. And so it may be said that men and women privileged to work in radio at its "cultural" best have been able to realize themselves truly and satisfyingly. At the same time, those who have excelled in the most popular types of programmes have won considerable monetary rewards.

The astonishing thing about Max Afford was that he,

unlike most of his fellow writers, managed to plant and keep one foot in each camp.

His qualities as a playwright were diverse. He developed over the years a supple workmanlike dialogue that could be sharp in comedy exchanges, or hair-raising in scenes of suspense and mystery, or earnest in passages of modern discussion. His capacity to objectify characters was freshened by observation of individuals he was acquainted with. As a colleague working in very close association I was often delighted to note how he would borrow a mannerism from the liftman or a telling phrase from a wharfie in the corner pub. He sometimes humorously took his revenge on a person who had irritated him – a pompous film executive or windy parliamentarian – by bringing that person, sufficiently disguised but not too much, into a satirical play scene.

Unlike so many would-be playwrights, he worked hard and long on the actual building of a play, whether for radio or stage, sometimes with half a dozen re-shapings. He understood the special needs in radio for immediate attack on the listener's attention, for limiting the number of characters in any one passage, for direct, uncluttered development of action. In theatre he understood the need for good entrances and exits, telling "curtains". The intangible quality which is called atmosphere and which seems to exist between, rather than in, the lines of speech belonged in high degree to many of his plays. Above all, he had an inexhaustible gift for inventive situation, for putting his people into interesting fixes from which it was his subsequent business to extricate them.

He was an indefatigable and true *tusitala* or songman or teller of tales, giving plenty of emphasis to plot. He could pitch the level of the tale as required, simple or complicated, and his tale telling never gave up. For twenty-five years Max Afford was virtually always writing a play.

Many were the tributes to the man and his work. Professor R. G. Howarth spoke of his "skill and liveliness as a dramatist". Ken Hall, the film producer, wrote: "Of all the men I have known in the writing profession, Max was the most sincere, the most genuine and certainly the most able." W. J. Cleary, formerly chairman of the Australian Broadcasting Commission, expressed his deep regard for Max's talents and character. 'He was one of the few unspoiled people I have met – modest, eager to learn, truly clean in heart and mind." The succeeding chairman, R. J. F. (later Sir Richard) Boyer, spoke of Max Afford as "a most valued contributor to some of the best of our broadcasts." T. Inglis Moore, the poet and critic, wrote: "He had outstanding gifts as a writer. He was at the top of his profession as a dramatic writer for radio, a first-class craftsman." Gwen Meredith, author of "Blue Hills" and a long-standing friend of both and Thelma Afford, wrote: "Max was one of the people whom success did not spoil. He was sincere and simple and lovable, blessed with a gaiety which he willingly shared both as a friend and as a writer. For me, and I am sure for many others, there will now be less laughter in the world." Others spoke of his active work as president of the Sydney P.E.N. club. Professional writers, such as Kathleen Carroll, Anthony Scott Veitch, Richard Lane, and Michael Noonan, combined in a tribute which emphasized the very high regard in which Max Afford was held: "In the hurly burly world of radio, Max always conducted himself with a dignity that commanded respect . . . Back in the early days of radio his attitude to his work and his constant refusal to lower his standards, plus his always pressing demands for better conditions, had an effect which the radio writers of today still feel. Max Afford played a most important part in establishing the radio writer as a person who matters."

His radio plays and serials are still heard over the Australian air, in periodic revival. His stage plays are still being produced by Australian and New Zealand little theatres. That is their truest outlet. But it is also fitting that some of them should be preserved within covers for the wider use of readers.

Leslie Rees
1960

RADIO PLAYS

Consulting Room

For my wife Thelma

Consulting Room

Characters and original cast

The play was first presented by the Australian Broadcasting Commission in 1948 with the following cast:

CLEM LASCELLES	Peter Bathhurst
CARLA, his wife	Elaine Montgomerie
SIR ERNEST BROWN, a famous specialist	Alfred Bristowe
MISS GWENNETH EDWARDS, a spinster	Nancye Stewart
DAVID FARRELL, her fiance	John Bushelle
DOCTOR	Richard Ashley
NURSE	Madge Ryan
VOICE	Tom Lake

Consulting Room

Fade in wild, tempestuous theme. Cross fade into the crash and beat of great seas. Establish. Then fade down to complete and absolute silence . . . A door opens off mike.

CLEM *(slightly off):* Carla . . .
CARLA *(also off):* Yes, Clem?
CLEM: This is the place right enough! See – here's the notice!
CARLA *(reading):* "Consulting Room".
CLEM: Let's go inside . . . (*Fading on*) I say, you're worn out.
CARLA *(slightly breathless):* It was that last steep bit. You're panting too.
CLEM: You held on to me. All the way up the hill!
CARLA *(laughing):* What's a husband for darling!
Pause.
CLEM: It was lovely coming up.
CARLA: That sunset! Remember it, Clem?
CLEM: Yes . . . the whole western sky was afire. Dark smoke and flames of orange and scarlet.
CARLA: And high up . . . those great distances of pale apple green . . . Clem . . .
CLEM: Yes?
CARLA: It was rather a strange sunset, wasn't it?
CLEM: Strange and . . . rather terrifying.
CARLA: I can't ever remember seeing such a sky before.
CLEM: We've never climbed as high as this before!
CARLA: We've never been able to!
CLEM: It's been a wonderful holiday, hasn't it?
CARLA *(slowly):* Yes . . .
CLEM: You don't seem too sure!
CARLA: Oh yes! I am really. But . . .
CLEM: But what?
CARLA: It's so hard to explain Clem. It's like . . . like . . .
CLEM: Yes?
CARLA: Like when you wake first thing on a lovely morning. A blue morning . . . with the sun all fresh and

golden. And you feel wonderful, but right back in your mind there's a dim kind of shadow. And . . . then you remember . . .

CLEM: Something unpleasant?

CARLA: Yes.

CLEM: Not this time, darling! We've had three weeks like a dream. Living in the lap of luxury!

CARLA: It's been awfully expensive, hasn't it?

CLEM *(grinning):* Ruinous! The Grand Palace Hotel caters only for millionaires . . .

CARLA: And crazy people . . . like us! But it's been worth it, Clem!

CLEM: Our own private suite on the third floor. Our name on a card in the door. "Mr. and Mrs. Clemont Lascelles". Lounge room . . . bedroom . . . bathroom . . .

CARLA *(smiling):* And what a bathroom! Water in three temperatures . . . ice . . . lukewarm . . . hot! Automatic hot air driers.

CLEM *(smiling):* Remember how annoyed you were when you couldn't find any towels? And you rang for the maid . . . and she showed you the automatic drier?

CARLA: I was so embarrassed! And you were a pig, Clem! You just stood there and laughed.

CLEM: You looked so young . . . and helpless!

CARLA: I was never so glad to get back to our lounge.

CLEM: Just as well we did! Smokey was kicking up the most unholy din . . . scratching at the door . . . mewing . . . It's partly your fault, darling . . .

CARLA: Mine?

CLEM: You've spoilt that cat hopelessly! Now he won't stay on his own for five minutes!

CARLA: You talk as though he were some ordinary cat!

CLEM: Well . . . isn't he?

CARLA: Smokey? Certainly not! He's a pure bred Persian with a pedigree as long as your arm – and a stack of blue ribbons to prove it! I wouldn't be separated from him for worlds. You know, I was rather scared they wouldn't let us keep him in the hotel . . .

CLEM *(grinning)*: A little extra money soon fixed that!
CARLA *(half-humorously)*: You know . . . sometimes I wonder if it wouldn't be cheaper to have a child . . .
CLEM *(sharply)*: Oh, no, it wouldn't!
CARLA *(quickly)*: Of course it wouldn't! I was only joking, darling.
Slight pause.
CLEM: I say, Carla . . . have you noticed? This room hasn't any windows.
CARLA: Strange! From up here, the view must be magnificent!
CLEM: Even better than our lounge. I'm thinking of that window looking across the water. You can see the breakers coming in for almost half a mile –
CARLA *(a sharp cry of terror)*: Clem . . .
CLEM: Carla – what is it?
CARLA: I . . . I don't know . . .
CLEM: But you're trembling! And you've gone white as a sheet! Sit down a moment . . .
CARLA: Yes . . . I . . . I think I will.
CLEM: Is it the pain?
CARLA: No.
CLEM *(gently)*: Darling, you don't have to be brave. Not with me . . .
CARLA: But it isn't, Clem . . . honestly! I'm all right now.
CLEM: Then . . . why did you cry out like that?
CARLA: I've told you . . . I don't know. Unless . . .
CLEM: Unless what?
CARLA: Remember what I told you about . . . the shadow?
CLEM: Yes?
CARLA: All this talk about our luxury hotel . . . living the life of millionaires . . .
CLEM *(quietly)*: You're thinking of the cost?
CARLA: Cost? Yes . . . yes, that was it! Clem . . . darling . . . how are we going to pay for all this?
CLEM: We can pay.
CARLA: But it will take all our money – every penny we've put by! Those savings . . . treasured over the past three years . . .

CLEM: It's going to take it all Carla.

CARLA: Clem . . .

CLEM *(gently):* That's how we planned it, Carla . . . remember? A month ago . . . just after you'd . . . you'd heard the news . . . from the doctor . . .

CARLA *(softly):* Yes . . .

CLEM: We were in that ghastly little flat looking out on the brick fields . . . and we were talking . . . talking . . . saying anything to keep our minds from the truth . . .

CARLA: And we mentioned dreams.

CLEM: You said dreams couldn't be bought with money. I said they could! And we agreed to try it. To purchase three weeks in heaven . . .

CARLA: The Grand Palace Hotel at Edgewater.

CLEM: Luxury! Three years' savings spent in three weeks . . . to buy an experience so magical that it seems hardly real! Until one pays their staggering bill.

CARLA: Clem . . . I'm scared . . .

CLEM: Why? We've lived our dream.

CARLA: I know. And it's been wonderful! But Clem . . .

CLEM: Well?

CARLA: What . . . what happens after?

A deep sonorous dramatic theme. As it fades . . .

CLEM: Never mind about the future! It's the present that matters now. And talking of that, shouldn't there be a nurse here?

CARLA: Perhaps one has to ring? Isn't that a bell-push by the door?

CLEM: Yes . . . (*Fading slightly.*) It says "Please Ring". *(Fading back.)* There now . . . that should bring someone.

CARLA *(nervous):* Clem . . .

CLEM: Yes?

CARLA: What will I say?

CLEM: Darling . . . this isn't the first time you've consulted a doctor!

CARLA *(bitterly):* No . . . but somehow, each time it gets harder.

Door opens.

CLEM *(softly):* Here's the nurse now . . .

NURSE *(fading in, kind and brusque):* Good afternoon.

CARLA: Good afternoon, nurse. I wonder if I could speak to Sir Ernest Brown?

NURSE *(frowning):* Sir Ernest? I'll have to see . . . he's a very busy man.

CARLA: Yes . . . we know that.

NURSE: Is it . . . urgent?

CLEM *(firmly):* Extremely urgent!

NURSE: I see. Tell me . . . what time was your appointment?

CARLA *(taken back):* Appointment?

NURSE *(a trifle sharply):* Naturally! Sir Ernest never sees anyone without an appointment! *(There is a slight awkward pause.)* You . . . *have* an appointment, of course?

CARLA *(helplessly):* I . . . I don't know. Clem, did you . . . ?

CLEM: I can't remember. Oh, but we must have one!

NURSE: We can soon find out! What is the name?

CARLA: Lascelles.

NURSE: Married?

CARLA *(smiling):* Oh, yes . . . Mrs. Clement Lascelles.

NURSE: Address?

CLEM: We're staying at the Grand Palace Hotel.

NURSE *(harassed):* Really? Now, I'm sure I'd remember an appointment made from there!

CLEM: Are you the only nurse?

NURSE: Oh, no.

CLEM: Then perhaps it was made with one of the other sisters?

NURSE: If so, it will be in the appointment book.

CLEM: I wonder if you'd be kind enough to look? It's really most important . . .

NURSE *(fading off):* Just wait here a moment . . .

CARLA: Clem . . .

CLEM: Yes?

CARLA: How dreadful if he won't see us!

CLEM: But he must! No matter how busy he is! We've got to

make that nurse understand that it's our last hope!

CARLA: Yes.

CLEM: So much has happened in the past few weeks, I'm getting things rather confused . . . We did have an appointment didn't we?

CARLA: I'm certain we did!

CLEM: But if you didn't make it . . . and I'm positive I didn't . . .

CARLA: No! I remember now . . . It was made *for* us! By someone back at the hotel.

CLEM: But who?

CARLA: It must have been someone we were talking to . . . down in the lounge. Old Mrs. Bettinson, perhaps . . . or that man who owned the department store. He's terribly rich . . . and he'd probably know Sir Ernest.

CLEM: But why should he make this appointment? You promised never to mention to a single soul about –

CARLA: But I haven't! Remember, we agreed we wouldn't even think about it again. Not for the whole three weeks!

CLEM: That's right.

CARLA *(slowly):* Then if I haven't told anyone, how could they –

CLEM *(sharply):* Ssssh!

NURSE: *(fading on):* Sorry to keep you waiting.

CLEM: Oh, that's all right.

NURSE: I had to find the appointment book. They never will put it in the same place. But I've brought it with me . . . Just to be sure.

CARLA: And you've found our appointment?

NURSE: No.

CARLA *(surprised):* No?

NURSE *(briskly):* I'm afraid there's been some mistake . . . some carelessness. There's no record of a Mrs. Clement Lascelles.

CLEM: But there must be! Otherwise, why are we here?

NURSE: You should know that better than I!

CLEM: Nurse . . . do you mind . . . could we see that appointment book?

NURSE: Certainly!

Rustle of pages.

And here's today's page.

CARLA *(suddenly):* But there is an entry written here!

NURSE: I'm telling you – it's not yours! Here . . . read it yourself!

CLEM *(reading slowly):* "Miss Gwenneth Edwards . . . aged fifty – spinster . . . train accident. Five o'clock."

NURSE: As you see, the rest of the page is blank. That means we're not expecting anyone else this afternoon.

CARLA *(disappointed):* Oh dear . . . I did want to see Sir Ernest so desperately!

CLEM: And we've come such a long way . . .

NURSE *(with sudden sympathy):* I'm sorry. I know just how you feel. And it is a long way from the Grand Palace Hotel . . .

CARLA: Yes . . .

NURSE: And you must have been very eager to get here to walk through all that rain . . .

CLEM *(sharply):* Rain?

NURSE *(slowly):* I noticed it when I first came in here. Why . . . you're both soaked through to the skin!

From somewhere a sudden wail of wind is heard. On it distant but clear a man's voice calls frenziedly.

VOICE *(off mike and carried wailing on the wind):* Mrs. Lascelles . . . Mrs. Lascelles . . .

CLEM: Carla . . . Listen!

VOICE *(off mike):* Try the other way! Mrs. Lascelles . . . *(Fading out on the wind.)* Mrs. Lascelles . . .

CARLA: It's old Major Perkins from the hotel!

CLEM: Are you sure?

CARLA: Yes . . . and he sounds frantic! Whatever can he want?

NURSE: Perhaps you'd better go and see.

CARLA: Clem – come with me!

CLEM: No. I want to stay and talk to the nurse. You can call if you need me.

CARLA *(fading):* I won't go very far . . .

NURSE *(briskly):* Now, Mr. Lascelles, I must ask you to excuse me . . .

CLEM: Nurse, just a moment.

NURSE *(frowning):* I'm sorry. But it's five o'clock . . . and we're expecting Miss Edwards any moment.

CLEM: But she's not here yet! Before this other patient comes . . . I've got to talk to you! You must let me see Sir Ernest!

NURSE: That's quite impossible!

CLEM: For five minutes . . . three! Just long enough to convince him he must talk to my wife!

NURSE: Mrs. Lascelles has no appointment . . .

CLEM *(in anguish)*: To a doctor, does that matter? If a person was brought in here . . . dying . . . in pain . . . and Sir Ernest could save that person's life, would he refuse because there was no appointment?

NURSE: That doesn't apply here!

CLEM *(desperately)*: But it does . . . I tell you it does!

NURSE: Why?

CLEM: Because Carla . . . my wife is dying! She has a little over . . . twelve months . . . to live!

Pause.

CLEM: Well?

NURSE *(quietly):* Why didn't you tell me this before?

CLEM: Because we agreed . . . both of us . . . that we'd never mention it again! We'd put it right out of our minds . . . we'd forget it completely during this holiday. *(With faint bitterness.)* Three wonderful weeks . . . with everything money could buy . . .

NURSE *(very quietly):* Except . . . forgetfulness?

CLEM *(staring at her):* Then . . . you know?

NURSE *(gently):* Not everything.

CLEM: Would it help if I told you?

NURSE: Perhaps.

CLEM: You see . . . we've been married almost three years. I'd just got out of the army . . . It must have been about twelve months later that Carla first noticed the pains . . . At first, she didn't worry about them. We were so happy . . . we laughed a lot . . . and there was so much else to think about . . .

NURSE: A family?

CLEM *(sharply)*: We have no family! Nor do we want children!

NURSE *(noncommittal):* No?

CLEM: I'd been through the war, remember – five years of it! Quite early we decided – Carla and I – that this was no world to bring children into! And now, thank heavens, we know how right we are!

NURSE *(without inflection):* Really.

CLEM *(softly):* Those first two years . . . I can't tell you how happy we were! I'm a writer of sorts . . . and I'd brought out two books of poems. The critics were . . . encouraging. Some were kind enough to say I had a future . . . *(Bitterly.)* I wonder what they're thinking now?

NURSE: And your wife?

CLEM: Carla never complained. Only sometimes when we talked of all the brave plans ahead . . . sometimes I'd see her face tighten . . . tighten with the clawing pain of it! Then I tried to make her tell me . . . but she wouldn't. And then . . . about six months ago . . .

NURSE *(softly):* Yes?

CLEM: I saw the change beginning . . . she was getting thinner . . . her face was pale, drawn . . . she wouldn't eat. And sometimes, in the night, I'd hear her cry out . . . and I'd feel her hand damp with sweat . . .

NURSE: But surely your wife saw a doctor?

CLEM: Not until after we . . . we'd almost quarrelled about it. I think Carla . . . knew. And she was afraid . . . desperately afraid that in some way, I'd . . . blame her . . . Then came that dark, rainy morning when we saw the doctor . . .

NURSE: Yes?

CLEM: I'll never forget his face as he came out of the surgery. It was even paler than Carla's . . . because, you see, we'd left it too late.

NURSE: And what was it?

CLEM: Cancer . . .

A sudden dramatic chord of music that dies away. In the silence, off mike, there comes a sudden wild, lost cry from CARLA.

CARLA: Clem . . . Clem darling . . . where are you?

CLEM *(alarm):* Carla . . . I'm here! Carla . . .

CARLA *(fading on):* Clem . . . oh Clem . . .

CLEM *(soothing):* There, sweetheart . . . there . . . It's all right. What was it?

CARLA *(in soft terror):* I couldn't find my way back . . . I was lost . . . I thought I'd never find you again. It was all so strange out there . . .

CLEM: But weren't you with old Perkins?

CARLA: Perkins?

CLEM: Yes . . . he was calling you . . . outside. You went to him . . .

CARLA *(slowly):* Clem . . . he wasn't there. He must have followed those men . . .

CLEM: What men?

CARLA: I couldn't see them. It was so dark outside. No trace of sunset now, Clem . . . the sky is like ink. Not even the faintest star shining. I walked a little way, calling Major Perkins's name. Then I heard voices . . .

CLEM: Men's voices?

CARLA: Yes.

CLEM: What were they saying?

CARLA: I think they were talking about . . . us.

CLEM: Us?

CARLA: I couldn't quite catch any words . . . except I'm certain that every now and then I heard something that sounded like our name. Oh . . . and someone mentioned the Grand Palace Hotel.

CLEM: But what were these men doing?

CARLA: I don't know.

CLEM: Didn't you look?

CARLA: I tried to, Clem. I began to walk through the darkness in the direction of the voices. But somehow I could never quite catch up with them. Then suddenly, they just faded away. And I heard the sea . . .

CLEM: Carla!

CARLA *(softly)*: The sound of waves . . . great waves crashing on to the beach. They seemed to be coming nearer . . . closer . . . There was the taste of salt in my mouth . . . the smell of the sea was all about me. And I was terrified . . . more terrified than I'd ever been before in my life.

CLEM: I heard you. It gave me a terrible shock.

CARLA: I was never so thankful in my life to see you there! But Clem . . . that sound of waves . . .

CLEM: Just your imagination, darling. Up here we're miles from the water.

CARLA *(quietly)*: Yes . . . Clem, let's go back!

CLEM: Back to the hotel?

CARLA: Yes. There's something . . . something about this place I can't understand . . . Clem, who were those men? Why couldn't I find them? Why was it suddenly so . . . black outside?

CLEM: It's night time, sweetheart.

CARLA: Look at your watch!

CLEM: Five o'clock . . . *(Sharply.)* But that's crazy! It was five o'clock when we came in here.

CARLA *(slowly)*: If you listen, you'll find your watch has stopped. At five o'clock . . . just like mine.

CLEM: We must have forgotten to wind them.

CARLA: We've never forgotten before!

CLEM: Then we'll find out the right time. We'll ask the nurse – *(He stops.)* She's gone! But I was just talking to her!

CARLA: About me?

CLEM: I had to tell her, sweetheart. I had to make her understand how urgent it was. And she seemed so sympathetic . . . I'm positive she's gone for Sir Ernest!

CARLA: But Clem . . . what if he asks me who sent us?

CLEM: We've got to remember.

CARLA: I've tried . . .

CLEM: Now, let's sit down and think back . . . quietly . . .

We shut Smokey in the kitchen. Then we let ourselves out through the lounge and went down through the main foyer.

CARLA: Wait a moment! We gave something to the clerk at the desk . . . a letter . . .

CLEM: That's right. A letter with some money and the keys of our rooms. Then you spoke to old Mrs. Atterbury . . .

CARLA: She asked me if we'd make up a four of bridge tonight. Somehow that seemed rather funny . . . I remember laughing . . .

CLEM: Then we came out on to the foreshore. Old Major Perkins was there . . . said he'd never seen such huge seas running. And then . . .

CARLA: Yes?

CLEM *(slowly):* Then we were outside this place, looking at the sunset . . . that strange unearthly sunset . . .

CARLA: But Clem . . . in between . . . what happened in between? When we left the hotel, weren't we going somewhere?

CLEM: Here?

CARLA: It could be. But I have a vague idea that this errand was . . . terribly important and . . .

CLEM: And what?

CARLA *(slowly):* Terrifying. I remember holding tight to your hand . . . all the way . . .

CLEM: Yes . . . and the sky was quite clear . . . except for that bank of clouds away in the west. There was no rain, Carla.

CARLA *(softly):* Then . . . how did we get so wet?

A long, dramatic chord of music. As it dies away, MISS EDWARDS *speaks off mike. She is a quiet, gentle little woman, but with enormous reserves of strength.*

MISS EDWARDS: Excuse me . . .

CLEM *(startled):* Oh . . . !

MISS EDWARDS *(fading in):* I'm sorry to startle you. I knocked, but no one seemed to hear. Is this the consulting room of Sir Ernest Brown?

CARLA: Yes.

MISS EDWARDS: I think I must have lost my way in the darkness. And to make matters worse, my watch seems to have stopped. I'm afraid I'm terribly late for my appointment.

CLEM: You're Miss Edwards!

MISS EDWARDS *(shyly)*: Yes . . . I . . . have we met before?

CARLA: No. But we heard all about you from Sir Ernest's nurse.

Far off, but approaching at great speed, the rush of a speeding train is heard.

MISS EDWARDS: How strange! I didn't think she knew anything about me. This is the first time I've been here and I –

The train is closer now. A shrill, urgent scream of a whistle is heard. MISS EDWARDS *gives a sudden cry of horror.*

Billy! Billy! . . . get off the line! The train's right behind you! *(Suddenly she screams.)* Billy . . . jump . . . Oh, my God, Billy . . .

Off mike there comes the harsh grinding of brakes and the pant of a train brought to a halt. Fade it under following dialogue.

CLEM *(sharply)*: Miss Edwards . . .

CARLA: Quick – she's fainting! Clem, help me . . .

CLEM: Get her on to the couch! Gently now . . . gently . . . gently . . . that's right . . . Where's the nurse?

CARLA: She must be just outside! Hurry, darling.

CLEM *(fading)*: Wait here with her . . .

CARLA: Miss Edwards . . .

MISS EDWARDS *(softly, moaning)*: A needle . . . ? Thank God! Quickly, doctor . . . quickly . . . Ah . . . ! No more pain now . . . just numb . . . and sleepy . . . sleepy . . . *(Her voice dies away in a sigh.)*

CARLA *(afraid)*: Miss Edwards . . .

MISS EDWARDS *(unsteadily)*: I . . . I . . .

CARLA: Are you all right?

MISS EDWARDS: Yes . . . yes . . . quite all right. I . . . I'm sorry. For a moment, I felt quite faint. I must have hurried up that hill. Silly of me . . . I keep forgetting I'm no longer a young woman . . .

CARLA: You . . . *walked* up here?

MISS EDWARDS: Of course.

CARLA: But . . . your injuries . . . ?

MISS EDWARDS *(politely puzzled):* Injuries? What injuries?

CARLA *(slowly):* So . . . you can't remember . . . either . . .

A slow ominous chord of music that rises until it is cut abruptly.

NURSE *(off mike, briskly):* Oh, there you are, Miss Edwards!

CARLA: Nurse . . .

NURSE: *(fading on):* One patient at a time, Mrs. Lascelles! You know, Miss Edwards, we've been expecting you for the past half hour!

MISS EDWARDS: I'm sorry, sister.

NURSE *(brisk professional cheerfulness):* Well, better late than never! Sir Ernest is waiting for you upstairs.

MISS EDWARDS: Is he . . . very angry?

NURSE: Sir Ernest? Oh, he never gets angry! Though heaven knows he's every right to lose his temper sometimes! Now . . . just sit down a moment . . .

MISS EDWARDS: But –

NURSE: He's asked me to check over this record. Just as well, I say. There's been two mistakes already today! Now . . . name . . .

MISS EDWARDS: Gwenneth Rosemarie Edwards.

NURSE: Spinster . . . aged fifty. Engaged in 1917 to a young man . . . killed in the First World War . . .

MISS EDWARDS *(softly):* His name was David Farrell. He lost his life in the battle of the Somme . . . April 3rd, 1918. I have his ring on a little chain around my throat . . . I'll show you . . . (*She stops in sudden panic.)* It's gone! I've lost it . . . David's ring . . . I've got to find it . . . I . . .

NURSE: Here it is.

MISS EDWARDS *(trembling):* Oh . . . thank you . . . thank you . . . It's all I have . . . I . . .

NURSE *(gently firm):* It was picked up a few yards from the crossing by one of the guards. Now . . . your profession?

MISS EDWARDS: I . . . I beg your pardon?

NURSE *(sharply):* Please, Miss Edwards! Put that ring away and pay attention! I asked you . . . your profession?

MISS EDWARDS: After David's death, I became a school teacher. Not that I'm clever or anything like that. I only taught the . . . very little ones . . .

NURSE: And then . . . ?

MISS EDWARDS: My father died. I was left some money . . . it wasn't much. But I managed to make a little extra.

NURSE: How?

MISS EDWARDS: As a nurse-maid. And sitting with children at night, while their parents were out. *(With a certain shy pride.)* I was a very good sitter . . . the children liked me. They cried when I went away. Sometimes . . . I . . . I cried, too . . .

NURSE *(gently):* Why?

MISS EDWARDS: I was living on . . . borrowed happiness. All my life I've longed and prayed for a child of my own. It was even worse after David was killed. There was this throbbing, aching pain . . . all this love and tenderness, locked up, wasted . . .

NURSE *(very gently):* Not . . . wasted.

MISS EDWARDS *(softly):* No . . . for so many children needed that love. The helpless ones . . . so tiny . . . so fragile. They'd smile up at me . . . and I'd know . . . peace . . .

Pause.

Nurse . . .

NURSE: Yes?

MISS EDWARDS: Whoever plans our loves sometimes makes very bad mistakes I think. Why was David taken?

NURSE: Perhaps that's why you've come here this afternoon . . .

MISS EDWARDS: Sir Ernest can tell me?

NURSE: If he wishes.

MISS EDWARDS: Do you know?

NURSE: I'm sorry, Miss Edwards. My job is to ask *you* the questions.

MISS EDWARDS: Forgive me. Please go on.

NURSE *(her old brisk manner):* Now . . . this holiday you took two weeks ago . . . ?

MISS EDWARDS: It was at Greenacres – my first holiday for five years. During my stay, I met Mrs. Archer – she has the small cottage near the railway line. And this afternoon . . .

NURSE *(as she pauses):* Go on . . .

MISS EDWARDS: But how strange . . . ! I . . . I can't remember very clearly. I think I promised to mind her little boy, Billy. She was going into the village to make some purchases and . . . *(Sharply.)* But what am I doing here?

NURSE: You can't remember?

MISS EDWARDS *(sudden alarm):* No . . . I must get back! I must have been crazy to come away like this! If anything were to happen to that child . . .

NURSE *(inexorably):* The child is safe . . . thanks to you.

MISS EDWARDS: To me?

NURSE: It is written in this record book . . . in Sir Ernest's own hand. At five o'clock this afternoon you took the child for a walk. He ran on ahead . . . picking wild flowers. You called. He took no notice. When you caught up with him, he was playing . . . on the lines.

MISS EDWARDS: No.

NURSE: It was impossible for the driver to stop the train in time. You acted in a split second! The child was bruised and shaken as you flung him clear. Shaken . . . but unharmed.

MISS EDWARDS *(softly):* Thank God!

Muted, fade in slow regular suck of the respiratory apparatus of an anaesthesia machine.

MISS EDWARDS: Whatever's that?

NURSE *(briskly):* No more questions! Sir Ernest musn't be kept waiting. Go through the door and up the stairs.

MISS EDWARDS *(fading):* Thank you, nurse.

CARLA: Nurse . . .

NURSE: Oh, yes, Mrs. Lascelles. I've spoken to Sir Ernest about you. It's highly irregular, but he's agreed to see you. Not I must go with –

CARLA *(urgently)*: Nurse – wait! There's just one more question . . . a most important one . . .

NURSE: No time now!

CARLA: But you must tell me – you must!

NURSE: What is it you want to know?

CARLA *(slowly, almost fearfully)*: Is . . . Miss Edwards . . . dead?

A strong, dramatic musical chord.

NURSE *(surprised)*: Dead? *(Lightly.)* Good gracious no! If she were dead . . . how could she be here?

CARLA: I . . . I don't know.

NURSE Is that all?

CARLA: Yes.

NURSE: Then I must get along to Sir Ernest . . . Oh, I almost forgot! He gave me this letter for you. *(Fading.)* Now, you must excuse me . . .

The soft regular breathing of the anaesthesia machine continues.

CARLA: That sound . . . It's so familiar . . . I've heard it before somewhere . . .

CLEM *(fading in)*: Carla . . .

CARLA: Sssh, Clem!

CLEM: What's the matter?

CARLA: That sound of soft, regular breathing . . . hear it?

CLEM: Yes. They must be operating upstairs.

CARLA: Operating? Of course! It's an anaesthesia machine! During the war, I did a first aid course . . . they took us through a hospital and –

CLEM *(interrupting)*: I say, Carla . . . what's that in your hand?

CARLA: A letter.

CLEM: Let me see. *(Sharply.)* Carla! Where did you get this?

CARLA: From the nurse. Sir Ernest gave it to her.

CLEM: But . . . where did he get it?

CARLA: What do you mean?

CLEM: This is our letter! The one we left with the clerk . . . back at the hotel! I can feel our keys inside the envelope . . . Wait a minute.

Rip of envelope.

See?

CARLA: There's a note inside! Clem . . . it's coming back! We wrote a note . . . It took us a very long time! Because it was most important. I remember we began it at least a dozen times . . .

CLEM: We'll see.

Rustle of paper.

Yes! It's my handwriting!

CARLA: What does it say?

CLEM: Listen . . . *(He reads slowly.)* "To Whom It may Concern . . . "

CARLA: Yes?

CLEM *(reading):* "This is the final statement of Clem and Carla Lascelles, both being completely sound of mind and in full possession of their faculties. For reasons given below, we have decided on this last grave and terrible step –

CARLA *(a husky horrified cry of realization):* Clem . . . ! Oh, Clem . . . !

CLEM: Carla . . . !

CARLA: Now do you remember?

CLEM: Yes . . .

CARLA: How could we have done such a terrible thing! To take our own lives! Clem . . . we must have been mad!

CLEM *(gently):* No, darling . . . perhaps we were just . . . too sane.

CARLA: But if only we'd thought clearly . . .

CLEM: The world's a very bitter place these days for people who can think too clearly! Don't you remember? We discussed all this so carefully . . . we weighed all the circumstances . . . the state of the world . . . your illness . . . the hopelessness of it all . . . and we found it . . . sadly wanting.

CARLA *(brokenly):* No . . . . .

CLEM: Yes, darling. Then we began it . . . three weeks of complete luxury . . . and then the jump . . . into the darkness.

CARLA: It was wicked . . . wicked . . .

CLEM *(gently):* Sweetheart, don't tremble so . . . You were brave enough . . . back there . . .

CARLA: Was I?

CLEM: We planned to do it on the last day at the hotel. Then this morning . . . those great seas . . . the biggest waves they'd ever seen! And you said . . . "Clem . . . let's not wait any longer!"

CARLA *(suddenly quiet):* And . . . that's why they weren't expecting us!

CLEM: Here?

CARLA: That's why we had no appointment! Don't you see, Clem . . . we . . . we came too soon! Clem, where are we? I'm afraid.

CLEM *(softly):* Yes . . .

CARLA: I'm more frightened than I've ever been in my life! Clem . . . take my hand . . . let's go back . . . quickly! There's the door . . .

CLEM: Come on!

NURSE *(slightly off, very sharply):* One moment!

CARLA *(terror):* Nurse!

NURSE: Where are you going?

CLEM: Back . . .

NURSE: Oh no you're not! Not after I've gone to all the trouble to persuade Sir Ernest to see you!

CARLA *(entreating):* Nurse . . . please . . .

NURSE *(like steel):* You wanted an appointment, didn't you? You begged for an appointment? Very well! *(She calls politely but firmly.)* This way, Sir Ernest! The young couple are waiting!

Dramatic chord of music. As it fades.

SIR ERNEST *(fading in):* Well, well! *(His manner is fatherly, brusquely benevolent.)* So this is the pair of youngsters that have caused us so much trouble! Well? What can I do for you?

Pause. He says, a trifle testily.

Well, speak up! Don't just stand staring at me!

CLEM: I . . . I'm sorry, sir. It's only that . . .

SIR ERNEST: That what?

CLEM: You're not in the least like what we expected . . .

SIR ERNEST *(brusque):* And what did you expect? Someone twenty feet high with a white beard down to their knees? Well, young lady . . . you were going to say something?

CARLA: Only . . .

SIR ERNEST: Only what?

CARLA: One of the reasons I stared so hard when you came in was that you . . . reminded me very much of someone I knew . . .

SIR ERNEST: And who was that?

CARLA *(simply):* My father. He died when I was twelve years old.

SIR ERNEST: Was he a medical man?

CARLA: No. He was a painter . . . an artist. He used to tell me the most wonderful stories. And when you came in like that . . . smiling . . . friendly . . . I thought for a moment you *were* my father and that . . .

SIR ERNEST *(as she pauses):* And what?

CARLA *(quietly):* . . . that it *is* true we're both . . . dead!

Pause.

CLEM: Are we, Sir Ernest?

SIR ERNEST: I can't answer that question.

CLEM: Why not?

SIR ERNEST: Because I don't know . . . yet.

CARLA *(tremulous):* But we . . . drowned ourselves . . .

SIR ERNEST: You tried to.

CARLA: Then . . . someone saved us?

SIR ERNEST: Three young men from the hotel pulled you out of the water.

CLEM: But there wasn't a soul about! We chose the loneliest part of the rocks . . .

SIR ERNEST: You forgot Major Perkins . . .

CLEM: The Major?

SIR ERNEST: When you passed him on the sea-front, he was alarmed by your strange faces . . . you both looked so strained . . . so desperate . . . After you disappeared over the rocks, he followed you . . .

CARLA: Yes . . . that's right! We heard him calling.

SIR ERNEST: His cries attracted the attention of the other men who were walking that way. Mr. Lascelles was saved first. It took them some time to find . . . the other . . .

CARLA: But . . . but if we're not drowned . . .

CLEM *(as she stops, quietly)*: Sir Ernest . . . where are we?

SIR ERNEST: In my consulting room.

CLEM: But sir . . .

SIR ERNEST *(gently and kindly)*: This is my consulting room, Clem. All kinds of people drift in here – to tell me their troubles – to ask my advice for what it's worth. Some I can send away . . . cured. Some require treatment that I must refer to a . . . *(He pauses for a split second.)* more gifted specialist. *(His voice slows.)* Others . . . just come to talk.

CARLA *(softly)*: And what do they find here?

SIR ERNEST *(simply)*: Comfort . . . understanding . . . hope.

CLEM *(bitterly)*: Is there any such thing left in this world?

SIR ERNEST: I think so!

CLEM: I'm sorry to disagree with you, sir. But we think differently! Look around you . . .

SIR ERNEST: I have.

CARLA: To see what, Sir Ernest! A world, wrecked and ravaged by two terrible wars . . . hovering on the brink of a third! Starvation in China! Racial war in Palestine! Capitalism and Communism with a death-grip on each others' throats. And over all the shadow of ghastly new weapons . . . the atom bomb . . . bacteria rockets – mutilations and slaughter and death . . . at the push of a button!

CLEM: And people wonder why we refuse to bring children into a world like this!

SIR ERNEST *(gently)*: Yet surely people can furnish their

own small world as they might furnish their own room . . . pleasant occupations . . . friends . . .

CLEM: No longer!

SIR ERNEST: But surely . . .

CLEM: We believe the essential decencies are drying up in the very hearts of the people! Even in one's own restricted circle, honesty is sneered at. Trust and friendship and honour . . . all swept aside in the cut-throat struggle for existence! The ruthless competition for money, and power!

SIR ERNEST: So . . . you decided that you wanted no part of such a world?

CARLA *(quietly):* No! Nor children to grow up in our image! To suffer as we have suffered . . . and to make the decision . . . we made!

SIR ERNEST *(gently):* So . . . you feel this is the sunset of our present civilization?

CLEM: We are certain of it!

SIR ERNEST: It is only the young who are so certain . . . like that southern boy I was talking to so recently.

CARLA: A southerner?

SIR ERNEST: A young aristocrat who had been fighting under General Lee in the American Civil War. He came from Virginia . . . had seen his fine old family home razed to the ground . . . his mother and brothers die under General Meade's bullets. Then both his legs were amputated . . .

CARLA: Oh . . . !

SIR ERNEST: Young, idealistic, sensitive . . . he saw nothing but his whole world crumbling and crashing down. He tried to take his own life. He was convinced that there was no future nor hope for the future . . . *(His voice rises, gains majesty and power.)* Yet . . . from that welter of pain and agony and bloodshed came that great and shining force that men call . . . Freedom!

CARLA: But that was in 1862! Yet you said you were talking to this man . . . only yesterday!

SIR ERNEST *(smiling):* Time . . . as you know it . . . does not exist here. You wondered why your watches had stopped. That is because here . . . the past, present, and future are as one. It merely means that one can see . . . a little further.

CLEM *(slowly):* So . . . you could tell this young southerner that hope was not dead.

SIR ERNEST: Just as I tell you! Every age has its fears, its terrors, its chaos! It took a great fire to sweep the city of London free from dirt and pestilence – to build a sweeter, cleaner city! It will be the same with this sick old world!

CARLA: If only we could be sure of that!

SIR ERNEST *(gently):* I *am* sure!

CARLA: How can you be?

SIR ERNEST: The chrysalis, trapped in its dark prison, cannot see forward to the moment it will emerge on spangled wings of a butterfly! Yet *we* know that time is coming – because we have seen it happen every year!

CLEM: But . . .

SIR ERNEST: And what is for the chrysalis a year is for you a lifetime. But here, a lifetime can pass like a flash! One thinks in terms, not of years, but of centuries . . . *(Gently.)* And that makes one . . . very wise . . .

CLEM: That's all very well, sir! There may be a new world ahead. But that's no use to us now . . . in our lifetime! We can't enjoy it!

CARLA: And we can't live in the future!

SIR ERNEST *(gently):* Your children can . . . and your children's children . . .

CLEM: We have no children.

SIR ERNEST: A pity!

CLEM *(sharply):* Is it a pity to raise children to be maimed and slaughtered in a third world war?

SIR ERNEST: You talk as though such a war were inevitable.

CARLA: The perils of peace can be just as bad, Sir Ernest! What of infantile paralysis? What of the unhappy children crippled . . . deaf mutes . . . imbeciles . . .

SIR ERNEST: All children are not born so.

CLEM: We prefer not to take the risk! There's enough pain

and sorrow in the world now, without adding to it!

SIR ERNEST: But why should such misfortunes happen to you two? You are both young . . . strong . . . healthy . . .

CLEM *(slowly):* You don't know so much, after all, Sir Ernest. My wife has just . . . twelve months to live. That was one of the reasons we . . . we . . .

SIR ERNEST *(with grave sympathy):* Is this true?

CARLA: Yes.

SIR ERNEST: What is it?

CARLA *(bravely):* Cancer.

SIR ERNEST *(softly):* Oh . . .

CARLA: You see, Sir Ernest . . . this is one time that all the talk in the world . . . can't help.

SIR ERNEST *(briskly):* I agree! You need practical advice! Fortunately, we've got just the right man here!

CLEM: A doctor?

SIR ERNEST: Brilliant man! Only young, but quite a genius in his way! I'll get him to see you.

CARLA: But can he do me any good?

SIR ERNEST: Certainly! He's discovered a complete and absolute cure for cancer in every form.

CLEM: You're joking!

SIR ERNEST: No.

CARLA: But . . . if this doctor had discovered this wonderful cure . . . why, the whole world would have heard about him!

SIR ERNEST: Oh, no they wouldn't!

CLEM: Why not?

SIR ERNEST *(smiling)*: You see . . . he isn't born yet!

Dramatic underlying chord . . . Fading.

Wait here . . . I'll tell him . . .

CARLA: Not yet born . . . Then how can he . ,. ?

CLEM: It's possible, Carla. If there's no such thing as time here, then there's no such thing as age . . .

CARLA: Then the unborn, the living, and the dead are all the same and –

CLEM: Sssh!

DOCTOR *(fading in – young, friendly):* Good afternoon. Sir Ernest told me you wanted to see me.

CLEM: Yes, doctor.

DOCTOR: It's the young lady, I believe. Now if you'll just lie down on that couch. Here! That's right! Now . . . tell me if you feel any pain where I press . . .

CARLA *(a gasp):* Yes . . .

DOCTOR: And there?

CARLA: Yes.

DOCTOR: I thought so! Tricky, but by no means hopeless!

CLEM: You mean . . . there's a chance?

DOCTOR: Every chance in the world! Pity I didn't see you sooner, though. It would have been much easier six months ago. Still, it's a fairly common formation.

CLEM *(bitterly):* Far too common where we come from!

DOCTOR *(sombre):* Yes . . . that's a great tragedy. Millions suffering and dying, I believe?

CARLA: Yes.

DOCTOR: It's incredible how strong a barrier selfishness can be! Take my case, for example. I have the knowledge and the power to bring comfort and happiness to all those poor sufferers. But I'm completely helpless! And all because two very selfish people stand in my way!

CARLA *(slowly):* Two . . . people?

DOCTOR: Young couple . . . like yourselves.

CARLA: And you think they're both . . . very wicked?

DOCTOR: Not really. It's just that . . .

CLEM *(quietly):* That what?

DOCTOR: When I see cases like your wife that other doctors call incurable . . . and I know I can heal so easily . . . naturally I get rather bitter! But this young couple aren't so bad. They've just got all their sense of perspective wrong! And the pity of it all is . . . they both honestly think they're doing the right thing by standing in my way!

CLEM: Doctor . . .

DOCTOR: Yes?

CLEM: What happens if this young couple . . . continue to do this?

DOCTOR *(shrugging):* There's not much I *can* do about it. Except wait until my turn comes round again.

CARLA: And when will that be?

DOCTOR: The next generation. Meanwhile, I must wait on here . . . and watch all that pain and agony and suffering . . . going on perhaps for another twenty or thirty years!

CLEM *(after short pause):* This young couple . . . do you know them?

DOCTOR: No. But Sir Ernest does.

CARLA: And is he very angry?

DOCTOR: Oh, no. Just rather sorry about such a tragic waste of affection. Because, you see, this couple have a terrific capacity for love and tenderness . . . but they'd rather lavish it all on a pet . . . Particularly the woman . . .

CARLA *(slowly):* What . . . sort of pet?

DOCTOR: You'll probably laugh when I tell you . . . It's a cat . . . a prize Persian they call "Smokey" . . . *(Slight pause.)* But there, I mustn't stand here gossiping! Just leave all the arrangements about your case in my hands. *(Fading.)* By the end of the year, I'll have you completely cured . . .

CARLA *(softly):* Clem . . .

CLEM: Yes, Carla . . . I'm just beginning to realize that we've made a very tragic blunder . . .

CARLA: What can we do?

CLEM: If only we could have one more chance!

CARLA: To go back?

CLEM: Yes! Perhaps we can! We've made a terrible mistake, but it was made in ignorance . . .

CARLA: And selfishness, Clem! This might be our punishment! To beg for a second chance . . . and be refused . . . all the time knowing . . .

CLEM *(interrupting):* We can only ask!

CARLA: Sir Ernest? He may not listen to us. But there's our . . . the doctor! He'd understand!

CLEM: Yes . . . we've got to find him! Come on . . .

CARLA: Wait . . . here's the nurse!

Consulting Room

NURSE *(fading in)*: I thought Sir Ernest was here . . .
CARLA. No . . .
NURSE: Then where are you going?
CLEM *(urgently)*: Nurse . . . that young doctor! Which way did he go?
NURSE: I passed him on the stairs . . .
CLEM: Thanks . . . *(Fading.)* Come on, Carla . . .
SIR ERNEST *(off mike)*: Nurse . . .
NURSE: Oh, there you are Sir Ernest!
SIR ERNEST *(fading on)*: You wanted to see me?
NURSE: These reports have just come through about the patients. Miss Edwards's operation is a complete success.
SIR ERNEST: That means we'll be losing her. Anything on the young couple?
NURSE: The young man is recovering.
SIR ERNEST: And the wife?
NURSE *(quietly)*: She died . . . exactly three minutes ago.
SIR ERNEST: I'm very sorry. They're so . . . very much in love.
NURSE: We don't arrange these things, Sir Ernest.
SIR ERNEST *(sighing)*: No . . . Well, I'd better see Miss Edwards. Will you call her in, nurse?
NURSE *(fading)*: Very good, Sir . . .
(Off mike, she calls.)
Miss Edwards . . . would you come in? Sir Ernest would like to see you . . .
MISS EDWARDS *(off mike)*: Coming nurse . . .
Slight pause. She fades in.
Are you going to scold me, Sir Ernest?
SIR ERNEST: Why should I?
MISS EDWARDS: For picking all these beautiful flowers. I've had the most heavenly morning in your garden. I just couldn't resist taking some of these blooms . . .
SIR ERNEST: I'd like you to accept them as a little farewell gift.
MISS EDWARDS *(slightly dismay)*: Farewell . . . ?
SIR ERNEST: Yes . . . you're got to go back . . . at once.
MISS EDWARDS: Oh . . .

SIR ERNEST: Is that so very alarming?

MISS EDWARDS: No. But it's so lovely here. The garden and the birds . . . the wide skies . . . the feeling of peace . . . contentment. I've been very happy here.

SIR ERNEST *(gently):* You can be very happy . . . back there. You'll find things rather different now.

MISS EDWARDS: In what way?

SIR ERNEST: You're a national heroine.

MISS EDWARDS *(sharply):* I? But how absurd! What have I done?

SIR ERNEST: Risked your life to save another. And the world still has a good heart, Miss Edwards. It can still respond to self-sacrifice and heroism. The newspapers and the radio are making quite an event about your recovery.

MISS EDWARDS *(frowning):* I'm not interested in that nonsense . . .

SIR ERNEST *(gently):* Would you be interested to learn you are to have your own institution for orphaned children?

MISS EDWARDS *(staring):* My . . . own . . . ?

SIR ERNEST: Three wealthy businessmen have already offered financial support. It is to be called the Edwards Home . . . and you are to have complete control.

MISS EDWARDS *(in slow, incredulous ecstasy):* Sir Ernest . . . !

SIR ERNEST *(smiling):* That makes all the difference, doesn't it?

MISS EDWARDS: But it's my dream . . . ! Something I've hoped and prayed for . . . and now . . . Oh . . . I . . . I don't know what to say . . . Sir Ernest . . . when can I go?

SIR ERNEST: This very minute, if you wish.

MISS EDWARDS: Oh . . .

SIR ERNEST: Aren't you going to . . . wish me goodbye? It will be a long time before we'll meet again.

MISS EDWARDS *(smiling):* Goodbye Sir Ernest. And thank you for –

CARLA *(fading in – wild with terror):* Sir Ernest . . . ! Sir

Ernest . . . Clem! He's gone . . . I can't find him!

SIR ERNEST *(gently):* My dear . . .

CARLA: We were outside . . . talking. Suddenly, his voice started to fade! I looked around . . . he'd gone . . . I searched everywhere . . . calling for him . . . he didn't answer . . .

SIR ERNEST: He'll never answer.

CARLA. Never?

SIR ERNEST *(gravely gentle):* No voice can carry across the gulf that separates the living . . . from the dead.

CARLA *(trembling):* You mean that . . . I . . . I . . .

SIR ERNEST: Yes.

CARLA *(a soft sobbing cry of grief):* Oh . . .

Pause.

SIR ERNEST *(the grave, stern judge):* Are you ready, Miss Edwards . . .

MISS EDWARDS *(distressed):* Sir Ernest, wait . . .

SIR ERNEST: Wait?

MISS EDWARDS: I can't go back right now. There is someone here who needs my comfort. This poor child . . .

SIR ERNEST: Very well. *(Fading.)* I shall wait for you . . . outside.

MISS EDWARDS: *(very gently):* Oh, my dear . . .

CARLA: Why did he have to go back? Just as we'd begun to understand . . . why did he have to go back?

MISS EDWARDS: In the beginning, it may be hard. But it can be very lovely here.

CARLA: Not without Clem!

MISS EDWARDS: I know how hard separation can be. I've been in love, too . . .

CARLA: Then help me! Go to Sir Ernest . . . make him see . . .

MISS EDWARDS: There are some things even Sir Ernest cannot do.

CARLA: Then there must be someone! Someone who'll listen to me! Someone who can give me a second chance . . . I'll do anything . . . anything!

MISS EDWARDS *(gently):* How did you come to be here at all?

CARLA: We were so unhappy . . . Clem and I. We both did something . . . something very wicked. So wicked that now I'm being punished for it.

MISS EDWARDS: No punishment lasts for ever . . .

CARLA: But it will be too late! That's what I've got to make them understand! There's only . . . twelve months . . . that's all the time I have left . . .

MISS EDWARDS: For what?

CARLA: To have my child . . .

MISS EDWARDS *(tender compassion):* Oh, my dear . . .

CARLA: He has the gift of healing . . . the power to relieve so much pain and agony! That's why I must get back! Because if I don't . . .

MISS EDWARDS: Yes?

CARLA: All this suffering must go on . . . year after year! While he waits . . . helpless . . . because of our selfishness!

MISS EDWARDS: Selfishness?

CARLA: Mine! Mine and Clem's . . . I . . . But we didn't realize what we were doing! We didn't know! And now . . . now it's too late!

MISS EDWARDS: No!

CARLA *(soft):* Miss Edwards . . .

MISS EDWARDS *(firm)*: You can get back! You must get back!

CARLA: But how?

MISS EDWARDS: Take my place!

CARLA: But you . . .

MISS EDWARDS: I will stay here! I am old – barren! I can give nothing to life! But you are young . . . in your hands is the greatest of all gifts!

CARLA: But Sir Ernest . . .

MISS EDWARDS: I will see Sir Ernest! He will understand.

CARLA *(softly):* You say you can give nothing to life . . . ? You are giving everything! This second chance . . .

MISS EDWARDS *(very gently):* Use it well, my dear. Try to

make others understand . . . back there. If only some of them realize . . . it will all be very worthwhile.

CARLA: I will!

MISS EDWARDS: Now . . . go . . . quickly. Goodbye, my dear.

CARLA: Goodbye . . . *(Fading.)* Clem will be waiting for me –

Pause.

SIR ERNEST *(slightly off)*: I thought you might like these roses . . .

MISS EDWARDS: Sir Ernest . . .

SIR ERNEST *(fading on)*: They're particularly lovely at this time of the year . . .

MISS EDWARDS: Is that all you have to say to me? No reproaches?

SIR ERNEST: Reproaches? What about?

MISS EDWARDS: That young woman . . .

SIR ERNEST *(laughing)*: Good gracious no! I knew from the beginning that you'd do this splendid thing!

MISS EDWARDS: You . . . knew?

SIR ERNEST: Of course! That was why I gave that young couple the silly letter they left at the hotel! Now everyone will think it was just another seaside accident.

MISS EDWARDS: Then . . . why didn't you . . . ?

SIR ERNEST: Give that girl her second chance? I couldn't! You see . . . that had to come from one of her own people – someone willing and ready to sacrifice their own happiness . . . for strangers . . .

MISS EDWARDS: I shall find my happiness here.

SIR ERNEST *(gently)*: Yes . . . I think you will . . .

Tap on door. He calls.

Come in . . .

Door opens.

DAVID *(slightly off, young)*: Gwenneth . . .

MISS EDWARDS *(incredulous happiness)*: David . . . ! Oh . . . David . . .

DAVID *(fading on, very gently)*: Darling, where have you been? I've waited . . . so long.

MISS EDWARDS: Oh . . . my darling . . .

DAVID: I thought I might find you changed. But you're just as I remember you . . . that night we said goodbye on the station . . . just the same . . .

MISS EDWARDS: No, David, I'm old . . . and faded . . .

DAVID *(smiling):* Faded? At nineteen? Darling, you're prettier than ever!

MISS EDWARDS *(choking):* Am . . . am I, David?

DAVID: Gwenneth . . .

MISS EDWARDS: Yes?

DAVID: Have you kept my ring?

MISS EDWARDS: Always! See?

DAVID *(gently):* Give it to me. Now . . . put out your hand . . . left hand. Now . . . the fourth finger . . . *(very gently.)* This is . . . forever, darling.

MISS EDWARDS: Yes, David. This is . . . forever . . .

Swell theme music . . . Fade.

Lazy in the Sun

Characters and original cast

The play was first presented by the Australian Broadcasting Commission on Saturday, 20 October 1951 with the following cast:

ARTHUR MORTON	Athol Fleming
ALICE MORTON, his wife	Enid Lorimer
CONSTANCE (27), their daughter	Ruth Cracknell
BILL (24), their son	Bruce Beeby
HAL BRODERICK (28)	Denys Burrows
GREG (32), his brother	Lloyd Berrel
VALERIE HICKMAN (30)	Ria Sohler
GRACE GALSTON	Ethel Lang
ANNA	Gloria Payton

The play was produced by Frank Harvey.

The action takes place in present-day Sydney.

ANNOUNCER: It was a rather nice thought on the part of Mrs. Alice Morton to ask her sister Grace down from the country to see the firework display on the eve of the Australia Day jubilee celebrations. But then the Mortons were nice people. Everyone said so – everyone, that is, except the envious few who resented the Mortons' comfortable place in the world – their three motor cars, their lovely home at Darling Point, Arthur Morton's solid but somewhat mysterious income from the city, Alice's place on her numerous committees, and daughter Constance's picture appearing so frequently in the social pages . . . On this jubilee night, three people sat in the lounge overlooking the garden which ran down to the harbour. A few minutes had elapsed since the last burst of fireworks. Arthur Morton, a well-dressed, florid man of sixty, moved in his chair, glanced across to his wife and sister-in-law, and remarked . . .

MORTON: Well . . . that seems all for the time!

ALICE: Yes dear. Pretty, wasn't it?

MORTON *(grunting):* Lot of tax-payers' money going up there!

ALICE: But, Arthur dear, it's a celebration!

MORTON: Yes. Have you seen the paper?

ALICE: It's there on the coffee table.

Paper rustle.

MORTON: The part I want isn't here.

ALICE: If it's the racing section, you took it up to your study just after dinner.

MORTON: Oh. *(He starts to fade.)* Excuse me, Grace.

ALICE *(a protest):* Arthur!

MORTON *(fading off):* Call me when the show starts again!

ALICE *(calling):* Arthur . . . really . . .

GRACE: Let him alone, Alice.

ALICE: Really Grace, it's too bad of Arthur. I scarcely see anything of him these days. He doesn't get home from town until after eight. By the time dinner is finished, it's nine. Then he just buries himself in his study until bed time.

GRACE: My Leo is just the same. I doubt if he's even missed me from home.
ALICE: But there's some excuse for the man on the land . . .
GRACE: Nonsense! Leo doesn't have to slave the way he does! Not with wool the price it is, anyway! I told him only last week that he could hire another dozen men.
ALICE: My dear, don't talk to me about trying to get labour! People just don't seem to want to work these days! Arthur says it's because there's far too much money around, bricklayers and hod carriers and people like that driving around in expensive cars! No wonder everyone's clamouring for migrant help!
GRACE: How is that girl of yours?
ALICE: Anna? Oh, she's a gem.
BILL *(fading in):* Did I leave my cigarettes in here, mum?
ALICE: I don't know, Bill.
BILL: Oh, here they are. Where's dad?
ALICE: He went to his study.
BILL: Good. *(Fading slightly.)* I'm going to lift a bottle of scotch from the cabinet.
ALICE *(a protest):* Bill dear, I don't think –
BILL: Don't worry, I'll put it back later. But Togo Martin's having the crowd over at his place at Elizabeth Bay. He just rang to say they've drunk him out of scotch.
ALICE: I suppose this means you'll be rushing out again?
BILL: Just as soon as I've filled my cigarette case.
GRACE: Alice . . .
ALICE: Yes, dear?
GRACE: Is that Doris Martin's boy?
ALICE: Yes.
GRACE: I haven't seen her for months.
ALICE: Neither have I . . . oh, we're still quite good friends, but she's such a queer person, so very touchy, you know. But she's never quite forgiven me about her garden party.
GRACE: Oh yes . . . you wrote to me about it. Didn't you slip her up or something?
ALICE: I did not! It happened months ago, Grace, when I

was on that committee of the Women's Overseas Aid. Lady Pinkerton was in the chair and at this particular meeting she said we weren't doing nearly enough about the food parcels for Britain. And, Grace, I felt so humiliated.

GRACE *(amused):* Why?

ALICE: Well, I hadn't done a thing about it! Oh, I'd meant to! Time and time again I'd said to Arthur that we *must* send a weekly parcel! But somehow . . . well, you know how it is . . . anyhow, just as soon as the meeting was over, I had Reynolds drive me straight to the bank and I sent a parcel from there.

GRACE: Only one?

BILL *(grinning):* The first and the last!

ALICE: My dear . . . the trouble it was! First I had to fill in some wretched form and halfway through I remembered I'd promised to open Doris Martin's garden party at three o'clock. And it was ten minutes past the time then! Next I had quite an argument with the clerk . . . I hadn't filled in the receiver's name! So I just said . . . "Oh, send it to anyone – I don't care!" Then Reynolds was held up in a traffic jam in William Street and I arrived at the wretched garden party half an hour late! And to this day, I'm certain Doris thinks I did it on purpose!

GRACE: Should I ring her while I'm down? Perhaps we could have dinner together . . .

ALICE: Not this week, Grace. I've a perfectly frantic time ahead! Tomorrow afternoon it's bridge! Then dinner with the Simpsons. Wednesday's races! Of course that means dinner at Tatts. Thursday there's a fashion parade at Princes . . . you know, that refugee woman with those divinely silly hats . . . and Friday there's a committee meeting with a card party later on and a sherry thing at five.

GRACE: My dear, how do you get caught up in such much?

ALICE: Oh, I don't mind! I think it's so much better to have a full, rich life, don't you?

ANNA *(off):* Excuse me, madame . . .

ALICE: What is it, Anna?

ANNA: A young lady at the door wishes to speak with you, please.

ALICE: A young lady?

BILL: Anyone we know, Anna?

ANNA: She says her name is . . . Miss Hickman.

ALICE: Hickman . . . Hickman . . . do we know any Hickmans, Grace?

GRACE: Wasn't there a Lady Hickman we met at the yearling sales last month? From South Africa, I think. I seem to remember she had a daughter with her . . . a rather attractive girl.

BILL *(grinning):* Anna . . . ask the young lady in at once!

ALICE: Bill dear, you'll be late for your party.

BILL: Don't hurry me, mum. I'm quite all right here.

ANNA *(off):* Miss Hickman.

VALERIE *(fading in):* Mrs. Morton?

ALICE *(slightly cold):* Yes . . .

VALERIE: It *is* . . . Mrs. *Arthur* Morton?

ALICE: That's right.

VALERIE *(smiling):* You see, I had to be sure. I didn't want to be . . . thanking the wrong person. I'm Valerie Hickman . . . from London.

ALICE *(at a complete loss):* How do you do?

VALERIE: About six months ago, you were kind enough to send me a parcel of food.

ALICE *(realizing):* Oh . . . ?

VALERIE: I realize that when you send out so many it must be very hard to keep a track of them. But that particular one meant a lot to me and I've come to thank you for it.

ALICE: Oh, that's quite all right.

BILL: Won't you sit down, Miss Hickman?

ALICE: Er . . . yes, of course. I should like to introduce my sister, Mrs. Galston, and my son William.

BILL: Bill for short. Tell me, how did you come to look us up?

VALERIE: The name and address of the sender was on the parcel. I've been thinking of migrating out here for some time, and your gift rather made up my mind. That's why . . instead of writing, I decided I'd thank you in person.

There is a short awkard pause.

GRACE *(filling it):* Where did you live in London?

VALERIE: Ave Maria Lane . . . near St. Paul's. Then I had a little place in Paris, close to St. Sulpice. Do you know Paris?

ALICE: Er . . . not very well.

VALERIE: Oh, I thought you might have gone there from London . . . so many Australians do.

BILL: We've never even *been* to England.

ALICE *(quickly . . . almost defensively):* Oh, we've talked about going . . . quite a lot. But it's just that I can't get my husband to budge! He says that Australia is good enough for him . . . and really, when you look around at the rest of the world, perhaps he's right.

VALERIE: Yes, indeed.

GRACE: You know, Alice, I was saying to Leo after the last wool cheque came in . . . *(To* VALERIE*)* we're on the land, you see . . . that we really should take a trip abroad. But what with the food shortage, though, mind you, that wouldn't affect us – we'd take plenty of food . . . and the climate . . . Leo said he'd never yet seen a film about England when it wasn't raining!

VALERIE *(smiling):* Oh, we do have some fine days.

GRACE: And then there's all the upheaval of getting away! It's not like just flying down to Melbourne for the Cup, I mean there's passports and luggage, and then there's all the fuss about getting a ship back gain. No, Leo wouldn't hear of it . . . although I pointed out that it would be nice to *say* that we'd been . . .

VALERIE: It's a very long way . . . you don't realize it until you get on the ship.

BILL: Which way did you come?

VALERIE: Around the Cape. Across the Indian Ocean there were three interminable weeks of nothing but water. We didn't even sight a ship.

BILL: We? Your family came with you?

VALERIE: No, I came alone. *(She pauses.)* I haven't any family. Dad died when I was quite young. My mother and elder sister were killed, in November 1940.

ALICE: Oh dear! An accident?

VALERIE *(clearly):* That was the night the Nazis tried to bomb St. Paul's.

ALICE: Oh! *(She adds.)* I remember that. We saw it on the news at the pictures.

There is another awkard pause.

VALERIE *(smiling):* Well . . . I must be going. It has been nice meeting you.

BILL: Where are you staying?

VALERIE: I have a room in King's Cross.

BILL: I'll drop you off in the car.

VALERIE: Oh, no.

BILL: No trouble! I'm going through the Cross to Elizabeth Bay.

ALICE *(genially):* Thank you for calling, Miss Hickman.

VALERIE: I have to thank you. *(Fading.)* Goodnight.

ALICE: Goodnight. *(Calling.)* Will you be late, Bill?

BILL *(well off):* Naturally!

ALICE *(after slight pause):* Well . . . of all the extraordinary things! Grace, it's like something you might read about! Fancy her calling on us . . . do you think we should have asked her to stay to supper?

GRACE: I shouldn't think so, Alice. After all, we don't know her.

ALICE: That's true. Besides . . .

GRACE: Besides what?

ALICE: I . . . I'm not too sure that I liked her. Oh, nothing that you could put your finger on . . . but somehow . . . I don't know . . . she made me feel uncomfortable. Know what I mean?

GRACE: Yes. Alice, I was just thinking . . . 1940 . . . wasn't that the year Old Roley won the Cup?

ALICE: Arthur would know.

GRACE: I'm certain it was. And we all drove down in the old Chev . . .

Distantly there comes the sound of a sudden whoosh.

ALICE: Oh look! They're starting again! Oh, isn't that beautiful?
She calls.
Arthur! Arthur, you're missing it all!
Another whoosh.
Arthur, do hurry!
ARTHUR *(fading in):* I might as well have waited down here!
ALICE: Why, dear?
ARTHUR: There's nothing on the radio but chaps describing all this hoo-hah outside there! I've been all round the dial trying to get the acceptances. *(Snorting.)* And the radio is supposed to cater for public entertainment.

Swell theme. Fade . . . Background sound of running car.
BILL: Miss Hickman . . .
VALERIE: Yes?
BILL: Did you get here today?
VALERIE: You mean . . . oh no! I've been here for almost a month. I should have gone out to see your mother before!
BILL *(quickly):* Oh, it wasn't that. But I thought . . . if you'd landed today . . . what with all the celebrations and fireworks and what-not, you might think that parties like this go on all the time out here.
VALERIE: They don't?
BILL: My word, no! This is a special occasion . . . it marks the jubilee of our federation.
VALERIE *(smiling):* You must put this down to sheer ignorance . . . but just what is this federation of yours?
BILL: Federation? *(Vaguely.)* Oh, it's some . . . some kind of political business between the states. I've forgotten the details. Anyway, it's an excuse for a lot of fun and games. Tell me, do you like parties?
VALERIE: Oh yes!
BILL: Why not join us . . . tonight?
VALERIE: I couldn't do that.
BILL: Why not? Were you doing anything else?
VALERIE: No.

BILL: Look here . . . I've heard about those single rooms in the Cross! To be in one is bad enough! But to be in one, and on your own, must be the very bottom. Particularly on a night like this, when everyone else is hitting the high spots.

VALERIE *(smiling):* It's very kind of you, but I'm used to being on my own. And there's another thing, Mr. Morton . . .

BILL: The name's Bill.

VALERIE: . . . even if I came to your party, I wouldn't know anyone there.

BILL: Leave that to me! My sister Connie's there with her fiance, Harold Broderick. And Togo's crowd are a friendly lot; you'll feel at home right from the jump! Besides, you'll be able to talk about England with old Hal . . . Hal Broderick, I mean.

VALERIE: He knows England?

BILL: Hal? He knows everything! Came back from a world trip about three months ago – England, France, Switzerland, Italy, and then through America. No trouble to Hal! When I said to him "How did you wangle the dollars?" he just grinned! It was money, of course!

VALERIE *(quietly):* He sounds a very lucky young man.

BILL: Lucky . . . and smart! Just bought a cracker new property at Palm Beach for his brother Greg. Greg's older than Hal, but he doesn't get about very much. Got himself shot up during the war, poor chap. Stays down at Palm Beach mostly.

VALERIE: How does this Mr. Broderick . . . the younger one, I mean . . . make his money?

BILL: Now . . . that's something one just doesn't ask! *(Quickly.)* Mind you, don't get the idea that Hal's crooked, or anything like that! But . . . when people want houses or flats or a new car in a hurry, and when they've got the cash to pay for it, well, that's where Hal comes in. A sort of . . . well . . . commission agent.

Fade in to subdued party background. There is a

murmur of voices against radio music and occasional shouts of laughter. Closer at hand cars are tooting horns and accelerating.

Well, here we are!

VALERIE *(dubiously):* Are you quite sure they won't mind a perfect stranger invading?

BILL *(interrupting):* But you're not invading! You're my guest!

Car slows down. Party background closer. Car stops.

Now, out you get!

Car door slams.

VALERIE *(a last protest):* Mr. Morton . . .

BILL *(firmly):* Bill!

VALERIE: Look here, I'm not at all sure that . . .

BILL *(interrupting patiently):* Valerie . . . you see that wide balcony above the lawn? That's Togo's flat. The parade of the boats begins in half an hour's time. Now, if you don't like the party, you can watch the procession from there! Now . . . what could be fairer than that?

VALERIE *(smiling):* Nothing, I suppose.

BILL: All right! Now, come on!

Swell theme. Fade down to:

Party background. Music. Murmur of voices. Laughter. Click of a door shutting. Fade down party background.

VALERIE *(softly):* I'm glad I remembered the balcony.

GREG *(slightly off):* I beg your pardon?

VALERIE *(surprised):* Oh! I'm sorry . . . I didn't notice you sitting in that corner.

GREG *(smiling):* Well, I'm sorry that you had to be sorry. I don't think we've met, have we?

VALERIE: I'm Valerie Hickman.

GREG: How do you do? I'm Greg Broderick.

VALERIE: Harold Broderick's brother?

GREG: Yes.

VALERIE: Oh, but I thought . . . (*She stops suddenly.*) It's rather lovely out here, isn't it?

GREG: My word! I say, you're English, aren't you?

VALERIE *(smiling):* Is that so obvious?

GREG: Only in your voice. Have you been out here long?

VALERIE *(after the slightest hesitation):* A . . . a few weeks . . .

GREG *(smiling):* Oh, then you're a very new Australian. Tell me, have they levelled out all the air raid trenches in Green Park yet?

VALERIE: Yes, but it's still a little . . . bumpy. *(Slight pause.)* You know London?

GREG: I was there during the war. February to May, 1944.

VALERIE: Did you like it?

GREG: Not at first. It seemed such a sad landscape. But then, almost overnight it seemed, the skies dissolved into the palest blue, and the trees took on the faintest greenish sheen . . . so vague and indeterminate you wondered if it was only in your mind. *(He adds . . . smiling.)* And suddenly, there were crocuses opening in Hyde Park.

VALERIE *(softly):* Yes.

GREG: I remember the window boxes in Mayfair . . . scarlet and gold, tulips and daffodils, like flames against the bomb-shattered buildings in Park Lane. But no one gave those ruins a single thought. It was another spring . . . a new miracle.

Pause. He adds lightly.

You'll find it different out here.

VALERIE: In what way?

GREG: Well, our spring gets along in a typically Australian manner . . . casually . . . lazily . . . slipping in because . . . well, it's time to arrive, anyway. The trees are still as green as they were in winter, but the days are warmer, longer, there's more time for swimming and sunbaking.

VALERIE: And racing and tennis . . . and yachting and cricket . . .

GREG *(smiling):* Cricket, particularly! But perhaps that's not being tactful.

VALERIE: Why not?

GREG: Well, after the last Test . . . it just fell right into our laps, you know.

VALERIE: Just as easily as that, eh?
GREG *(quickly):* I say . . . I didn't mean to sound smug . . .
VALERIE: You didn't.
GREG: Then why did you say that?
VALERIE *(gently):* Perhaps . . . envy. Out here so many other things fall into your laps . . . without opposition or struggle. So many things other people only dream about . . . here you're born into them . . . and grow up accepting them as part of your heritage. *(She stops.)* Really, I've no right to talk like this . . .
GREG: No. Go on . . .
VALERIE: I'd rather not . . .
GREG *(quietly):* What you're saying actually boils down to the old proverb . . .
VALERIE: What's that?
GREG: "Easy come . . . easy go."

Pause.

That's what you meant by . . . envy, wasn't it?

On his last word there comes another whoooz of a rocket.

VALERIE: Look! More fireworks!
GREG: You can't change the subject like that.
VALERIE: We can talk about it some other time.
GREG: When?
VALERIE: I don't know.
GREG: Look here. Some of the crowd are coming down to my place at Palm Beach for the weekend.
VALERIE: Yes, Mr. Morton's already asked me.
GREG: Splendid!
VALERIE: But I've refused.
GREG: I say – you can't do that! If you come down I'll show you some of my weaving. I'm pretty good at it. Won some prizes.
VALERIE *(surprised):* At weaving?
GREG: Is that so strange?
VALERIE: No . . . except that . . .
GREG: Well?
VALERIE: All this talk of outdoor sports . . . and swimming

. . . and sunshine . . . somehow I didn't think . . .

GREG *(as she pauses, smiling)*: . . . that I was the type, eh? Well, that just goes to show that you can never tell with the Aussies! But Hal bought me a loom about six months ago . . . and honestly . . . I *am* quite good at it! So . . . will you come?

VALERIE *(smiling)*: I'll see. *(She stops.)* Hello . . .

GREG: What is it?

VALERIE: The parade of the boats. It's just starting! Shall I call the others?

GREG: They'll know soon enough.

VALERIE: Here comes the first one . . . like a huge white swan. It's just rounding the bend . . . see it?

GREG: No.

VALERIE *(laughing)*: Well . . . there must be something very wrong with your eyes.

GREG *(simply)*: Yes. *(A slight pause.)* I'm blind.

VALERIE *(a tiny shocked gasp)*: Oh . . .

GREG *(cheerfully)*: Now please don't apologize . . . I don't know why it is that people get such a shock about blindness. Believe me, there are plenty of worse things.

VALERIE *(quietly)*: When . . . did it happen?

GREG: Bomber raid over Breman . . . just after my London leave. I was with the R.A.A.F. We caught fire . . . some of the other chaps . . . *(He pauses.)* Oh yes, there are worse things than blindness.

VALERIE: I can imagine . . . nothing worse.

GREG: Don't you believe it! Take tonight for instance. When Hal suggested driving me up, I was as keen as anyone! And ourselves . . . out here . . . until you knew, there was nothing to suggest that it wasn't a most interesting conversation between two . . . ordinary people. *(Cheerfully.)* Was there now?

VALERIE: No.

GREG: So let's keep it that way! Now, suppose you tell me –

Door opens, releasing a wave of party sound.

BILL *(fading in)*: So there you are! I've been looking

everywhere for you. Oh . . . so you've met Greg?
VALERIE: Yes.
GREG: You'd better tell the others that the parade's started.
BILL: Crikey, yes! I'll give them a yell.
VALERIE *(interrupting quietly):* Oh, Mr. Morton . . .
BILL *(firmly patient):* Bill!
VALERIE *(smiling):* All right, Bill. Remember your invitation for the weekend?
BILL: Too right I do!
VALERIE: Well . . . if I may . . . I'd like to . . . change my mind and accept it.

Swell theme. Fade . . .
ANNA *(fading in):* Mister . . . Morton . . .
MORTON *(brusque):* Yes, Anna?
ANNA: Reynolds says to say that the car is ready.
MORTON: Good! I'll be along in a few minutes. Is my briefcase in the hall?
ANNA *(fading):* Yes, sir.
A deep-toned clock strikes quarter hour.
ALICE *(fading in):* Oh, there you are, Arthur . . .
MORTON: Alice . . . is that clock right?
ALICE: Quarter-past ten? I think so, dear. Arthur, could I talk to you for a few minutes?
MORTON: Not now, Alice.
ALICE: But Arthur . . .
MORTON: There are four big meetings tomorrow . . . two in Sydney, one in Melbourne, and one in Adelaide! This Friday is going to be one of my busiest days! You'll have all the weekend to talk to me . . .
ALICE: With four meetings? I won't even see you tomorrow!
MORTON: Well, Sunday then! The kids will be away for the weekend and we'll have some peace.
ALICE: But this is important . . .
MORTON: So's my work! *(Fading.)* Goodbye, dear . . .
ALICE: Arthur . . . wait!
Door slams off.
Oh dear!

CONSTANCE *(fading in):* Mum dear . . .

ALICE: Yes, Connie?

CONSTANCE: Have you seen the *Globe?*

ALICE: Your father took it.

CONSTANCE: Blast! Mum, why don't we get three or four papers?

ALICE: There's the *Newsprint.*

CONSTANCE: I don't want the *Newsprint!* I want the *Globe!* They had a photographer at the Crocodile Club last night, he took some pictures of Hal and me.

ALICE: I didn't notice them.

CONSTANCE: You saw the paper?

ALICE: Just the social stuff. Mind you, I only glanced through very hurriedly.

CONSTANCE *(grimly):* They'd better be in! Hal could just about have bought the paper with the drinks he gave that photographer! Hal's not going to like it if they've missed out!

ALICE: Connie dear! Was Bill with you last night?

CONSTANCE: For a while.

ALICE: Alone?

CONSTANCE: Do you ever see my young brother alone these days . . . or nights? Of course not! That Hickman girl was with him. But they left early . . . about half-past one, I think it was. Mum, where's Anna?

ALICE: In the kitchen.

CONSTANCE: I want her to go out and get me a *Globe.*

ALICE *(absently):* Yes dear.

CONSTANCE: Because you might as well know the worst! Bill got into a fight at the Crocodile last night! If they haven't printed my picture, that's probably the reason . . .

ALICE: A fight? But how?

CONSTANCE: It was all very stupid, really. Bill and that girl were at a table with Togo and Peter Hannaford and Larry King . . . Larry was drunk, as usual. That Hickman girl was wearing one of those bare-shouldered, strapless cocktail frocks. You know, with the little bolero jacket. I had one a few seasons ago.

ALICE: But what about this fight?

CONSTANCE: Well . . . Larry kept pestering Miss Hickman to take off the jacket . . . he kept drooling about it being so hot in the club and wanting to see her shoulders. You know what a fool Larry can be! And she refused . . . anyhow, Larry crept up behind her and tried to slip it off.

ALICE: But surely that wouldn't start a fight?

CONSTANCE: Didn't it just? Miss Hickman wrenched away, clasping the jacket around her shoulders . . . and she was as white as death, mum . . . I've never seen anything like it! Then Bill jumped and hit Larry and Larry hit him back and waiters came running from everywhere . . . and old Pietro came along clucking like a hen . . .

ALICE *(dismay)*: Oh Connie . . . !

CONSTANCE: Anyway, Hal, bless his heart, smoothed them all down and everything would have been all right . . . except that this girl insisted on Bill taking her home. But Evan Beaufort saw it all . . . and you know that he's a spy for that social woman on the *Globe* and . . .

HAL *(fading in)*: Hello . . . hello . . . hello . . . !

CONSTANCE: Hal!

HAL *(grinning)*: Never expected to see the boy friend so bright and early, eh? Hello Alice. Where's the old man?

ALICE: You've missed him, Hal.

HAL: Never mind. I'll phone him up. Got a straight tip on Fast Flyer for the three-fifteen at Flemington! Well, Connie old girl, we didn't make the papers, but your brother did.

CONSTANCE: That business last night?

HAL: You bet! I've brought it along.

Rustle of paper.

HAL: Just listen to this! *(He reads with obvious enjoyment.)* A boisterous young colt connected with a family well known for their deep interest in the gee-gees kicked over the traces last night at the Crocodile Club. The dispute arose over the unharnessing of a pretty little filly by a young trainer who had been celebrating not wisely but too well and –

BILL *(fading in):* All right, Hal! Give it away!

ALICE: Bill! Oh, Bill, this is too bad!

BILL: I can't see what all the fuss is about! I've read that tripe myself. No names are mentioned . . .

ALICE: But everyone will know! I mean . . . everyone at all interested in racing . . .

BILL: That doesn't include the whole world, you know! So just let's forget it.

ALICE *(indignantly):* We'll do no such thing! Even before this happened, I was going to talk to your father . . .

BILL: What about?

ALICE: You and this girl!

BILL: Now, just a minute, mum! I'm old enough to look after these things for myself.

CONSTANCE: You're twenty-four! And she's at least thirty! Perhaps even more . . .

BILL *(flashing out):* So what? You're darn near thirty yourself!

CONSTANCE *(hotly):* I'm twenty-seven next birthday and you know it! And I think it's downright rotten of you to talk like this in front of Hal!

HAL *(grinning):* Don't mind me, old girl. It'll be on the marriage lines, anyway. But talking about this other dame . . .

BILL *(shortly):* She isn't a dame!

CONSTANCE *(still rankling):* That's just what we all want to know. Who is she?

BILL *(patiently):* She's a very nice girl just out from England.

CONSTANCE: She told you that?

ALICE: Yes, dear.

CONSTANCE: Then she's a liar!

BILL *(hotly):* Now look here Connie . . .

CONSTANCE *(interrupting):* You tell them, Hal! Perhaps he'll believe you!

HAL *(smugly):* She's been pulling your leg, old boy! She's been living in the Cross about six months.

BILL: How do you know?

HAL: Funny how things come out, y'know. A few weeks ago, I decided on a bit of investment at the Cross. One of the prospects was a residential in Darlinghurst Road. The joker who's running it gave me the books to look over. Among the tenants there's a Valerie Hickman from England. *(Grinning.)* I dunno what she told you, old son . . . but she's had that same room for the past six months.

BILL *(incredulous):* You've made a mistake . . .

CONSTANCE: You're the one that's made the mistake! Tearing around the place with some strange woman you picked up . . .

BILL: I didn't "pick her up"! She came here . . . to this house . . .

ALICE: Why? That's what worries me. Oh, I know the excuse of the food parcel, but surely that's all plain nonsense.

CONSTANCE: Of course it is! She came here with one purpose in mind . . . to get in with our set! She'd read all about us in the newspapers . . . she knew we had money and position!

HAL *(facetiously):* Bill . . .

BILL: Well?

HAL: Hope you've been watching your step, old boy! Dames like that make a packet out of blackmail!

BILL *(boiling):* You shut your mouth!

CONSTANCE: Bill!

BILL: He needn't go round judging everyone by himself!

CONSTANCE *(trembling with anger):* Now you've gone just a little too far! Mum, I'm not going to sit here and listen to him insult Hal!

HAL: Take it easy, Connie. I'm used to hard words.

CONSTANCE: At least you work for a living! He does not a darn thing but fritter away dad's money! Cars and drinking and night-clubs . . .

BILL *(sneering):* Look who's talking now!

ALICE: Children . . . children . . . !

HAL: I think I'd better break this up by taking myself off. I've got to look at a couple of cars in town this morning.

CONSTANCE: I'll come with you, Hal. I've got a hair appointment for three o'clock.

ALICE: But Connie . . . what will you do between times?

CONSTANCE *(bitingly):* Well away from home sweet home! *(Fading.)* Come along, Hal.

HAL *(cheerfully, fading):* See you two later.

Door closes off.

ALICE: Oh, Bill . . .

BILL: Now, don't start all over again, mum.

ALICE: But to talk to Hal like that! And in front of Connie, too! You know how she hates any reference to Hal's business.

BILL: But that doesn't stop her marrying into it, does it? She won't face the ugly fact that Hal's a snide black marketeer . . . yet she can't wait to take his name and share in the spoils.

ALICE: What an extraordinary way of putting it! When I married your father, I didn't actually approve of him being a bookmaker, but then if every young woman questioned the source of her future husband's income, wherever would we be? Why . . . our . . . our world might just stop dead!

BILL: And you're just as bad as Connie, because you encourage it.

ALICE *(gently):* Bill dear . . . you're so very young. When you're older, you'll understand better. Now about this girl . . .

BILL: I said I didn't want to talk about her.

ALICE: But we *must* talk about her! Don't you see there's something very peculiar going on? Her odd behaviour at the club last night . . . and now all these lies . . .

BILL *(doggedly):* I'll ask her about those myself!

ALICE: You're seeing her again?

BILL *(clearly):* We're driving down to Greg Broderick's place at Palm Beach for the weekend! Hal and Connie are coming, too . . . at least, they *were* coming!

ALICE *(for her, very quietly):* Bill . . .

BILL: Yes?

ALICE: You're not being very . . . foolish with this girl?

BILL: Foolish?

ALICE: You know perfectly well what I mean.

BILL: No, mum. I'm not being . . . foolish, as you call it. I happen to be in love with Valerie.

ALICE *(a protest):* Bill! Don't talk such nonsense.

BILL: And quite possibly, if the opportunity comes up over this weekend, I'm going to ask her to . . . marry me.

Swell theme. Fade down . . . A nearby radio blares out hot jive music.

VALERIE: Do you mean to say that you actually wove these lovely things yourself?

GREG *(smiling):* All my own work! Just like the pavement artists outside St. Martin's-in-the-Fields!

VALERIE: But these scarves . . . and this rug! I've never seen more perfect weaving!

GREG: Give most of the credit to the old loom. It's here in the corner. I say, is that radio worrying you?

VALERIE: A little.

GREG: I'll turn it off.

VALERIE: No. Let me –

GREG *(smiling):* Don't worry. I know every inch of this house. And it's only out there in the living room. *(He fades off.)* Excuse me a moment.

Pause. There is a click and the radio is shut off. GREG *fades back talking as he comes.*

Like atomic energy, you know.

VALERIE: The radio?

GREG *(grinning):* A wonderful power being misused. Or perhaps they'll have more sense with atomic energy. Now, come over and see the loom.

VALERIE: What's this you're making?

GREG: Another rug. There's a handicrafts school quite near here. A clever young lady comes up and does the colour matching for the wool.

VALERIE: The shades are so delicate.

GREG: Yes . . . so everyone tells me. Pastel colours, aren't they? *(Pause.)* Aren't they? *(Pause.)* Val . . . what's the matter?

VALERIE *(quietly):* All this lovely work . . . so beautifully done . . . and you've never seen it . . .

HAL *(slightly off):* I say, I say! Who turned off the music-box?

GREG: We did, Hal. It was worrying us.

HAL *(gently chiding):* Break it down, old man! I want to get the results of the three-thirty! If a certain gee-gee romps home, I stand to win a packet!

GREG *(in an elder brother, indulgent tone):* All right. But for Pete's sake, keep that door closed.

HAL: Okay!

Door closes. The music starts again . . . muted this time. It continues for a minute then, likewise muted, fade in raucous running racing commentary.

VALERIE: I thought your brother had gone swimming with Constance and Bill.

GREG: Not while he's got money on a horse! *(Pause.)* What are you thinking?

VALERIE: How strange that two brothers can be so different!

GREG: In a way, I'm to blame. I'm seven years older than Hal. Our parents died when we were kids . . . we went to live with an aunt. I sort of brought Hal up . . . we had some very good times together.

VALERIE: And he's still very fond of you.

GREG: When I came back from the war . . . when Hal saw what had happened to me, it changed him completely. He's never quite got over the shock of it.

VALERIE: And now . . . he's taking it out on the rest of the world?

GREG: Something like that.

Pause. The muted race commentary continues.

GREG: Don't blame him too much. He's grown up in an era of easy money and weakest to the wall. My brother's determined the wall's the place for other people . . . not for him! Yet he's been very good to me. This house and everything in it I owe to Hal . . . although I realize to get it he may have cheated his closest friends.

VALERIE: And he has no pity for them?

GREG: He doesn't know the meaning of the word.

VALERIE: Yet . . . toward you . . . his brother . . .

GREG: Hal has sympathy, because that's something every decent person is born with. But pity – real pity – can only spring from deep personal suffering. But in time, Hal will learn that, too.

The race commentary is shut off suddenly. The door opens.

HAL *(fading in):* It's paid off! Boy – how it's paid off!

GREG *(drily):* I gather Fast Flyer lived up to his name.

HAL: What a horse! My lucky day, I reckon. Well now, I think I'll toddle down and join Connie and Bill for a dip. Sure you won't change your mind, Val?

VALERIE: Quite sure.

HAL *(fading):* Ta-ta. See you in time for drinks . . .

Door closes.

GREG: What did he mean about changing your mind?

VALERIE: Bill had asked me earlier. I told him I wasn't very keen on swimming.

GREG *(smiling):* I wondered what had upset that young man!

VALERIE *(gently):* Bill's very used to getting his own way. And this was his second refusal.

GREG: What was his first?

VALERIE: Coming down here in the car, he asked me to marry him.

GREG *(almost incredulously):* No . . . !

VALERIE: Don't laugh, Greg. He was very serious about it. As serious as only a boy of twenty-four in love for the first time can be.

GREG *(warmly):* But of all the cheek! Only a silly young goat without a brain in his head would entertain the idea in the first place! How did he take the refusal?

VALERIE: Not very well, I'm afraid. I'm sorry, because I like him. I like his kindness . . . his easy friendly acceptance of people. There's not a shred of suspicion or distrust in Bill.

GREG: Sometimes, you know, that can be a bad thing.

VALERIE: It makes one too vulnerable?

GREG: Yes. And the truth can be rather a shock. And brother Hal's an example of what shocks can do to people.

A telephone rings abruptly.

GREG: Oh, excuse me.

He fades off slightly. The telephone stops.

Hello . . . oh, hello Molly. What – right now? *(Pause.)* It's a bit difficult, what about the morning? Splendid! All right, that's a date! About eleven . . . yes, I'll be there. Goodbye, Molly.

Hangs up and fades back.

Some friends wanted me to go over for a drink.

VALERIE: And I'm keeping you here.

GREG: Oh, no! I wouldn't have gone in any case. Not this afternoon – it's far too hot. And they live up the side of a hill with dozens of steps to climb. Now you know one of my faults . . . I'm bone lazy!

VALERIE *(laughing):* You look fit enough!

GREG: Comes from that lazy Australian habit of sunbaking.

VALERIE: A delightful habit. I've acquired it myself.

GREG: Might do a bit of it right now. Have you a costume?

VALERIE: Bill suggested I bring one.

GREG: Slip into it and I'll meet you in the patio in five minutes. We might as well be out there as stewing inside here. Don't forget now . . . five minutes.

Swell theme. Fade down . . . Tap on door.

VALERIE *(calling):* Is that you, Greg? I'm just putting on my wrap. *(Slight pause.)* Come in!

Door opens. She starts in surprise.

BILL *(fading in):* So you've decided to go swimming after all?

VALERIE *(shortly):* Don't be silly, Bill.

BILL *(doggedly):* I don't know what you mean by silly! It seems you'll do anything that Greg asks you, but I just get the polite brush-off. You only came down here at all because Greg wanted it. Now you're going on the beach with him.

VALERIE *(patiently):* I'm not going swimming. I'm meeting Greg out on the patio.

BILL: In a swimsuit and bathing wrap?

VALERIE: I believe that's the regulation uniform for sunbathing! Now . . . would you mind!

BILL *(interrupting):* Just a minute, Val! I want to talk to you.

VALERIE: What about?

BILL: A lot of things that have been boiling up in me all day. Things I should have said to you . . . coming here in the car this morning. For instance, this story of yours about being in Australia only a few weeks.

VALERIE: Bill, I . . .

BILL *(talking her down):* You've been here six months! It doesn't matter a row of pins to me . . . but why lie about it? Why make me look such a fool in front of Connie and Hal?

VALERIE *(quietly):* If I did that, I'm sorry. As for the lie . . . it was one of those stupid things done on the spur of the moment – one never thinks of the consequences, I'm afraid. From the very first week I arrived, I'd meant to thank your mother for that parcel. But I kept putting it off . . .

BILL: Why?

VALERIE: I'd seen your pictures in the papers, read about you all. Put it down to shyness, if you like. But I was terrified you'd think I was trying to . . . crash in. When I finally made up my mind, I was ashamed to admit that it was so long.

BILL: Then why do it at all?

VALERIE: It was a case of now . . . or never. You see, Bill, I'm going away.

BILL: Where to?

VALERIE: Back to England.

BILL *(in dismay):* But you can't do that!

VALERIE *(steadily):* I must. When I arrived here, I had just enough money to last me six months – that and my return fare. Now, there's only the fare . . . and there's another reason.

BILL *(interrupting):* But surely you could step into a very good job?

VALERIE: I don't want a job! Not out here!

BILL: So that's it! The old, old story! Nothing in this country is good enough!

VALERIE *(softly):* Good enough! Bill . . . if poor broken, half-starved England had one-tenth of the physical advantages of this country, she'd be Shakespeare's demi-paradise come true! Not good enough . . . ? Why, there's so much material good out here, packed down and running over, that when people like myself first arrive we can't believe it! It's only after we've been here a few months, when we've started to take the bounteous food, the sunshine, the easy living for granted, it's only then that we begin to look beneath the surface . . . *(Slowly.)* And that's when we begin to get . . . frightened.

BILL: Frightened?

VALERIE *(gently):* You can't understand that, can you?

BILL: Hanged if I can! What's there to be frightened about? Going hungry? No one ever starves in this country! Losing your job? There's not half enough people to fill the posts advertised! Loneliness? Well, there's always a crowd of good sports somewhere having a party!

CONSTANCE *(fade in cheerfully):* Who's having a party?

VALERIE: Hello, Connie.

CONSTANCE: I say, what's the matter? Have you two been scrapping?

BILL: Val's criticizing the way we live!

VALERIE *(crying out):* No . . . that's not true.
BILL: Then why are you clearing out of the country?
VALERIE: I'd rather not talk about it any more.
BILL *(hotly):* Oh, no! You can't wriggle out of it like that! You told me you were afraid . . . all right! Afraid of what? Give it a name!
VALERIE *(quietly):* Very well, Bill. It's called . . . blind indifference!
CONSTANCE: Indifference? Indifference to what?
VALERIE: To your duty as landlords of a really great continent! Because it hasn't the slightest value to you!
BILL: I say, Val . . .
CONSTANCE *(stung to anger):* I've never heard of anything quite so stupid . . .
VALERIE *(after a slight pause, quietly):* Perhaps you're right, Connie. Perhaps I am being stupid.
CONSTANCE: Of course you are!
VALERIE: Stupid in ignoring a self-evident fact . . . that no ones values a thing until it has some importance to them. Therefore, why should this country have any value to you? Have you ever had to fight for it? To really suffer for the soil as people in other countries have suffered for theirs? This land that supplies so much to so few . . . there's never even been a serious attempt to wrest it from you.
BILL: We had the Japs pretty near . . .
VALERIE: But how near? A bombing raid on your Darwin which most people read about in the newspapers . . . or saw on the newsreels! But down here in the cities . . . you were still isolated from it all! You've never seen your homes burning, your skies blackened, people you loved maimed and crying out for death! You've yet to see blood in your streets . . . like the streets of Guernica, Rotterdam, Coventry, London . . . *(Her voice slows and softens)* . . . and, please God, you never will. *(Pause.)* But if it does come . . . I . . . I don't want to be here. I'd rather be among my own folk . . . people who've already been through it. Been tried and

tested . . . and come out . . . finer.

BILL *(sombre):* And you don't think . . . we will?

VALERIE: That's for you to say, Bill.

BILL: But it's the reason you're afraid, isn't it? It's the reason you won't stay on here?

VALERIE *(quietly):* Yes.

CONSTANCE *(suddenly brittle with dislike):* So you've decided to go home?

VALERIE: I'm going back to England. But home . . . *(She pauses.)* . . . where my home stood there's nothing but ruin, crumbling walls and empty windows staring out across wide spaces of rubble to the cathedral. Even after ten years, it's still the same. Yet, in the centre of this desolation there's a tiny garden with wall flowers climbing around a tablet. And on that tablet the words . . . "This garden is maintained in the belief that beauty will some day return to a bomb-torn city." *(Pause.)* When it comes again, I want to be among people like this . . . where gentle stubborn courage rises strong and free and invincible.

CONSTANCE *(slowly):* You know . . . you've got a brazen nerve!

BILL: Connie . . .

CONSTANCE: If this place is so bad, why did she come out here in the first place? And why stay on here? She wasn't forced!

VALERIE: No. Because that's something else you have . . . perhaps the most precious thing of all. Freedom . . . to live as you please . . . to say what you please . . .

CONSTANCE *(brittle):* Even to running down the very people who've been kind to you!

VALERIE *(hurt):* Oh, you don't understand . . .

CONSTANCE: Because we *have* been kind to you!

VALERIE: I'm not denying that! Not for one moment!

CONSTANCE: All right! Then stop trying to live our lives for us! We're getting along all right out here. And how would you like it if we sailed into your country – accepted your hospitality, and then turned around and criticized every single thing you did?

VALERIE *(quietly):* I'm sorry. I suppose it did sound like that. But I ask you to believe it wasn't meant that way. And it's only because you've been so kind that I felt free . . . to talk as I did.

GREG *(away):* Val . . . what's keeping you?

CONSTANCE *(ignoring this):* We know how you must feel . . . losing your home and all that in the war. But all that's in the past! One can't go on brooding about it forever! The best thing is just to forget . . .

VALERIE *(almost passionately):* It isn't so easy to forget! The fire and the bombing, yes, they destroyed only the material things. But there were other forces, more cruel and deadly . . . that planned the destruction of the will and the spirit! It's easy to talk of forgetting when there's nothing to remember! But just try to wash out the memory of the human will breaking under torture and pain . . .

GREG *(off, impatiently):* Val . . . are you coming?

VALERIE *(quiet again):* I must join Greg. *(Fading.)* Excuse me . . .

There is a pause. It is broken by BILL.

BILL *(uncomfortably):* What did she mean by torture?

CONSTANCE: Oh, she's just a little hysterical! Too highly strung, you know. Otherwise she'd never have put on that absurd scene at the Crocodile, when Larry King tried to . . .

Interrupting her – off – comes a scream and a crash.

BILL *(sharply)*: What's that?

HAL *(off, alarm):* It's Val! She tripped on the steps . . . that gown . . .

BILL: Come on!

Running footsteps.

GREG *(fading in, alarm):* What's happened?

HAL: Val's come a cropper on the stairs.

GREG *(alarm):* Val . . . ?

HAL: Now . . . take it easy, Greg! And watch your own step . . . we don't want another accident.

GREG *(impatiently):* I'm all right!

HAL: Not on these steps. I told you we should have had a rail put there months ago. Now, take my arm, old man . . .

GREG: Never mind about me! It's Val . . . is she badly hurt?

HAL *(a question):* Bill . . .?

BILL *(subdued):* I don't know, she's on the landing. One foot seems twisted.

GREG: But how did it happen? Wasn't anyone with her?

HAL: No. It was the gown . . . she tripped . . . now stay where you are, Greg. Don't move. I'm going to give Bill a hand. *(Pause.)* Can we lift her, Bill?

BILL: Get this dressing gown out of the way first. Careful now . . . slip it off her shoulders . . .

CONSTANCE *(a sick gasp):* Look! Look at her back!

BILL *(swallowing):* Good – grief! *(Huskily.)* No wonder she wouldn't let anyone see it . . .

GREG: What's wrong?

CONSTANCE *(ignoring him):* She . . . she must have been in some dreadful accident . . .

BILL: What kind of accident would leave scars like that?

CONSTANCE: I don't know. I . . . I . . . *(Her voice trails away.)*

GREG *(crying out):* What's wrong? Won't somebody tell me? What's wrong with her back?

HAL: Steady, old man! Maybe it's as well you can't see it!

GREG *(on edge):* See what, for heaven's sake?

HAL: Her back's all scarred . . . long red weals . . . like . . . like . . .

BILL *(as he hesitates, grimly):* Why don't you tell him, Hal? Long red weals . . . just like the marks . . . of a whip!

Swell theme quickly. Fade down . . . Tap on door.

VALERIE *(calling):* Who is it?

GREG *(off):* It's Greg . . .

VALERIE *(quietly):* Come in.

Door opens. GREG *fades in.*

GREG *(smiling):* Well . . . a fine old fright you gave us!

VALERIE: Greg, I feel awful about this. To cause such trouble.

GREG: You're very lucky . . . taking a header like that and coming out with nothing worse than a turned ankle. It could have been so much worse!

VALERIE: Yes. The doctor says I should be walking by the end of the week.

GREG: And he means walking . . . not running, particularly down steep stairs.

VALERIE: That's the last thing I remember. Hearing you call and running out to join you.

GREG: Well, we carried you up here . . . at least Bill and Hal did. Then Connie put you to bed while Bill rang the doctor. Of course he wasn't in. So Hal got in his car and scouted the neighbourhood until he found one . . .

VALERIE: Hal did that?

GREG: Yes. And brought him back post-haste! Did you like Dr. Ramsay?

VALERIE: Very much.

GREG: Good type. Ex-army man. He was telling me he'd been with the occupation forces in Germany for a long time. Your case interested him very much.

VALERIE *(laughing):* A sprained ankle?

GREG *(quietly):* Something else.

VALERIE'S *laughter dies away . . . Pause.*

Val . . . why didn't you tell us you'd been in the hands of the Gestapo? *(Pause.)* Well?

VALERIE *(slowly):* Would you have believed me?

GREG *(gently): I* would have.

VALERIE: You . . . yes. But the others . . . Connie, your brother . . . Bill. Oh, not that I would have blamed them! Out here . . . half a world away, sometimes it doesn't seem true, even to me. In Australia, the Gestapo is something to be read about in books or seen on the films or heard on the radio. It's an enthralling adventure that happens to fictional characters, so removed from the life you live here as to be fantastic, like King Solomon's mines or the Mountains of the Moon.

GREG *(quietly):* Not to me. Nor to Dr. Ramsay.
VALERIE: So that's how you knew?
GREG: Yes. *(Pause.)* How did it happen?
VALERIE *(quietly):* It was after the November blitz. On that night, I lost everything . . . everything except a kind of blazing berserk rage against the creatures who could do such things. I was just twenty . . . the age when it seems so easy to take the law of retribution into your own hands. So I went to Paris . . . to live with a cousin.
GREG: But surely France was occupied?
VALERIE: Oh yes. But I didn't go to Paris on a pleasure trip. I went because my cousin's husband was the head of an underground movement, meeting twice a week in a cellar under a bistro near St. Sulpice. It was sabotage work . . . you do that kind of thing when you're twenty and you feel that life has stopped for you. Anyhow . . . but it wasn't any glorious adventure. Most of the time I was terribly afraid, and only the determination to balance an injustice kept me going. *(Her voice slows.)* But in time . . . even that began to fade.
GREG: Yet you stayed in this dangerous work?
VALERIE: Yes. I stayed.
GREG: Because, I suppose, there was nothing else you could do?
VALERIE: Oh no. I could have gone back to England . . . one of our sidelines was the smuggling out of refugees. No, it wasn't that, Greg. By this time I'd found that there was something deeper than mere hate . . . more lasting than the thrill of adventure. Something not as pompous as patriotism . . . not as grand as love of country . . . yet combining, somehow, the two . . . combining it with a quiet, steady courage of a people willing to fight and suffer and die for soil made almost holy by such sacrifice. It made me marvel where such courage came from . . . until I understood.
GREG: What?
VALERIE: That these little people . . . the peasant and farmer . . . had been fighting all their lives. Fighting for

a bare living from his handful of land! Fighting sickness from his goat and his cow, fighting the wind that sought to unroof his house, the rain that flooded the seed from his field, the sun that burnt his land and the frost that blackened it! So that the land, his land, became part of him, part of his strength and hope and future! To yield that piece of soil to a conqueror would be like yielding his own heart . . . *(Pause.)* Some of these people even did that. One day we were raided. The men were killed. The women . . . *(She pauses.)* After four months, another underground movement arranged my escape to England. *(Simply.)* That's all.

GREG *(quietly):* No wonder you feel so very deeply about conditions . . . out here.

VALERIE: You heard what I was saying to Connie?

GREG: No.

VALERIE: Then how . . . ?

GREG: Bill told me.

VALERIE *(quietly):* That's a pity.

GREG: Why?

VALERIE: Isn't there some cliché about regretting words spoken in anger?

GREG *(gently):* You had every right to be angry with them.

VALERIE: No, Greg. Not with Connie and Bill . . . nor with anyone else. But . . .

GREG: Well?

VALERIE: I . . . I don't quite know how to say this. *(Pause.)* Greg, why do you think I came out to Australia?

GREG: There could be a dozen reasons.

VALERIE: One was enough for me. I wanted something to believe in, Greg, something to hope for! I wanted to be able to see into the future . . . clearly . . . without fear.

GREG: But surely in England . . .

VALERIE: Yes . . . there's a future there. England is building it now . . . but slowly . . . painfully almost, because her people are tired. My country needs half a century of peace to restore her greatness . . . her dignity.

GREG *(gently):* Yet you came away . . . ?

VALERIE: I ran away! Away from the shabbiness and insecurity . . . away from the threat of a third world war! I was terrified, Greg . . . more afraid than I'd ever been during the resistance in France. I felt I just couldn't go through it all again. You may call it cowardly . . .

GREG: Or very human.

VALERIE: So I came here . . . to a country where I felt the future was as boundless as the horizons.

GREG: Was? *(Pause.)* Or . . . is?

VALERIE: You know how I feel about that, Greg. Perhaps that was what made me so angry. You said a moment ago that cowardice was human. Isn't it just as human to be disappointed in a broken illusion . . . and to let that disappointment rankle? *(Pause.)* Why are you smiling?

GREG *(gently)*: "Bring me my bow of burning gold;
Bring me my arrows of desire!
Bring me my spear: O clouds unfold!
Bring me my chariot of fire . . . "

(He pauses.) You know how it goes on?

VALERIE: "I will not cease from mental fight
Nor shall my sword sleep in my hand
Till we have built Jerusalem
In England's green and pleasant land."

Pause.

GREG *(gently)*: Val . . .

VALERIE: Yes?

GREG: When Blake wrote these lines . . . Australia was barely ten years old . . .

VALERIE: Meaning that I'm an idealist . . . asking for the impossible?

GREG: Not impossible . . . just . . . premature. Thinking people have been trying to build a new Jerusalem for two thousand years. *(He smiles.)* Out here, we're very new at the job.

VALERIE: A century and a half . . .

GREG: We've done quite a lot in that time. We've spanned the gulf between the Stone Age Aborigine and the television set. It's taken the Old World a great deal longer than one hundred and fifty years to do that! And give us another century and a half . . . let us be as old as America is now . . . perhaps you'll find your new Jerusalem right here.

VALERIE: Perhaps . . .

GREG: A doubtful word . . .

VALERIE: Only because I feel so many things must come to this country . . . a new trial of strength.

GREG *(quietly):* We'll meet it, Val. Oh, I know you can talk of Poitiers and Crecy and Inkaman, but we have our own achievements, too. They're not as star-studded, because our history's too new for that. You might call ours a sort of catalogue of . . . of grimy courage. Anzac, the Somme, El Alamein and the Kokoda Trail. If the rest comes, Val . . . we'll come through.

VALERIE: Greg . . .

GREG: Yes?

VALERIE: Aren't you thinking personally . . . judging the morale of a country by the courage of a few like yourself?

GREG *(softly):* The morale of the country . . . Val, did Bill ever tell you of the time when the Japs were practially on our doorstep?

VALERIE: Yes.

GREG: There were no parties then. People forgot about being lazy in the sun. Arthur Morton was an air-raid warden. His wife was making bandages in a Red Cross depot. Bill was giving blood donations. Connie and her friends were emergency ambulance drivers . . . studying first aid and gas treatment. And this was typical of the whole country! Suddenly the population closed together as one solid unit . . . inspired perhaps not by patriotism as by fear . . . but inspired as never before!

VALERIE: Inspiration through fear . . . yes . . . it was like that in the resistance.

GREG: Have you ever travelled beyond our cities?

VALERIE: No.

GREG: You speak of the French peasant fighting for his land. In our outback country there's a never-ending resistance movement . . . the battle with drought and flood and soil erosion tragic enough to break the toughest man. Yet these chaps go on, year after year, because they, too, were born to the land and love it and are prepared to battle for it.

VALERIE: Even against Nature . . .

GREG: And here in Australia, she can be the toughest of them all!

Pause.

VALERIE: Greg . . . forgive me.

GREG: Why?

VALERIE: For being foolish and impetuous . . . forming hasty judgments with so little knowledge.

GREG *(smiling):* It's so easy to do that out here. You're by no means the first person to fall into the trap. And you know the reason? It's because we're a simple people set down in a vast and complex country. And our distances are so broad that the visitor like yourself sees only one small facet of our existence at one time!

VALERIE: If only I could have met you before. I realize now that there's so much I have to learn.

GREG: There's still time.

VALERIE: A few weeks . . .

GREG: No, Val. All the rest of your life . . . here!

VALERIE: Here? You mean . . . I should stay?

GREG: Yes. Because we need you.

VALERIE: So far I've given nothing but criticism.

GREG: Better that than apathy, surely! We need people like yourself . . . people who, although they've suffered, still burn with the fierce flame of national freedom. Not only you, Val, but hundreds, thousands like you! To argue and debate and question . . . without fear or favour. And to bring the experience of the old world to the optimism of the new! Don't you see, Val . . . more than anything that's what we need?

VALERIE *(slowly):* All this would have been so worthwhile

. . . if what you say is true!

GREG: Find out for yourself! Stay on here.

VALERIE: And you'll help me?

GREG: If you'll accept the burden of a blind man.

VALERIE *(softly):* A *blind* man? Oh, Greg my darling . . .

GREG: Val . . .

VALERIE: To call yourself a burden . . . you who have a clearer, wider vision . . . than any of us . . .

Swell theme . . . Fade out to end of play.

STAGE PLAYS

Awake My Love

(A romantic drama based on
the life of Colonel William Light,
first Surveyor-General of
South Australia)

Preface

The colony of South Australia was founded on the dream of one man. Edward Gibbon Wakefield, convinced that settlement by convict stock was a mistake, visualized a colony of wealthy English squires and free English labourers. Instead of wide grants, the land was to be bought by the rich. Thrifty labourers, saving their wages, could in turn also purchase land. Thus colonization would flourish – the rich bringing a steady supply of capital to the colony, which would in turn be followed by a stream of industrious labour.

But, like all Utopian dreams, this one failed. Wakefield had considered every factor save the human element of blunder. The main power of the colony was in the hands of a Board of Commissioners in London. It was this body which sent out to the new colony two men completely different in temperament, in nature, and in ideals, both to highly important appointments. Surveyor-General Colonel William Light sailed for South Australia in May 1836. Eight months later, John Hindmarsh arrived as Governor of the new colony.

Light, with two surveying vessels and a handful of men, found his equipment totally inadequate for the enormous task ahead. He had scarcely begun his work when the Commissioners in London, having sold allotments, landed the immigrants in the new colony. This body of men discovered they had paid for land not even surveyed, since Light could not do the impossible. Then the South Australian Company, formed in London for the purpose of buying large tracts of land, found fault with Light's choice of the capital. In this, they were firmly supported by Hindmarsh, who disliked the Surveyor-General and was prepared to obstruct him in every way.

By the beginning of 1837, the new colony was torn with bitterness and rancour that must have appalled Wakefield. Quarrels were frequent; the Colonial Treasurer and the Colonial Secretary fought each other with bare fists in the street! The Resident Commissioner was threatened with a public horsewhipping. Meanwhile, the temper of the settlers rose until there was the near threat of civil war against the Governor! Matters became so dangerous that in 1838, both Colonel Light and Governor Hindmarsh were recalled to England. Light, resigning, stayed in the colony, to die of consumption a year later. Hindmarsh was replaced, in October 1838 by Governor George Gawler.

It is against the tempestuous background of these two years that this play is placed. Light's tragic career, with its uphill fight against jealousy and obstruction, is historically correct in every detail. His unflagging faith in the future of the capital of Adelaide, his tender idealism, his bitter rancorous battles with the irascible Hindmarsh, his resignation, the terrible loss of his documents by fire, and his pitiful death are factual incidents. Fictional liberty has been taken with the Manners family and the character of the woman, Linda, whose unswerving affection consoled Light's hardships and gave him tender comfort in his last dark hours.

Historians may question this dramaturgical licence, but before proceeding with its defence let us look at the character of the man.

William Light, born 1788, was a son of Francis Light, Governor of Penang. When that gentleman married Martina Rozells, princess daughter of the Rajah of Queda, the latter presented the island of Penang to Britain as a wedding gift to Francis Light. From this strange and colourful background came William, eldest of the five Light children. At the age of six, the boy William was sent to England to be educated. At twelve, he entered the British Navy and, during the next ten years, this "son of an Eastern prince" was prominent in court circles. He was a guest of the Prince Regent, later George IV, and a lifelong friend of the Duke of Wellington. Gracious, cultured, artistic, and sensitive, Light married Mary Bennett, daughter of the Duke of Richmond and three children were born of the union.

Light's sudden decision to leave the luxurious life of English society – to part from his wife and family – is not easily understood. History remains mute as to the reason, but theories abound. The chest complaint which was to end the colonel's life may have been the cause of his sailing for the new – and sunny – colony, and, if he believed his residence in South Australia but temporary, it explains why Mrs. Light did not accompany him. But another story stirs murkier waters: it suggests that the dark strain in the colonel's blood reappeared abruptly in one of the children – a discovery which resulted in an estrangement between husband and wife. One thing is certain – that in the new colony this proud, artistic, idealistic man was intensely alone.

Records discreetly suggest that Light turned to his housekeeper, Miss Maria Gandy, for companionship. So there is actual foundation for the romantic angle of this play, even though the characters of Linda, her mother, and her father are purely fictional. Or perhaps semi-fictional, for is it too much to believe that among the wealthier land owners in the new colony there was some such woman as Linda Manners, gentle, artistic, and even as the colonel himself "standing like Ruth among the alien corn"? And is it not likely that these two people should be drawn together, first in companionship, then as close friends, and later in a hopeless, tragic, frustrated love?

Colonel William Light remains one of the most colourful and interesting figures in Australian history. Yet a line in a history book, and a bronze effigy are all that remain to perpetuate his name. These – and the city of Adelaide – into which Light built the strength of his own body, and which in turn became his monument and his sepulchre.

Max Afford
Sydney 1947

Thelma Alford
1960.

Thelma Alford
1960.

Amelia and Mrs Orchard
Thelma Alford
1960.

Linda and Mrs Manners

Amelia and Algernon

Characters and original cast

The play was first presented at the Independent Theatre, Sydney, on 4 September 1947, for an extended season of six weeks, with the following cast in order of appearance:

MRS. CHARLES ORCHARD	Catherine Foa
AMELIA, her daughter	Pamela Bromley-Smith
MRS. HENRY MANNERS	Enid Lorimer
CHARLES ORCHARD, manager of the South Australian Company	Desmond Retallic
TRAVERS FINNIS	John Cameron
DIXON, a housekeeper	Dulcie Stark
COLONEL WILLIAM LIGHT, Surveyor-General of South Australia	Paul O'Loughlin
HENRY MANNERS, Advocate-General of South Australia	Charles Tasman
GEORGE STEVENSON, Secretary to the Governor	Raymond Irons
JOHN HINDMARSH, first Governor of South Australia	Kevin Brennan
OSMOND GILLES, Colonial Treasurer	Donald Bear
MARIA GANDY, a housekeeper	Fay Grieye
CAPTAIN HERBERT FYFFE-LOMAX	Kevin Healey
CAPTAIN ALGERNON D' CREPNEY	Ronald Frazer

The play was produced by Doris Fitton, and the decor and costumes were designed by Thelma Afford.

The melody for Linda's song was composed by Henri Krips, whose score is in manuscript form in the Fryer Library, University of Queensland.

The action takes place during 1837–39 in the newly settled colony of South Australia.

Act One

SCENE 1

Living room of the Manners home in Adelaide, South Australia, on an evening in September, 1837.

A large room in which good taste and comfortable furnishings have to some extent overcome the crude construction. The walls are of wood, covered with rough plaster, but their harshness is softened by the draping of curtains and several good pictures.

There are two entrances to the room, one down right which leads to the rest of the house, another up left which connects with the front door and main entrance. In the centre back wall is a fireplace and over this a mantel with red bobble braiding. Over this again is a large mirror, also ornamented with the bobble braid. On either side of the mirror are two candelabra with lighted candles. Between them an erection of wax fruit, covered by a glass dome. On either side of the fireplace are miniatures, and framed silhouettes. Beyond these are two large French windows. These have heavy curtains looped back on either side. Outside are green shutters, which, like the windows, open down the centre. These are closed when the play opens. On the side walls hang portraits of the Manners family in circular gilt frames. Up from the right-hand entrance stands a small piano with a red cover on the top. On this stands an oil lamp, lit in the night scenes. In the opposite corner is an old-fashioned work basket of cedar with a small table nearby. Several chairs and a couch, a brass fender and coal scuttle, and several kangaroo skins on the floor, complete the furnishings. About the whole apartment there is an air of picturesque roughness combined with comfort.

When the curtain rises, it is about nine o'clock of a cold spring night. There is a log fire blazing in the fireplace. A sheaf of wattle decorates the tall vase on the table. Outside the spatter of rain is heard. The sound of voices precedes the entrance of three women, who come through the door down right. MRS. CHARLES ORCHARD *enters first: a plump, gossipy little woman in her early fifties. She has a certain faded prettiness marred by a bitter, discontented mouth.* MRS. ORCHARD *is followed by her daughter,* AMELIA, *an over-feminine, fluffy little creature.* MRS. HENRY MANNERS *enters last of all. She is a tall gracious woman nearing sixty, with charm and distinction. She stands just inside the door, smiling as her guests peer around with surprise and delight. Then* MRS. ORCHARD, *gushing, turns to her.*

MRS. ORCHARD: What a lovely room, Mrs. Manners! I declare! Not even the new Government House will compare with this!

MRS. MANNERS: The credit is entirely due to Mr. Manners . . .

MRS. ORCHARD: Really?

MRS. MANNERS: He had the labourers working on this place months before Linda and I arrived. We brought most of the furnishings from home.

She comes down and gestures to the couch. MRS. ORCHARD *sits, but* AMELIA *is flitting around examining each fresh object with little twitters of pleasure.*

MRS. ORCHARD: And that lovely dinner! What a shame Mr. Manners had to miss it!

MRS. MANNERS: It was to be a small celebration. But contrary winds delayed his return from Kangaroo Island.

MRS. ORCHARD *(sighing):* Somehow, nothing ever seems to go right in this horrible place! You know, when Charles was offered the position of manager out here, we were delighted! The South Australian Company . . . well . . . it's got standing, as you might say!

MRS. MANNERS: Of course.

MRS. ORCHARD: Little did we think we'd rue the day we

ever left England! I hadn't been out here three weeks before . . . Amelia!

This to her daughter who, pausing in her explorations, has lifted her dress and is industriously rubbing right shoe against left ankle.

How many times have I told you not to DO that?

AMELIA *(pouting)*: But mama . . . I am bitten all over!

MRS. ORCHARD: So am I! But I do not make a common spectacle of myself by scratching in public!

AMELIA *(sullenly)*: The Governor's wife has them . . .

MRS. ORCHARD: Amelia!

AMELIA: So she has, mama! I was sitting behind her at Trinity Church on Sunday! I could see them hopping . . .

MRS. ORCHARD *(outraged)*: That will do, pertness! Oh, if only your father would come away from the table . . .

MRS. MANNERS *(smiling)*: Don't reprimand the child. I'm afraid we're all suffering.

MRS. ORCHARD: It's disgusting! At home, I would have gone cold with the very thought of such creatures! But here . . . the whole colony crawls with the pests!

MRS. MANNERS: Have you tried paraffin?

MRS. ORCHARD *(bitterly)*: We've tried everything!

And now AMELIA *has discovered the piano.*

AMELIA: Mama! Mama! . . . look!

MRS. ORCHARD: Yes, angel. But come and sit down.

AMELIA *crosses and sits on a small hassock near the fireplace. She arranges her frock to form a pretty picture.*

AMELIA: Mama . . . we had a piano at home . . .

MRS. ORCHARD: Yes.

AMELIA: Why not here?

MRS. ORCHARD: Your dear papa considers the instrument to be extravagant in a new colony.

MRS. MANNERS: Perhaps Mr. Orchard is right. But Linda would not be happy without her piano.

MRS. ORCHARD: I am told your daughter has a great talent for music?

MRS. MANNERS *(quietly):* She has a great love for it.

AMELIA: But the whole colony talks of Miss Linda's cleverness! There is that poem she is setting to music . . . the poem written by Colonel Light . . .

MRS. ORCHARD: Hush, Amelia!

MRS. MANNERS *(smiling):* It's no secret. A few weeks ago the colonel heard Linda sing at an evening given by Captain Lipson. He asked my daughter if she would care to compose a melody for certain verses he had written.

AMELIA: Where is Miss Linda?

MRS. MANNERS: When Mrs. Hindmarsh was called away so suddenly, I promised her a pattern. Linda is looking for it.

MRS. ORCHARD: Don't tell me Mary Hindmarsh means to appear in another new dress!

MRS. MANNERS: Oh, no! Mrs. Hindmarsh wants to make some garments for the blacks outside the settlement.

AMELIA *gives a lady-like shudder.*

AMELIA: Nasty naked savages . . . living in those dirty wurlies with their dogs! No wonder we scratch all day and night!

MRS. ORCHARD: Yes, indeed! I can see nothing picturesque in them!

MRS. MANNERS *(gently):* Who can?

AMELIA *(promptly)*: Colonel Light! Only yesterday, he was down at the river bank with his sketching pad!

MRS. ORCHARD *(with a swift glance around):* It would seem that the colonel is rather versatile. Surveyor-General, an artist with the brush, and now . . . a poet!

AMELIA: And so handsome! That dark, curling hair greying at the temples . . . so distinguished! And what a leg the man has!

MRS. ORCHARD: Amelia!

AMELIA: Mama! Darling mama! Have I said anything unmaidenly?

MRS. ORCHARD: You have overwhelmed your mama with shame! Such fervent declarations – in public – from a child of your age!

MRS. MANNERS *covers the situation with ready tact. She says, half-jokingly.*

MRS. MANNERS: It is as well that the colonel is happily married!

MRS. ORCHARD *gives that furtive glance right and left, the preliminary to a confidence.*

MRS. ORCHARD: Did you say . . . "happily" married?

MRS. MANNERS: Surely he is?

MRS. ORCHARD: Not if rumours are true, my dear! The colonel has a wife and three children in London. Yet . . . he sails out here alone! Why?

MRS. MANNERS: It may not have been convenient for Mrs. Light to leave London.

MRS. ORCHARD: In this heathen colony, a wife's place is by her husband's side! But there it is! What is good enough for us doesn't suit the daughter of the Duke of Richmond! If I can put up with hardships, why can't she?

AMELIA *(innocently)*: Because she's a lady, mama!

The right hand door opens and two men enter. CHARLES ORCHARD comes first, a loud-mouthed pompous man of middle age. His companion is younger, in his early thirties. TRAVERS FINNIS is a quietly spoken man, with an air of suppressed energy and vitality.

ORCHARD *(speaking as he enters):* . . . and I say the fellow's made a complete mess of everything! And nothing you say will convince me otherwise.

He stops, nods to the women, and comes down.

ORCHARD: We're talking about this man Light!

FINNIS: I think your husband's rather hard on the colonel, Mrs. Orchard.

ORCHARD: Piffle! I'm giving you facts, man! Here we have a new colony, swarming with settlers waiting to claim the land they've bought . . . and Light hasn't even completed his surveys!

FINNIS: Because the commissioners in London didn't give him time!

ORCHARD: That's his story!

FINNIS: And it's true! The colonel had scarcely set foot in the colony before the first boat load of settlers arrived!

ORCHARD: He's a muddler! A confirmed muddler.

MRS. ORCHARD: Charles!

ORCHARD *turns to her.*

ORCHARD: Would anyone but an incompetent bungler put the capital city six miles from the seacoast?

FINNIS *(warmly):* That's only your opinion, sir! Personally, I don't know . . .

ORCHARD *strides to him and taps him on the chest.*

ORCHARD: Then let me tell you, sir, I DO know! Didn't my own company lose hundreds of pounds when our stores were ruined, because they were landed so far from the capital? Farming land! That's what this should be!

FINNIS: I agree with Light that this is the only possible place for the capital!

ORCHARD: And what about Port Lincoln?

FINNIS: Completely unsuitable!

ORCHARD: Well, young man, I'll tell you something! I'm recommending that my company buy no more acres on this present site! That's how confident I am that the capital will be moved!

MRS. MANNERS: But surely Governor Hindmarsh would never do that?

ORCHARD: He'll do it quick enough!

MRS. MANNERS: But all these settlers had bought their land before they left England! If the capital is moved, it means ruin for them!

ORCHARD: Then they can thank your precious Colonel Light for their predicament!

FINNIS: What rot you talk!

ORCHARD *(affronted):* I beg your pardon!

FINNIS *turns to* MRS. MANNERS.

FINNIS *(quietly):* You need have no fear that the capital will be moved. The colonel means to stand by his decision. And I agree with him.

ORCHARD: You would! You're Light's friend!

FINNIS: And proud of it!

ORCHARD *(ugly):* You'd better be, my lad! It's as much as your billet's worth!

MRS. ORCHARD: Oh, Charles . . .

ORCHARD: There's far too much favouritism here! Light's nose has been out of joint ever since he couldn't name this new capital Wellington – after his friend the Duke!

FINNIS: It's Hindmarsh who annoys the colonel! Agitating to have the capital moved to Encounter Bay . . .

ORCHARD: Where it should be!

FINNIS: Nonsense! Light considers the seacoast too dangerous – too exposed!

ORCHARD *(hotly):* He CONSIDERS it! Why the fellow didn't even trouble to examine the location closely! Just came here and dumped the capital in the worst possible spot!

FINNIS *(coldly):* Perhaps, sir . . . in the light of your great knowledge, you might care to take over the appointment of surveyor-general yourself?

ORCHARD: I couldn't possibly make a damn worse mess of it!

MRS. ORCHARD: Charles . . . !

ORCHARD *(rounding on her):* And don't keep squeaking "Charles"!

LINDA MANNERS *enters through the left hand door. She has her mother's grace and dignity – a girl in her late twenties. She has a rather pale oval face with large dark eyes and a well-formed mouth. But the full red lips might be almost sensuous in features less finely chiselled. Into the brooding strife of the room, she brings something very calm, distant, and rather aloof. She smiles, and it has the effect of lighting her face with an almost youthful radiance.*

LINDA: Forgive me being so long . . .

MRS. MANNERS: You found the pattern, Linda?

LINDA: Yes. And Mrs. Hindmarsh sent her apologies again. She has no idea why the governor should send for her.

MRS. ORCHARD *(darkly)*: I suppose it's more trouble.

MRS. MANNERS: Is it still raining?

LINDA: Not at the moment. But I'm afraid we have a wild night ahead.

MRS. ORCHARD: Charles dear, do you think we should go while it's still clear . . . ?

She turns to her hostess.

Would you mind? It is getting late and the roads are in such terrible condition.

AMELIA: I lost a shoe in King William Street! If it had not been for papa's strong arm, I would have sank almost to . . . to . . .

Her words are lost in a wide yawn. She drops her head, and places two fingers to her mouth.

Oh dear . . . the heat of the fire has made me so drowsy . . .

ORCHARD: Past your bedtime, young lady!

FINNIS: If we could be excused, I think we had all better go. If this rain continues, the river will be over the stepping stones!

MRS. MANNERS: I only trust you get home without a drenching . . .

The ladies have risen. MRS. MANNERS *takes the candelabra from the mantelpiece.*

FINNIS: Goodnight, Miss Linda.

The others make their farewells, which LINDA *acknowledges with a smile.* MRS. MANNERS *ushers them toward the left hand door.*

MRS. ORCHARD: Thank you for a most enjoyable evening, Mrs. Manners. We are only sorry we could not hear your daughter sing to us . . .

MRS. MANNERS *(as they exit):* You must come again soon. When Mr. Manners is here . . .

They exit left hand door. The room is now lit only by the gentle radiance of the candelabra on the piano. LINDA *stands for a moment then, crossing to the window, pulls back the curtain and looks out into the night. Returning, she goes to the piano and picks up a sheet of manuscript music from the top. She runs her eyes over the notes, smiling slightly. Then, almost on a sudden impulse, she sits at the piano and, propping up the music before her, runs her fingers over the keys. The quaint, sad little melody sounds through the silent room.* MRS. MANNERS *returns through right door. She stands just inside, listening. Presently,* LINDA *sees her and stops.*

MRS. MANNERS: Go on playing.

LINDA *continues. Then as she finishes, she looks up.*

LINDA: You like it, mama?

MRS. MANNERS: I do. Who is the composer, Linda?

LINDA *rises and smiles.*

LINDA: It's my music for the Colonel's poem.

MRS. MANNERS *(pleased):* Why, Linda . . .

LINDA: I can take little credit. The music was already there . . . penned into the words . . .

She places the music on the piano and turning, crosses to the fire, spreading her hands to the warmth.

Mama . . .

MRS. MANNERS: Yes?

LINDA: How long have we been in the colony?

MRS. MANNERS: Almost three months.

LINDA: Are you ever . . . sorry we left England?

MRS. MANNERS: Isn't it a little early to ask that question? Perhaps in twelve months.

LINDA *turns.*

LINDA: Would twelve months change the Orchard family? Would twelve years?

MRS. MANNERS *(gently):* You're very lonely, aren't you, child?

LINDA: Not lonely, mama. But . . . lost, I think. So many faces . . . so few friendly. So much struggle . . . and so little understanding. Or perhaps it is my fault?

MRS. MANNERS: I think it is ours. We should never have brought you out here.

LINDA *(smiling):* I refused to stay behind! Back there it seemed all so strange and magical — a garden of Hesperides beyond the far horizon. I think I almost expected the golden apples . . .

MRS. MANNERS: Linda . . .

LINDA: You see, mama . . . deep down, I suspect I'm quite as romantic as little Amelia . . .

A tap sounds at the right hand door. The two women turn as it opens to admit the housekeeper. She looks at MRS. MANNERS.

DIXON: If you please, ma'am, the colonel would like to speak to you.

LINDA *(surprised):* Colonel Light?

MRS. MANNERS: Ask him to come in, Dixon.

The housekeeper exits. A moment later COLONEL WILLIAM LIGHT *enters. He is tall and slim and in his mid-forties, though his vigour and charm give him the appearance of a much younger man. His face is interesting; there is intellect in the broad brow, sensitivity in the mobile mouth, but the nose and chin are those of a man ready to fight to the last for his ideals. His manners, his speech, his bearing all reflect his gentle birth. He stands just inside the door for a moment, smiling at the two women.*

LIGHT: My apologies for this late visit . . .

MRS. MANNERS: Come inside, colonel . . .

LIGHT *comes down, moving with a slight limp.*

LIGHT: I would not have troubled you – but I understood Mr. Finnis was dining here tonight.

LINDA: You have missed him by a few minutes.

LIGHT: Then he must have crossed the river by the stepping stones.

MRS. MANNERS: If the matter is urgent, Dixon can go after him . . .

LIGHT *(quickly):* No, no . . . ! It is no night to send anyone on an errand! The streets are inches deep in water. But I noticed some disturbance outside the governor's house . . .

MRS. MANNERS *and* LINDA *exchange a quick glance.* LIGHT *sees this.*

You knew of it?

LINDA: We suspected something. Mary Hindmarsh was

dining here. She would have stayed, but her husband sent his groom to bring her away . . .

MRS. MANNERS: I hope it's not more trouble! There's talk of civil war . . .

And now LINDA *cries out with sudden bitterness.*

LINDA: A fine end to Mr. Wakefield's brave brave plans This was to be a model colony, with no taint of convict labour! Every man free and happy, with holdings paid out of his own pocket!

LIGHT *(grimly):* Would you prefer slave labour? The scum of Portsmouth's rotting hulks . . . chained in our streets like wild beasts!

LINDA *(passionately):* Yes . . . yes! Rather than bloodshed . . . yes!

LIGHT *(gently):* There will be no rebellion here, Miss Linda. We have no hotheaded rum corps as opposed the man Bligh in New South Wales! There is a conflict between two men. Hindmarsh and myself and we shall fight . . .

Something chokes suddenly in his throat. He is racked by a sudden fit of coughing that brings his handkerchief to his lips. He turns away, struggling to control the spasm. As it passes, he turns and looks rather shamefacedly at the two women.

Forgive me . . .

LINDA *(anxious):* Colonel . . .

LIGHT: A mere passing indisposition. I must be on my way . . .

LINDA: That cough grows no better, colonel.

LIGHT: It's stubborn . . .

LINDA: Nor will you help it by going out into the storm!

LIGHT: Dr. Woodeforde tells me a few Australian summers will cure it completely.

LINDA: Shall I give you my prescription?

LIGHT *(smiling):* If you wish.

LINDA: A glass of wine and a warm by this fire!

LIGHT: No, no . . . the hour is late! I could not dream of putting you to such trouble!

MRS. MANNERS: It's no trouble. I'll see to it myself.

She exits down right. LINDA *goes to the fire and pokes*

at the coals. She turns as LIGHT *limps across to the fire.*

LINDA: Your wound troubles you?

LIGHT: Like my chest, that Corunna bullet hole will never accustom itself to these wintry conditions!

He looks around the room, sees the open piano.

Did you play for your guests tonight?

LINDA: No. I was strumming when you came in.

LIGHT *walks across to the piano and sees the manuscript. Turns, delighted.*

LIGHT: This is the melody for my verse!

LINDA: I finished it this afternoon.

LIGHT: How splendid!

He takes up the manuscript and looks at it.)

"Melody by Seiglinda Manners . . ." Is that your full name . . . Seiglinda?

LINDA: Yes.

LIGHT: And I have to know you three months to discover this!

LINDA *(smiling):* Few people know it at all. It was mama's choice. But papa considered it too much of a mouthful. He shortened it to Linda.

LIGHT: But it's so right for you!

LINDA: Seiglinda?

LIGHT *(softly):* Seiglinda . . . (*He lingers on the syllables.)* It reminds me of some still, quiet pool – a deep pool, with the surface tranquil and calm under the evening shadows. Yet gleaming and rippling with a million facets of silver when the sun strikes it . . .

There is a little silence.

LINDA: Would you like to hear the melody?

LIGHT: Very much.

She stretches out her hand for the manuscript, but LIGHT, *his eyes on her face, does not seem to notice it.* LINDA *smiles.*

LINDA: May I have the music?

LIGHT: Your pardon!

He hands her the manuscript. LINDA *moves to the piano while* LIGHT *lowers himself into the chair near the fire, his eyes never leaving her.* LINDA *sits, places the music in position, and runs her fingers over the keys. She has a charming voice, untrained, but sweet and full.*

LINDA *(sings):* I saw you on a blue Spring day
At dawn.
The little birds a-flutter at your
Feet.
You smiled; and then the blue was turned
To gold . . .
Because you smiled on me — that sweet
Spring morn.

I met you when the Autumn tints were
Red . . .
And silvered was your hair and grave
Your eyes.
But when you smiled, the blue of Spring
Was nigh . . .
And we were young again — and so in love.

The piano notes die away. The silence is broken by LINDA *who turns.*

You like it?

LIGHT *rises slowly to his feet.*

LIGHT: You gave my poor lines a beauty undreamt of when I penned them!

The deep sincerity of his tone holds LINDA *for a moment. Then she speaks quickly.*

LINDA: I have made two copies . . .

She starts to move to the left hand door when LIGHT'*s quiet voice stops her.*

LIGHT: Miss Linda . . . please do not go.

LINDA: But your song . . .

LIGHT: First I must tell you something. I did not come here tonight to meet Mr. Finnis . . .

LINDA: No?

LIGHT: I delayed my visit purposely, hoping that your guests would have gone . . .

LINDA: But why . . . ?

LIGHT: I think I hoped for something like this . . . to talk with you . . . not among groups of people, but alone like this. But I never thought to hear you sing . . .

LINDA *(gently):* You have heard me sing before.

LIGHT: Yes . . . at Captain Lipson's house . . .

LINDA: I had hoped you might forget that! I still blush when I think how badly I played . . .

LIGHT: It was the wretched piano!

LINDA: In this climate, it's almost impossible to keep an instrument in tune . . .

LIGHT *speaks with sudden bitterness.*

LIGHT: Is anything in tune here? *(Then he smiles.)* Forgive me! I should not have said that!

LINDA: Why not? You have no easy task in this colony!

LIGHT: And today has been particularly irksome! I found a hundred petty irritations that left me worried . . . depressed! Times like this, I find walking the best medicine!

LINDA: In the rain?

LIGHT: Anything was better than sitting alone! I wanted to get away – leave behind all the treachery – the false promises! That was why I chose to walk in the bush. But tonight, even the bush seemed desolate, weeping, darkly ominous. In all the colony, there seemed no place of sanctuary! But now . . . I know I was wrong.

LINDA: You have found it?

LIGHT: Yes! In this room! Listening to your song, I knew something of the healing peace that comes in great cathedrals . . . *(He smiles.)* Tonight you have done me a very great serivce, Linda.

LINDA *(quietly):* You are welcome here whenever you please.

LIGHT: Thank you. And now –

He breaks as MRS. MANNERS *enters left.*

MRS. MANNERS: Mr. Finnis is here, colonel.

LIGHT: Finnis?

MRS. MANNERS: He wishes to speak with you urgently . . .

LIGHT: Ask him to wait. I am just going.

LINDA: No, no. Mama — ask him in.
LIGHT: But —
LINDA: You have not yet had your wine. And I must get your music . . .

She crosses to the door left, and exits with her mother. LIGHT *stands irresolute, his lean face shadowed, almost as though he has a premonition of what is to come.* TRAVERS FINNIS *enters left.*

FINNIS: Colonel . . .
LIGHT: Yes, Travers?
FINNIS: Houghton told me you were here. It's a bad business, Will! The settlers are demonstrating outside the governor's house!
LIGHT: Why?
FINNIS: Hindmarsh believes he has discovered a new location for the capital!
LIGHT: Again?
FINNIS: It's no mere talk this time! News has come of a natural harbour near the Murray mouth at Encounter Bay. Hindmarsh has prepared a request for Strangways and Hutchinson to head a land party to examine the site! And Captain Crozier is to survey the seacoast!
LIGHT: Hindmarsh must be mad!
FINNIS: He cares nothing for the ruin of the settlers here! Small wonder they are angry! You must do something, Will!
LIGHT: In good time.
FINNIS: But we must act now!
LIGHT: How?
FINNIS: You have the settlers of the colony behind you! These men have put every penny they own into the land! They will prevent the governor from changing the capital!
LIGHT: By insurrection?
FINNIS: Yes! All they lack is a leader! If you were to but say the word . . .

LIGHT *goes to* FINNIS *and puts his hand on his shoulder.*

LIGHT *(quietly):* No my friend. We have been sent out here to build up a new colony, not to have it laid waste with bloodshed. The troubles of the capital, black as they are, have yet fallen short of civil war.

FINNIS: The powder is very dry . . .

LIGHT: Mine will not be the hand to touch the spark! Nor yours, Finnis! We are builders – not destroyers!

FINNIS: But Hindmarsh . . .

LIGHT: I will deal with Governor Hindmarsh! Now . . . return to your lodgings – sleep well – wake refreshed. That is what I intend to do!

FINNIS *looks at him for a long moment, then shrugs his shoulders.*

FINNIS: I thought it only right to warn you, colonel . . .

LIGHT: I understand.

FINNIS *goes to left hand door. There he turns.*

FINNIS *(very quietly):* Take care, Will. There are people in this colony who lack your tolerance. I feel we tread on very dangerous ground . . .

He remains looking at LIGHT *as the curtain falls.*

Act One

SCENE 2

Living room of the Manners home, one month later. The room is similar to the setting of the previous scene, but the curtains are looped back, and the green shutters open to admit the bright noonday sun. In one window hangs a cage containing a Rosella parrot. The centre of the room has been cleared and a massive table stands there. Six chairs have been placed around it — two at either side, one at each end. There are ink pots, pens, and papers on table. The time is shortly before noon.

When the curtain rises, HENRY MANNERS *is discovered putting papers at the head of the table. The Advocate-General of South Australia is a tall, heavily built, rather commanding man nearing sixty. Yet there is nothing overbearing or pompous in his manner. He is a just, kindly man, with a respect for authority. If Henry Manners has a fault, it is his trace of snobbishness, for here is an individual proud of his position in the colony, a man who values above all things his reputation and the social standing of his family.* MRS. MANNERS *enters down right. There is about her expression and movements a certain air of excitement mingled with apprehension.*

MRS. MANNERS: Henry dear . . .

MANNERS: Yes?

MRS. MANNERS: I am certain the clock in the kitchen is slow!

Very deliberately, MANNERS *takes from his pocket a large, turnip-faced watch and consults it.*

MANNERS: Ten minutes to the noon hour!

MRS. MANNERS: Then it IS right!

MANNERS: I trust so, my dear. If not, I must speak to Dixon about it.

MRS. MANNERS: No, no . . . it is just that the time seems to crawl so slowly . . . How are the arrangements?

MANNERS: I have decided that Gilles will sit here . . . *(He indicates the chairs as he speaks.)* Orchard opposite him. Stevenson I've placed at the governor's right hand. Now . . . how is the wine?

MRS. MANNERS: I am having it chilled in the water cooler.

MANNERS: It must be just the right temperature, Rose. Hindmarsh has been known to fling tepid wine across the room!

MRS. MANNERS *does not answer for a moment. She is straightening a cushion, then . . .*

MRS. MANNERS: Henry . . .

MANNERS: Yes, my dear?

MRS. MANNERS: Don't you think it's rather a mistake to hold this meeting here?

MANNERS: Now, Rose, we have been all over that subject!

MRS. MANNERS: But –

MANNERS: Where else could it be held? The new Government House isn't finished . . .

MRS. MANNERS: But this is a private house . . .

MANNERS *(firmly):* It is the home of the advocate-general of South Australia, Rose! If the governor of the colony chooses to convene a meeting here, it amounts to an order!

MRS. MANNERS: I suppose so.

MANNERS: I prefer the subject closed!

He takes out his watch again, consults it.

The meeting should be concluded within half an hour. That will give us time for a stroll in the garden. Luncheon must be served at one o'clock.

MRS. MANNERS: Yes, Henry.

MANNERS: After the meal we will return here. While we are resting, Linda may care to sing for us.

MRS. MANNERS: No, Henry . . .

As her husband looks up in suprise.

Linda won't be here.

MANNERS: And why not?

MRS. MANNERS: She has gone to lunch with the Peters.

MANNERS: And you let her go?

MRS. MANNERS: Come, Henry dear. Linda is no longer a child!

MANNERS: You realize that this is merely a stupid excuse? Because the girl is opposed to this scheme to move the capital?

MRS. MANNERS: She told me so.

MANNERS: Told you?

MRS. MANNERS: Linda said she could not stand by and see such injustice done to an old friend.

MANNERS: Close that door . . .

MRS. MANNERS, *a trifle surprised at the request, crosses and closes the right hand door. When she returns,* MANNERS *speaks quietly.*

MANNERS: Ever since I returned from Kangaroo Island I have meant to speak to you on this matter, Rose. I am not sure I approve of this close friendship. How long has it been going on?

MRS. MANNERS: Two or three months. Perhaps longer. I've given it no thought.

MANNERS: Why not?

MRS. MANNERS: The colonel is an honourable man . . .

MANNERS: He also happens to be married!

MRS. MANNERS: But, Henry . . .

MANNERS: Wait! There are stories circulating in this colony – gossip concerning Light and our daughter – which I have thought it better to ignore. But I can do this no longer. Now the place is buzzing with some sly story about a musical composition . . .

MRS. MANNERS: But surely that was harmless enough?

MANNERS: It is not the fact, Rose. It is what people make of it! In our position we cannot afford such gossip.

MRS. MANNERS: But this tittle-tattle . . .

MANNERS *(quietly):* Tittle-tattle has dragged more than one good name into the mud, Rose! In a colony of this size, where everyone's movements are known, we cannot afford to be less than above suspicion.

MRS. MANNERS: How are you going to stop it, Henry?

MANNERS: Linda must see the colonel only at this house!

Surely that is not asking too much? It makes no bar to their friendship.

MRS. MANNERS: Then you will speak to Linda?

MANNERS: Tonight! I should have brought up this matter before, but business . . .

A tap on the door interrupts him. He calls.

Come in!

The right hand door opens. MRS. DIXON, *the Manners's housekeeper, enters right.*

DIXON: If you please, sir – Mr. Orchard and Mr. Stevenson have arrived.

MANNERS: Have the gentlemen come in.

As the housekeeper goes, he turns to his wife.

Now, I'm sure you have much to do . . .

MRS. MANNERS: Indeed, yes. I trust everything will be to your liking, Henry.

She goes upstage and exits left. MANNERS *arranges an ink pot here, a paper there.* CHARLES ORCHARD *enters with* GEORGE STEVENSON. *The governor's secretary and first editor of the* "South Australian Register" *is a burly, ruthless man. He carries in one hand a roll of paper.*

ORCHARD: So we're the first?

MANNERS: Yes. Is that the document, Stevenson?

STEVENSON: This is it!

He hands the document to MANNERS, *who unrolls it and runs his eyes over the lettering.* ORCHARD, *meanwhile, essays one of his witticisms.*

ORCHARD: Nice Christmas present for our clever surveyor-general! Hindmarsh should have entwined a holly wreath through it – and added the usual festive greetings!

STEVENSON *(cold – unamused):* This is serious business, Orchard!

MANNERS *moves to the head of the table and places the document there. Speaks rather worriedly.*

MANNERS: Serious, indeed, gentlemen. How do you think Light will take this?

STEVENSON: What can the man do? An official order from

the governor remains an official order!

MANNERS: Even when it carries the intention of shifting the capital?

STEVENSON *looks him straight in the face. He replies coldly, firmly.*

STEVENSON: Even when it carries the intention of shifting the capital!

There is a moment of small tension. It is broken by a tap on the door. The housekeeper enters, announces.

DIXON: Mr. Osmond Gilles.

OSMOND GILLES *enters. The colonial treasurer is a lean, quiet man. He nods as he enters.*

GILLES: How d'you do . . . how d'you do . . . Everything in order?

STEVENSON: Even to the document!

He nods to the head of the table. GILLES *crosses and looks at the document. He nods gravely.*

MANNERS: We might as well sit down.

He gestures the men to their seats. As they sit . . .

GILLES: I wish Jeffcott could have been here. He'd have been a tower of strength!

STEVENSON: The judge had to go to Encounter Bay with Captain Blenkinsop.

ORCHARD *(sourly):* Don't mention that man's name to me! He's responsible for all the fuss!

MANNERS: Wasn't there a shooting?

ORCHARD: Yes.

MANNERS: I heard rumours of trouble while I was away on the island . . .

ORCHARD: Then I'll tell you what happened! You know that my company has fisheries at Encounter Bay . . .

MANNERS: Yes . . . Stephens is in charge.

ORCHARD: Was in charge, you mean! There was some trouble with the labourers. Blenkinsop says that Stephens lost his head and shot at them. Stephens, arrested on a capital charge, denies it!

MANNERS: And Jeffcott?

ORCHARD: My company employed the judge to go down to

Encounter Bay with Blenkinsop and get the truth!

GILLES *(shaking his head):* I wish he could have put off the journey until later!

STEVENSON: Why?

GILLES: In a sticky business like this, it's impossible to have too much backing!

STEVENSON *(coldly):* You have the governor's approval! Isn't that enough?

ORCHARD: I see what Gilles means. Light may have all kinds of tricks up his sleeve.

STEVENSON: No. There is only one way Light can sidestep this order.

GILLES: How?

STEVENSON: By a direct refusal to obey!

ORCHARD: He'd never dare! That's outright mutiny!

MANNERS *(quietly)*: We cannot be too sure, gentlemen. Remember, the colonel takes his orders from the commissioners in London.

STEVENSON *(icily):* I would not advise you to remind Hindmarsh of that fact!

There is an awkward silence in which the worried tension grows. MANNERS *looks at his watch gain.* ORCHARD, *on tenterhooks, rises and walks to the window.*

ORCHARD: He may not show up . . .

GILLES: That would not surprise me in the least! Light has declared that, regarding the choice of the capital location, no power on earth can alter his decision!

STEVENSON *taps the document.*

STEVENSON: We'll see what this does!

ORCHARD *turns from the window.*

ORCHARD: If you ask me, it's more than time someone put this damned upstart in his place! Coming here with his high-and-mighty airs! Just because he's been a guest at the royal court!

STEVENSON: It takes no great wit to crawl into royal favour these days!

GILLES *(sharply):* Hindmarsh couldn't do it! And he tried for years!

ORCHARD *gives a sudden snigger.*

ORCHARD: Our governor in a court ball room! Talk about a bull in a china shop!

There is a tap on the door. It opens to admit the housekeeper again. She announces.

DIXON: His Excellency the Governor!

The four men rise to their feet. CAPTAIN JOHN HINDMARSH *enters. Stocky, red-faced, with surly lines around his mouth which tell of an ugly temper when roused, with an arrogant beak of a nose betraying his domineering nature, Hindmarsh looks just what he is: a bluff, dictatorial old sea-dog, better fitted for the quarter deck than the governor's chair. He is in full official uniform and he stands glaring around the room, his glass eye fixed, acknowledging the greetings with a grunt.*

HINDMARSH: Where's Light?

STEVENSON: He should arrive at any moment now, sir.

HINDMARSH: So . . . ! The Governor of South Australia must await an officer's pleasure! *(To Stevenson.)* You've made out that order?

STEVENSON *gestures to paper at head of table.)*

STEVENSON: Just as you ordered, sir.

HINDMARSH *crosses the room to head of table and, sitting, takes up the document and runs his eye over it. The other men sit and eye their superior cautiously. It is* ORCHARD, *fawning, who breaks the silence.*

ORCHARD: Sir . . . we were saying that it's a pity Judge Jeffcott could not be present . . .

HINDMARSH *slowly raises his little eyes from the document and fixes them on the unfortunate* ORCHARD.)

HINDMARSH: What the devil do you mean, sir?

ORCHARD: Only . . . er . . . we . . . we think he should be here . . .

HINDMARSH *(with terrifying quietness):* And why, pray? I can do my own business in my own way! Do you imagine Jeffcott has to hold my hand in everything I do? *(His voice rising.)* I'm the Governor of South Australia – not Jeffcott!

ORCHARD *(cringing):* Naturally, but . . .

HINDMARSH *jumps to his feet, glaring at* ORCHARD.

HINDMARSH: But – but . . . ! You think I'm incompetent, don't you? You believe I daren't make a single move without Jeffcott's advice! Well . . . I can guide this colony without the advice of any damned outsider!

He thumps the table.

Understand that! All of you!

During this undignified harangue, LIGHT *has entered with the housekeeper. He waves her aside and, as she exits hurriedly, he stands listening to the governor's bull-roarings with an expression of mingled amusement and distaste.* LIGHT, *like* HINDMARSH, *is in full uniform. And now* HINDMARSH *has paused. As he sits, glaring around the table,* LIGHT *gives a polite cough . . . The governor and the men swing around.* HINDMARSH *glares at* LIGHT *for a long moment, then speaks with repressed savage geniality.*

HINDMARSH: Well . . . sir!

LIGHT *crosses to the table.*

LIGHT: You sent for me, sir?

HINDMARSH: I did! And the appointment was for twelve noon!

LIGHT *(calmly):* It has just this minute struck the hour.

HINDMARSH *glares at him then, defeated, waves to a chair.*

HINDMARSH: Sit down, man – sit down!

LIGHT: Thank you. I prefer to stand . . .

HINDMARSH: I said . . . SIT DOWN!

LIGHT *hesitates for a moment, then shrugs elegantly and drops into the vacant chair at the foot of the table.*

And now to business! You know why you've been summoned here?

LIGHT *(casually):* I fear 'tis something to my detriment . . .

His eyes flick over the table.

I notice the opposition out in almost full force. I can

only wonder why you omitted Judge Jeffcott.

ORCHARD *(stiffly):* The judge has business at Encounter Bay . . .

LIGHT: Oh yes . . . I remember. Your company manager has been exposed for the lying trickster that he is . . .

ORCHARD: Look here –

LIGHT *(smiling):* The unfortunate Stephens had not sufficient intelligence to cover his crooked dealings in the manner of other colony officials!

ORCHARD *(hotly):* Sir . . . !

LIGHT: Does the cap fit so well, Orchard?

ORCHARD *wheels on the governor.*

ORCHARD: Your Excellency –

But HINDMARSH *waves an impatient hand.*

HINDMARSH: Enough of that! Argue at your leisure!

He draws a deep breath and looks up.

Colonel Light . . .

LIGHT: Sir.

HINDMARSH: I have called you here because of the report made by Captain Crozier and Mr. Strangways on the new harbour discovered at the Murray mouth . . .

LIGHT: I take it the report was favourable?

HINDMARSH *(heavily):* Most . . . favourable!

LIGHT: In spite of the fact that when Sturt examined the Murray mouth, he condemned it . . . because it was exposed to the full force of the southerly gales? Because, as a general rule, rivers which terminate in broad, shallow lakes, have no navigable channels to the sea?

STEVENSON *(thinly):* May I remind you colonel . . . we are discussing the Crozier-Strangways report! Not that of Captain Sturt!

HINDMARSH: You have it there! Read it to him!

STEVENSON *picks up another document from the table. He reads carefully, in his thin, dry tone, pausing from time to time to raise his eyes to* LIGHT's *face.*

STEVENSON: Crozier speaks of the new harbour at Encounter Bay as being a really fine port . . . with good lands and fresh water. Strangways reports it would make an ideal commercial centre for goods shipped along the Murray . . . a great site for a principal town! It has rich soil and fresh water . . . with an anchorage that could be made safe and navigable.

LIGHT: No!

STEVENSON: He also states that the mouth of the Murray could be navigated by small draught ships.

He lays down the document. As he raises his eyes, LIGHT *speaks with gentle irony.*

LIGHT: Is that all?

HINDMARSH, *stung by the veiled contempt in his voice, leaps to his feet.*

HINDMARSH: Isn't it enough, sir? Doesn't it make it plain how you've blundered – placing the capital where it is now – miles from the sea coast! Here we have a splendid site . . . on the banks of a safe and navigable harbour . . .

LIGHT: No, sir!

HINDMARSH: What do you mean?

LIGHT: Your informants err greatly when they call that harbour safe and navigable! I tell you, sir . . . Encounter Bay is a veritable death trap!

HINDMARSH: Words! Mere empty words!

LIGHT *jumps to his feet. His gentle, ironic mood falls like a cloak. There is tension in his attitude – fire in his voice.*

LIGHT: Unfortunately, sir . . . I can produce something more tragically tangible than mere words! I can produce evidence of smashed and battered vessels – drowned men – hundreds of thousands of pounds of good money – washed deep into the sands of your safe and navigable harbour! I can show you wrecks like the barque *South Australian* . . . driven ashore by the fury of the storm – smashed beyond repair! Can you waive tragedies like that away with a gesture?

HINDMARSH *(shrugging):* Such accidents can be helped. We shall make ample provision for the protection of vessels once the new capital is started on its way!

LIGHT: Sir . . .

HINDMARSH: Well?

LIGHT: You speak as though the removal of the present capital has already been decided upon?

HINDMARSH *(deliberately)*: It has! I have decided it shall be moved!

LIGHT: Sir – you cannot . . .

HINDMARSH *(snapping)*: I can do as I please! I'm recommending to the secretary of state the removal of the present capital – and announcing my intention of doing this immediately!

LIGHT *stares at the governor, his face pale and tight.*

LIGHT *(very quietly)*: In which case, sir – why is my presence here so necessary?

HINDMARSH: Because I have an official order for you!

With eyes still on LIGHT's *face, he reaches out a hand.* STEVENSON *picks up the document he brought with him and puts it into the governor's hand. Without moving his eyes,* HINDMARSH *passes it across the table. It is placed in front of* LIGHT, *who ignores it.*

HINDMARSH: That document, colonel, demands that you drop your present survey work here. And that you proceed to Encounter Bay, there to survey the site for the new capital!

LIGHT *(very quietly)*: I am to take this as an official order from the governor?

HINDMARSH: You are! I am waiting for your answer!

LIGHT: I definitely and absolutely refuse!

There are little alarmed ejaculations from the men at the table. HINDMARSH, *purple in the face, stares at* LIGHT *as though unable to believe his ears.*

HINDMARSH: You . . . WHAT?

LIGHT *rises in his chair. He grips the table and, facing the governor, speaks very quietly, but with a passion of sincerity that trembles the very words.*

LIGHT: I must remind you, sir, that the South Australian commissioners gave me complete power to select the capital of this colony! "Not merely in a good position, but in the best position!" Those were my orders . . . word for word! And I have carried out those orders to the letter! I have chosen the only possible location where the capital can grow and expand! I am not thinking of this year or next year or even a decade hence! I am thinking of a hundred years from now when this barren site will be a widespread city, stretching and lapping to the very edge of this seacoast you now condemn! I am thinking of the generations unborn who will load me with the full responsibility for this present site!

HINDMARSH: A pretty speech, colonel! But I have given you an order! As governor of this colony, I demand that you carry it out!

LIGHT: There are some things more awe-inspiring than the commands of a governor! One of these is the trust of the people!

HINDMARSH: People?

LIGHT: Yes . . . the land-holders in this colony, who have justified their faith in my choice by spending thousands of pounds on their holdings! They are confident in the future of this capital! The removal of the city site at this late hour will mean ruin and bankruptcy for these good folk . . .

HINDMARSH: Nonsense . . .

LIGHT: Will you think it nonsense, sir, if they rise up against you and show . . . perhaps by bloodshed . . . what I am trying to proclaim in peace?

HINDMARSH *(rising temper):* You dare threaten me?

LIGHT: Threaten you? No, sir! I am trying to protect you . . .

HINDMARSH: Protect me?

LIGHT: From your own jealous and selfish whims! From the consequences of your own obstinacy!

HINDMARSH *jumps to his feet, almost apoplectic with rage.*

HINDMARSH: Do you realize whom you're addressing? I

happen to be GOVERNOR of this bloody colony!

LIGHT: One would never suspect it by your language, sir!

STEVENSON: You must not talk to His Excellency like that!

LIGHT: Then let His Excellency address me in a manner befitting his position!

HINDMARSH, *having recovered his breath, thumps the table in his anger.*

HINDMARSH: I . . . I . . . I'll clap you in irons! I'll order you flogged! How dare you flout my authority . . . you impudent . . . hopping . . . landlubber!

LIGHT *reddens at this jibe at his infirmity. He stiffens with anger; his face sets; he bows to the assembly.*

LIGHT: I wish you all good afternoon! We will, I presume, continue this discussion when His Excellency recovers his temper – and his dignity!

He wheels and strides from the room. The men spring up in their seats.

MANNERS: Colonel – Please –

HINDMARSH: Step from this room and I'll order your arrest!

MANNERS: Colonel – wait – please . . .

He moves quickly to LIGHT's *side and lays a hand on his arm.* LIGHT *halts.*

LIGHT *(coldly):* Am I to understand that His Excellency regrets the expression . . . impudent, hopping landlubber?

He speaks without turning. The men look at HINDMARSH, *who sinks back in his chair and grunts.*

HINDMARSH: Yes . . . yes . . .

MANNERS: Come back and sit down . . .

LIGHT *returns and takes his seat. The men do likewise. Although the tension has eased, the room is still tight with the clash of personalities.* STEVENSON *clears his throat.*

STEVENSON: Colonel . . .

LIGHT: Well?

STEVENSON: His Excellency has given you an order –

LIGHT: Which I refuse to obey!

STEVENSON: Because of the people . . .

LIGHT: Not only the people! The prerogative of moving the capital remains with a higher power than the governor!

HINDMARSH: I have full power of control in this colony!

LIGHT: The commissioners have full power of control! They gained this shortly after your sailing in the *Buffalo!*

GILLES *(to Hindmarsh):* Is this true, sir?

HINDMARSH: A pack of lies! An excuse to side-step my order!

MANNERS: Have you proof of this, colonel?

LIGHT: Summon the resident commissioner here!

HINDMARSH: Piffle! Fisher would have let me know before this! I am not to be fooled, Light. This is a malicious invention bred by your jealousy of my position here!

LIGHT *(quietly):* Whatever jealousy exists between us is solely on your side!

HINDMARSH: Prove it!

LIGHT: You have been jealous of my rank and my position from the first moment you set foot in the colony! Nor have you ever forgiven the commissioners for leaving the selection of the capital site to me! But . . . unable to vent your spite on the board, you have shown it by attempting to belittle me in every way!

HINDMARSH: Lies . . . !

LIGHT: I say that in every possible way you have deliberately held up the survey of the town!

HINDMARSH *(slowly):* Take care, Light! Such words bring you dangerously near to sedition!

LIGHT: It is more than time, sir, that we knew where we both stand! Your jealousy of me – aided by Stevenson's venomous pen and poisonous press – has gone on too long!

STEVENSON *leaps to his feet.*

STEVENSON: This is too much! I demand, sir, that your order this man's arrest! If not for your own safety – then for the safety of the colony you rule!

LIGHT *wheels on him, his voice like steel.*

LIGHT: Be warned, Stevenson! Do not fly too high! You have embroiled your governor in enough trouble! Would you add civil war to his sorrows?

STEVENSON *turns to* HINDMARSH.

STEVENSON: Sir . . .

HINDMARSH: Shut up and sit down . . .

STEVENSON, *panting with rage, resumes his seat, watching* LIGHT *with open malevolence.* HINDMARSH *addresses* LIGHT.

HINDMARSH: I've been very patient with you, colonel! I've ordered you to survey the new location at Encounter Bay! What's your answer?

LIGHT: Until I receive orders direct from the commissioners – no!

There is a small agitated pause. HINDMARSH *rises slowly to his feet . . . and his tone is like the roll of drums.*

HINDMARSH: Colonel William Light! As Governor of the Colony of South Australia, I order your arrest on three charges! Of insulting a superior officer in the execution of his duty to the Crown! Of deliberate and calculated disobedience to your Governor's orders! Of making libellous statements against the Crown and attempting to undermine its authority!

He raps the words.

Stevenson! Call a marine!

STEVENSON *springs quickly to his feet and crosses to the right hand door. But, as he reaches it, it opens. The housekeeper pushes a paper into his hand with a whisper. During the ensuing dialogue,* STEVENSON *opens the enclosure and reads it. Meanwhile,* LIGHT *is on his feet.*

LIGHT: One moment, sir! I have no doubt that this is as good a way as any to rid yourself of a very irritating thorn in your flesh! But have you considered the commissioners . . .

HINDMARSH: I'll take full responsibility!

LIGHT: Already they are gravely displeased with many of

your actions in this colony! I urge you to think carefully before –

And now STEVENSON, *at the door, gives a cry of dismay.*

STEVENSON: Sir . . .

He is staring with ashen face at the message. Slowly he looks up at the governor.

HINDMARSH: Man! What ails you? What is it?

STEVENSON: This note . . . a runner just brought it from . . . Encounter Bay . . .

HINDMARSH: Encounter Bay?

STEVENSON *(huskily):* There's been an accident . . . Judge Jeffcott . . . Captain Blenkinsop . . .

HINDMARSH: What about them?

STEVENSON: They had concluded their business and were intent upon exploring the Murray mouth. A sudden gale sprung up and . . . their boat overturned . . .

As they stare at him, he comes slowly forward and puts the note in front of HINDMARSH.

HINDMARSH *(sharply):* Were they . . . injured?

STEVENSON: Dead . . . ! Both drowned . . .

With a sharp breath, HINDMARSH *scoops up the note and glances at the message. The men have risen to their feet in consternation. Very slowly,* HINDMARSH *crumples the note in his fingers and slumps down in his chair. He tries to speak, then licks his dry lips and mutters.*

HINDMARSH: Jeffcott . . . dead . . . ! Of all places . . . Encounter Bay . . . !

There is a moment of complete stillness. Then LIGHT *picks up the survey order and tears it in half – in quarters. He faces* HINDMARSH *and speaks very slowly.*

LIGHT: And that, sir . . . was your idea of a safe and navigable harbour!

No one moves . . . the curtain falls slowly.

Act Two

SCENE 1

Bank of the river Torrens, six months later. From a grove of gum trees and stunted yucca, a green bank is seen. The time is about four o'clock in the afternoon.

LINDA *and* LIGHT *are discovered. She is standing against a tree stump, holding a bunch of wattle bloom.* LIGHT *is some little distance away, putting quick, deft finishing touches to a drawing on a sketching pad. He looks older, more tired. The gentle hush of late autumn is spread over the scene.* LIGHT *lifts his pencil, scrutinizes the sketch, then shakes his head.*

LIGHT: It's hopeless!
LINDA: Let me see it.
LIGHT: No, no . . . it's nothing but a poor caricature!
He whips the paper from the block and tears it in half, dropping the pieces beside him on the bank.
LINDA: Try again.
LIGHT: No. You must be tired, Linda. And the light is fading. Come . . . rest a while.
LINDA *corsses and sits on the grass beside him. There is a comfortable little silence. Presently she speaks.*
LINDA: Isn't it quiet, Will?
LIGHT: Wonderful! I never realized there could be such peace . . . such stillness.
LINDA: We might be a thousand miles away from the colony . . .
LIGHT: How I wish we were!
As LINDA *looks up.*
Oh, Linda – I'm so desperately tired of it all! So weary of the bitterness – the jealousy! Perhaps I'm getting old – losing fire . . .
LINDA *(smiling):* Nonsense . . .
LIGHT: This is all I want now . . . peace . . . stillness . . . pause to rest and talk and listen.

LINDA *(gently):* Will . . .

LIGHT: Yes?

LINDA: You're working too hard.

LIGHT: Perhaps . . .

There is a silence. LINDA *speaks a trifle anxiously.*

LINDA: Is it your health, Will?

LIGHT: No . . .

LINDA: Sure?

LIGHT: In truth, Linda – I am not sick so much in body as in mind. Time was when I took pride in my work – when I welcomed each new day for my labour. But now . . .

LINDA: Now?

LIGHT: I cannot shake off a depression. A sense of utter futility . . .

LINDA: Futility? Oh, Will . . . has overwork sapped your imagination as well as your strength? What of your dreams?

LIGHT: A frail foundation for happiness!

LINDA: Not when they come true! Why, from this very struggle you are raising a lasting monument to your name!

LIGHT: Who will remember a poor surveyor . . . a petty official?

LINDA: They will remember his work!

LIGHT: Oh, Linda . . . if only it grows as I planned! A white city of wide streets, set against the hills and swept clean with the fresh sea winds! A city of sunshine and freedom and the laughter of little children . . . If only I can carry it out!

LINDA: You will!

LIGHT: If only I could be sure!

LINDA: Within a few days, Mr. Kingston returns with the extra help you sought from the commissioners in London.

LIGHT: Yes! With this behind me, nothing can stand in my way!

LINDA: There is the governor . . .

LIGHT: Hindmarsh? He may not be here to oppose me!
LINDA *(surprised)*: Why not?
LIGHT: When my deputy-surveyor sailed for London, he had two duties to perform. One was to obtain additional help for the surveys . . .
LINDA: And the other?
LIGHT *(slowly):* Kingston was to place a record of Hindmarsh's muddling incompetence before the commissioners – and ask for his recall!

He is excited, eager. But there is no enthusiasm in LINDA*'s face. She rises slowly to her feet.* LIGHT *says in surprise.*

Linda . . .
LINDA: Yes?
LIGHT: I thought you'd be delighted at the news! With Hindmarsh gone, my biggest obstacle is removed.
LINDA: True . . . but . . .
LIGHT: But what?

LINDA *turns to face him. She speaks quietly.*

LINDA: Such a pity it could not have come about some other way. Like this, it seems to smack of . . . treachery.
LIGHT: But surely you realize this colony will never progress while Hindmarsh remains governor?
LINDA: I realize it very well.
LIGHT: Yet you disapprove of what I've done?

LINDA *makes a little puzzled, bewildered movement with her hand.*

LINDA: I don't know. Once everything was so clear in my mind. Now . . .
LIGHT: Yes?
LINDA: Affection and principle oppose each other so bitterly. I am confused . . .

LIGHT *rises to his feet and crosses to her. He speaks gently.*

LIGHT: Linda . . .
LINDA: Yes?
LIGHT: Can I ever hope to match your perfection?
LINDA *(half smiling):* You can ask that? Knowing me all these months?

LIGHT: I have valued your friendship much too dearly to search for faults.

Some hidden meaning in his tone causes her to turn away. She speaks quickly.

LINDA: It has been all so pleasant, our liking the same things. Books, and music, and poetry. It has been a true companionship . . .

LIGHT *(quietly):* No, Linda . . .

He turns her round very gently.

For me . . . all this has gone deeper than mere companionship . . .

She does not look at him.

I have been waiting to tell you this for so long . . . since that night, months ago, when you played my song. I knew . . . then . . .

LINDA: Will . . .

LIGHT: When I told you I was sick in mind, it was the truth! I have had no peace, sleeping or waking! *(His voice slows.)* I love you very deeply, Linda.

She stands with bowed head and LIGHT *cries out, almost in pain.*

Have you nothing to say?

Slowly LINDA *looks up. Her voice is quiet, too quiet, as though she kept too tight a rein on herself.*

LINDA: Between us, there can be no talk of love!

LIGHT: You must know how I feel!

LINDA: If there is love, we must be strong! We must cast it out . . .

LIGHT: No, Linda, no! Oh, my dearest one, there is so little happiness in life! Love makes that happiness! If we cast out love, what remains?

LINDA *cries out, almost harshly.*

LINDA: Trust remains! And honour!

LIGHT *(bitterly):* Trust! Honour! To you those words come so easily!

LINDA: How can you say that!

LIGHT: You talk of companionship! What use is that to me? Oh, Linda! If you could but know the strength of my love — the agony and bitter hunger of it! Could you be so steadfast then?

LINDA *looks at him and there is gentle pain in her voice as she speaks.*

LINDA: And you think I know nothing of these things?

LIGHT: How can you?

LINDA: Dear God! Am I hewn out of solid rock! I have thoughts and desires and passions even as you! Oh, Will . . . now I will tell you something I have never breathed to a living soul . . .

LIGHT *(softly):* Yes . . . ?

LINDA: Ever since I was little, I have read my Bible before I slept at night. Once there was a time when I read the simple childish verse . . . but that time is gone.

She looks at him, head high, almost challengingly and the burning naked passion in her tone quivers and trembles.

Shall I tell you what I read now? The Song of Solomon! It has the very words that keep singing in my heart! "Let him kiss me with the kisses of his mouth, for thy love is better than wine!" Oh, my dearest heart, see how I know . . . chapter and verse! "His left hand is under my head and his right hand doth embrace me . . . "

She stops, head high, her breast rising and falling.

LIGHT *(gently):* Oh, my darling . . .

LINDA: Now do you understand!

LIGHT: Yes . . . but before . . . How could I when you gave me no sign?

LINDA: And you think it was simple! To feel your touch on my arm set my blood pounding . . . to talk of companionship . . . when my very soul cries out for the strength of your love!

Suddenly, she buries her head in her hands, almost in sudden shame at her confession. She turns away as LIGHT *speaks gently.*

LIGHT: Linda . . .

And when she does not speak.

You have known of this . . . for long?

LINDA *(a whisper):* Weeks . . . months . . .

LIGHT: Why didn't you tell me?

LINDA *turns to him, speaks with trembling fervour.*

LINDA: What right had I?

LIGHT: Don't speak of rights!

LINDA: We must!

LIGHT: What are petty rights and wrongs compared to our love! In the past, I made a mistake! Is my punishment to continue?

LINDA: There is nothing we can do.

LIGHT: Yes! We can start afresh! Take our happiness together!

LINDA: Such happiness is not for us!

LIGHT: We love each other!

LINDA: But you are not free to love . . .

In passionate agony, LIGHT *thrusts out both hands.*

LIGHT: Dear God! Are there chains about my wrists?

LINDA *(slowly):* No . . . only about your heart!

LIGHT, *stricken at the bitter truth of her words, turns away. Linda says gently.*

I should not have said that . . .

LIGHT: It is I who should ask your forgiveness. I forgot your greatness, Linda . . .

LINDA *(slowly):* Yet at this moment, I would change places with the meanest wench in the colony!

As LIGHT *turns slowly and looks at her, she goes on.*

Then I could come to you boldly, regardless of the consequences . . . the shabby wreck of two lives . . . yours . . . mine . . .

There is a pause. Then LIGHT *speaks, his tone sombre with humility.*

LIGHT: Help me, Linda. Tell me what I must do.

LINDA: You must promise me one thing. This must never happen again.

LIGHT: I cannot promise that . . . I cannot!

LINDA: You must!

LIGHT *(in bitter agony)*: Do you ask me to be more than human!

LINDA: I ask you to think of me! Rather than endure this scene again, it would be better never to meet . . .
LIGHT: No!
LINDA: Then you promise?
LIGHT *(slowly):* If it must be so . . . yes.

She reaches forward and presses his hands, a little gesture of comfort. Then, crossing to the tree stump, she picks up her parasol. Then she turns.

LINDA: It is late. I must hurry home.
LIGHT: Wait . . .

He picks up his sketching pad from the grass.

LINDA: No, Will, I must go alone.
LIGHT: Alone? But it grows dark . . .
LINDA: I can find my way easily.
LIGHT: I would not dream of such a thing! Let me . . .
LINDA: We must not be seen together!
LIGHT: Why not?
LINDA: It is papa. He has forbidden that I see you except in our house.
LIGHT: But –
LINDA: Had papa not been away, I would never have dared come here alone this afternoon.
LIGHT *(slowly):* It is this gossip?
LINDA: Yes.
LIGHT: But surely your father trusts you . . . ?
LINDA: It is not so much papa . . .
LIGHT: Well?
LINDA: These whispered stories of our meetings have reached the ears of the governor . . .
LIGHT: Hindmarsh?
LINDA: A vindictive man, Will . . . and dangerous! This gossip could give him a weapon against which we have no defence!
LIGHT: No . . . Even Hindmarsh could not stoop so low . . .
LINDA: We must give him no opportunity! That's why I must go back . . . alone.
LIGHT: But . . . when will I see you again?
LINDA *(smiling):* Very soon.

LIGHT *(insistent)*: Yes . . . but when?

LINDA: Papa will be home in a few days. Perhaps we could arrange some music at our house. I will ask mama.

LIGHT: I cannot wait that long. Could I call tomorrow evening?

LINDA *(gently):* You must be patient, Will. All the years are ahead of us . . . there is so much time to plan and . . .

She stops abruptly as something catches in LIGHT*'s throat. Again his body is racked with the stifled paroxysm of coughing. He fumbles for his handkerchief, presses it quickly to his lips, wiping them rapidly, furtively. Still holding the handkerchief, he turns, breathless, husky.*

LIGHT: This . . . this chill night air . . .

He stops, conscious of LINDA*'s horror-stricken eyes fixed on the handkerchief in his hand. He makes a movement to stuff it in his pocket, but* LINDA *springs forward.*

LINDA: Will . . . ? *(sharply)* Will . . . show me that handkerchief?

LIGHT *turns from her and thrusts it into his pocket, speaking as he does so . . . almost harshly.*

LIGHT: No, no . . . ! *(then, as though realizing the futility of subterfuge, he says slowly)* There's . . . nothing we can do . . . Dr. Woodeford said so himself . . . weeks ago . . .

LINDA *(slowly)*: Oh, my darling . . . ! But . . . why didn't you tell me?

LIGHT *turns to her. He smiles gently.*

LIGHT: Of what use, Linda? You could have been no . . . kinder?

LINDA *stares at him. She says very quietly.*

LINDA: No . . . only . . . wiser . . .

Her eyes look steadfastly into his face as the curtain falls slowly.

Act Two

SCENE 2

Interior of LIGHT*'s cottage, one week later. A room built of weatherboard, lined inside. It has few furnishings, but these show taste and discernment. There are several good water-colours on the walls. The furniture is massive and somehow suggestive of a ship. Against the back wall is a sideboard on which stands a jug of water and several glasses. A fireplace is downstage left and near this is a heavy seaman's chest. On the table, near centre, a large paraffin lamp burns. A small fire is blazing in the fireplace. There are two entrances – right wall upstage and left down past the fireplace.*

When the curtain rises, it is about nine o'clock of an autumn night. A woman is bending over the fire, poking at the embers. This is MARIA GANDY, LIGHT*'s housekeeper. She rises, stands looking around the room then brings a chair close to the fire. At that moment, a knock comes to the door up right. She moves across and opens it.* LINDA *enters, followed by* TRAVERS FINNIS. *Their faces are set . . . worried . . .*

FINNIS: The outer door was open, Maria . . . we came straight through . . .

LINDA: Did the colonel get our note?

MARIA: Yes, Miss Linda. He should be here directly. But you are early.

FINNIS *(sombre):* I know.

LINDA: How is the colonel?

MARIA: Far from well. He rose from his bed but ten minutes ago.

FINNIS: His wound troubles him?

MARIA *(shakes her head):* It is the cough . . . this morning he could barely speak. He caught a chill a week ago, sketching on the river bank. It settled on his chest.

FINNIS: I wondered why he didn't get down to the boat to meet Kingston this morning.

MARIA: This morning, the pain was too great for him to move across the room.

LINDA: Has he been like this very long?

MARIA: It was bad yesterday. Then, this afternoon, your message came. It was wonderful to see the difference it made . . . he seemed like a new man!

FINNIS *turns miserably to the fireplace.*

FINNIS: God help me . . .

MARIA: I'll knock on the colonel's door and tell him you're both here.

She crosses and exits down right. LINDA *moves around the room, then takes off her shawl and hangs it on the back of a chair near left hand door. Meanwhile* FINNIS *stares unhappily into the fireplace. Suddenly he takes from his pocket an official envelope.*

FINNIS *(bitterly):* If only I had the courage to burn this thing.

LINDA *(wearily):* Someone else would have to break the news to him. You are the colonel's best friend. It will come easier from you than from Hindmarsh.

FINNIS: It's because I'm his best friend I find it so devilishly difficult! Why else do you think I called on you to help me?

There is a pause, heavy . . . brooding with anxiety. LINDA, *standing with clasped hands, speaks quietly.*

LINDA: Mr. Finnis . . .

He turns.

There is no chance whatsoever of this cruel order being rescinded?

FINNIS: No.

And suddenly he bursts out.

Miss Linda, I can't do this thing! It's asking too much of me!

LINDA: I loathe the task even more than you do. But rather than let Hindmarsh announce this news, I'll tell the colonel . . . myself!

She puts out her hand.

Give it to me!

FINNIS *hesitates, then slips the document back into his pocket.*

FINNIS: I'll do it.

The opening of the right entrance door attracts their attention. LIGHT *enters. He has dressed hurriedly and untidily. He limps forward, his face grey and drawn with pain. Only his eyes are bright and burning as with some inward fire. About his whole appearance is a forced, unnatural animation, as though some feverish anticipation is urging his sick body on to this great moment. His face lights as he comes down.*

LIGHT: Finnis! And Miss Linda! I did not expect such a pleasure!

FINNIS: I asked Miss Linda to come with me . . .

LIGHT: Naturally! It is only right my two closest friends should be present on such a grand occasion . . .

And now he is moving chairs to the fire, fussing with his jacket, all the time keeping up a running fire of eager, excited chatter.

And how is Mr. Kingston, Travers? I must present my apologies for not being down at the boat to meet him. But this wretched chill continues to trouble me, somehow I cannot throw it off! But it's this wretched inactivity that has fostered my illness . . . now that Kingston has returned with all the help I need, we can get to work again! I'll forget this ailing body in the planning and building ahead!

And now he turns to them.

Now, tell me the news! I suppose it would be too much to expect that the commissioners have agreed to my full complement of surveyors?

No one speaks. For the first time, LIGHT *sees their dark and shadowed faces.*

Is anything the matter? It . . . IS good news?

Slowly, FINNIS *shakes his head.* LIGHT *gives a little gasp of dismay and, reaching out an unsteady hand, grips the top of the chair. He speaks quietly.*

Travers . . . ? The commissioners haven't . . . refused?

FINNIS *(slowly):* Yes, Will. I'm afraid they have.

LIGHT *stares at the couple incredulously. One sees that this is the last possible thing he expected. He speaks unsteadily.*

LIGHT: Some mistake . . . surely . . . ?

FINNIS: No.

LIGHT: Then what . . . what . . . ?

His voice trails away. FINNIS *starts to speak, but the look on his friend's face silences the words on his lips. It is* LINDA *who speaks quietly . . . bravely.*

LINDA: Mr. Fisher sent you a letter, Will. From the commissioners. It . . . explains everything. Mr. Finnis has it.

LIGHT *turns to* FINNIS, *who takes the document from his pocket and hands it to his friend.* LIGHT *takes it, breaks the seal and opens the document. He slants it toward the lamplight, closes his eyes, shakes his head, then hands the document to* LINDA.

LIGHT: Read it for me. My eyes are weak tonight. And Fisher's handwriting was always execrable!

LINDA *takes the document and begins to read in a low, clear voice.*

LINDA: To Colonel William Light, Surveyor-General of South Australia . . .

Acting under orders from the commissioners I am addressing this letter to you, calling on you to state in writing, within one week, whether you will undertake to effect a running survey of a hundred and fifty square miles . . .

LIGHT: Running survey? What is Fisher talking about? I am not surveying a local fair ground.

FINNIS *(quietly):* There is more to come . . .

LIGHT *turns to* LINDA, *who continues gently.*

LINDA: The commissioners trust that Colonel Light will pledge himself to obey the required conditions. But, if it is not done in the week allowed, Mr. Kingston is to be notified that the supervision of the entire survey has . . . devolved on him . . .

A gasp from LIGHT. LINDA*'s tone trembles ever so slightly as she continues.*

LINDA: . . . and that Mr. Kingston is henceforth to act on all instructions given from time to time to the surveyor-general . . . and exercise all powers attached to that appointment . . .

Her voice dies away. LIGHT *is open mouthed, almost gaping in his incredulous amazement. When he speaks his voice is a dry croak.*

LIGHT: What does all this mean?

FINNIS *does not look at him as he replies.*

FINNIS: The commissioners consider your present method of survey too slow and too costly, Will. Unless you are prepared to change it, you are to be suspended from your position of surveyor-general . . . and Kingston assumes full control in your place.

There is a moment's pause, then LIGHT*'s whole body sags limply into a chair. He covers his face with his hands.* LINDA *and* FINNIS *spring to his side.*

LINDA: Will . . .

FINNIS: Are you all right?

LIGHT *removes his hands from his face. He makes an obvious effort at self-control and when he speaks his voice is steadier.*

LIGHT: It was just . . . the first shock . . .

He raises a haggard face to FINNIS.

So . . . Hindmarsh has the last laugh, after all?

FINNIS: If it is any comfort to you, Hindmarsh goes too! The commissioners intimated that much to Kingston!

LIGHT *(bitter):* My clever deputy-surveyor appears in very good favour!

FINNIS: Small profit he will make from it, Will! I can speak for the entire staff when I say there isn't a single man who will take orders from Kingston!

LIGHT: They may think differently when his appointment is announced!

He stands suddenly upright.

You may take this message back to Kingston – that I do not need five minutes to consider such a proposal, let alone a week! I would never dream of continuing office under such humiliating circumstances!

He turns away. LINDA, *suffering with him, cries out bitterly.*

LINDA: So much for justice! So much for honourable reward! You have lived for this colony – built into it the very strength from your body! And this is how you are repaid!

LIGHT: Hush, Linda . . .

LINDA *wheels on* FINNIS.

LINDA: Did Mr. Kingston tell the commissioners the true reason for these delays they criticize? How the colonel had to fight the governor every step of the way? How most of the journeys had to be done on foot, cutting through the tangled scrubland? Did Mr. Kingston explain how bad food and poor wages turned the survey workers from willing labourers to discontented ruffians – and how the colonel, in a desperate effort to push on the surveys, paid the men out of his own pocket?

FINNIS: Have no fear, Miss Linda! If Kingston has not explained these things, I certainly will!

LIGHT *(wearily):* I doubt if it will do much good, Travers . . .

FINNIS: Why not?

LIGHT: The commissioners have already made up their minds I have neglected my duties and bungled my appointment!

FINNIS: It's shameful!

LIGHT: Please – let us talk no more about it. I am weary of the whole sorry business!

He resumes his seat and sits staring into the fire. A silence falls on the little group. It is FINNIS *who breaks it, speaking rather hesitantly.*

FINNIS: Will . . .

As LIGHT *raises his head.*

Forgive an old friend this liberty. But . . . what are your plans?

LIGHT: No doubt something will turn up for me.

FINNIS: And until then?

LIGHT: I shall write my defence of these charges so that the commissioners may know the truth!

FINNIS: Of course, but . . . what about money?

He pauses and, as LIGHT *does not speak, he hurries on.*

When carrying out your duties, you've sacrificed your personal fortune. How are you going to live now?

LIGHT: Once my name is cleared, I can go to work.

FINNIS *(quietly):* Colonel – in my pocket are two letters – resignations – mine and Mr. Houghton's. They were written this afternoon. They go to Fisher first thing tomorrow.

LIGHT: But what will you do?

FINNIS: Nixon and Jacob are resigning with us. Together we mean to start a private firm. We should like to name it . . . "Light, Finnis and Company".

LIGHT *does not speak, but slowly he gets to his feet.*

Well?

LIGHT *puts out his hand and* FINNIS *grips it.* LIGHT *says very simply.*

LIGHT: My friend. My very good friend.

There is a moment's silence, then almost an embarrassment. FINNIS *drops the hand and speaks quickly to cover his emotion.*

FINNIS: Then it is settled! I am to see Houghton tonight . . .

LIGHT: You waste no time . . .

FINNIS: Why delay once the course is decided?

He turns to LINDA.

Thank you, Miss Linda – and have no fear about tonight.

He crosses to the door.

Take courage, Will. I think this is the beginning of better times. And watch your health! Now we need you more than ever!

He exits. As the door closes behind him, LIGHT *turns to* LINDA.

LIGHT: What did he mean?
LINDA: Now that you are free from interference . . .
LIGHT: No, no! His other remark. That you must have no fear about tonight?
LINDA *turns away.*
LINDA: It was nothing.
LIGHT *(quietly):* Linda . . .
She turns.
LINDA: Yes?
LIGHT: Does Mr. Manners know you are here?
LINDA: Papa was summoned to the Government House . . .
LIGHT: And during his absence, you came?
LINDA: Yes.
LIGHT: And against your father's wishes. Linda, that was so very foolish . . .
LINDA: Not for me, Will. The issue was simple. You needed me.
She takes his hand and leads him to his chair.
And so . . . I am here.
LIGHT: So . . . from the bitterest misfortune, some good comes. Have I not found my truest friends?
LINDA: There should be so many more!
LIGHT: Two faithful friends are as much as any man can ask . . . or deserve!
LIGHT *is seated.* LINDA *drops on to the hassock at his feet.*
LINDA: I have done so little . . .
LIGHT: You have done everything, Linda.
LINDA: You give me too much honour, sir.
LIGHT: No. These past days, lying in that quiet room, I have come to know the truth. One man's strength is only so much – and I have reached the limit.
LINDA: I will not listen to such nonsense! This is not the man I know!
LIGHT *(gently):* Tonight, Linda, you see me for what I am! No brave figure of defiance, but a poor creature near broken by ill health and misfortune. A man clinging desperately to the one unchanging thing in a world of deceit and treachery!

LINDA: Deceit and treachery cannot last, Will! Your work will remain . . . long after men like Fisher and Hindmarsh are forgotten!

LIGHT: So I must live in the future? I cannot do it, Linda . . .

LINDA *(gently):* Will . . .

LIGHT: Surely it is not too much to ask for some little happiness now? Am I always destined for discouragement?

LINDA *reaches up and takes his hand in hers.*

LINDA *(very gently):* Every great and lasting achievement is born of sorrow and heartbreak. Lift up your eyes, Will! The very mountain tops in all their majesty were but wrought by the tortured agony of the earth!

LIGHT *(softly):* Linda . . .

LINDA: Shame on you, sir. Are you the first man to suffer persecution for your ideals? Think of Michelangelo – blinded, deserted, yet hewing in stone beauty matchless and unconquerable! And Shelley, reviled by his fellows, snared by his passions, embittered . . . lonely! And Keats – unhappy Keats – shackled by ill health, driven to his grave by callous critics, who in their jealousy shut their ears to words that echoed the very music of the spheres!

LIGHT *rises slowly to his feet. Gently, still holding her hands, he brings* LINDA *up with him. The inspiration has flooded back into his face.*

LIGHT: You believe in me . . . as much as that?

LINDA: More! Much more!

LIGHT: And you say you've done so little? Is it so little to fill a barren, empty life with the new inspiration to live . . . to fight?

LINDA: That quality was yours long before you met me!

LIGHT: And you think it could have stood alone under such adversity? Oh, Linda dearest . . . if anything were to take you from me . . .

LINDA: Nothing will take me from you, Will. Whenever you need me, I will be here . . . always . . .

There comes a light tap on the door. LIGHT *and* LINDA *exchange a look. The tap sounds again.* MARIA*'s voice sounds offstage.*

MARIA: Colonel . . .

LIGHT: What is it, Maria?

MARIA *(offstage):* His Excellency is here, sir.

LINDA *(soft alarm):* Hindmarsh!

LIGHT: He must not find you here!

LINDA *(steadily):* I do not fear the governor's malice . . .

LIGHT: You cannot afford to be mixed up in any trouble, Linda! Go home as quickly as you can . . .

The tap on the door sounds again.

MARIA *(offstage):* His Excellency is waiting, sir.

LIGHT *(softly):* Annie is in the kitchen. She will take you across the paddock. Now . . . hurry!

He presses her hands and ushers her quickly through the other door. The tap on the door, more urgently.

MARIA *(offstage):* Sir . . .

LIGHT *(impatiently):* One moment . . .

From offstage comes HINDMARSH*'s impatient voice.*

HINDMARSH: Stand aside, woman!

MARIA *(offstage):* But, your Excellency . . .

HINDMARSH *(offstage):* I'm going in!

HINDMARSH *enters. It is obvious that the governor has been drinking. His small eyes are bloodshot and there is the faintest slurring of his speech when he talks. He stands just inside the door, hands behind his back – the captain on his quarter-deck, balancing himself on his stocky legs. He looks steadily at* LIGHT *and speaks with a slow malevolence.*

HINDMARSH: A word with you!

LIGHT: Well, sir?

HINDMARSH: No doubt you wonder why I'm here?

LIGHT *(wearily):* If you have come to acquaint me with the commissioners' ultimatum, then, sir, you are too late!

HINDMARSH: Apparently bad news travels fast?

LIGHT: Aye . . . even to the position of governor!

HINDMARSH: What do you mean?

LIGHT: Since Kingston's return, I understand that we are both in the same unhappy position!

Now HINDMARSH *strides forward. He is smouldering with the blackest of rages, all the more dangerous for its repression. He speaks slowly.*

HINDMARSH: This was to have been a great occasion for you, Light . . .

LIGHT: In what way, sir?

HINDMARSH: Do you deny that my deposition is due to any other cause but your lies? Lies which Kingston has placed, at your bidding, before the commissioners? Do you imagine I am blind to the fact that all this is but the fruits of months of intrigue?

LIGHT: I deny that, sir!

HINDMARSH: Why? I'll tell you why? Because the whole dirty plan has suddenly recoiled on your own head! Because, in setting a snare for another's feet, you've fouled your own!

LIGHT *turns away. He speaks quietly.*

LIGHT: I have no wish to discuss the matter.

HINDMARSH: Because the words leave a bitter taste in your mouth?

LIGHT *swings round on his tormentor, his face pale and angry.*

LIGHT: Sir – I beg of you! State your business and go away!

HINDMARSH: When I choose!

LIGHT: In God's name! Can't you see I am not myself tonight?

HINDMARSH *(with slow venom):* I scarcely imagined you would be! Malice and enmity are slow poisons, my fine fellow! But they wither the soul, not the body!

LIGHT: How well you state it, sir!

HINDMARSH: State what?

LIGHT: Your own pitiable case! You talk of poisons that wither the heart – when your own soul is curdled black with hatred!

HINDMARSH: That's enough!

LIGHT: Even now – with the tide of adversity rising above

your own head – you come here to gloat! To wring the last drop of bitter relish from a companion's misfortune!

HINDMARSH *(snarling):* Companion? Never!

LIGHT *(turning away):* I assure you, sir . . . a figure of speech.

HINDMARSH: To the devil with your figures of speech! I'll have none of them! I call a spade a spade!

LIGHT *wheels back on him.*

LIGHT: And you have very successfully dug your own grave with it!

HINDMARSH: If I have, you lie deep beside me!

LIGHT *stares at* HINDMARSH, *then he speaks very quietly.*

LIGHT: Aye . . . there's the tragedy of it. So much we might have accomplished together! Here we had virgin soil – to till and sow and watch grow fruitful! But in their blindness, the commissioners must needs yoke alien beasts to the plough, so that even the first furrows were twisted . . . useless . . .

HINDMARSH, *listening to this, waves a contemptuous hand.*

HINDMARSH: Spare me the pious prattle, colonel! I've not come here to listen to that!

LIGHT: Why have you come?

HINDMARSH: To give you warning!

Something in the other's tone makes LIGHT *say slowly.*

LIGHT: What now?

HINDMARSH: In spite of your studied knavery, I must remind you that I am still governor of this colony until such time as Gawler arrives here . . .

LIGHT: Does anyone dispute the fact?

And now HINDMARSH *is watching him closely with those small, red eyes.*

HINDMARSH: In such capacity – however temporary – I am responsible for the . . . morals of the officers who serve under me . . .

LIGHT: I no longer serve under you!

HINDMARSH *(pouncing):* Then you accuse yourself?
LIGHT: Sir . . .
HINDMARSH: Out of your own mouth, Colonel Light! Out of your own mouth!
LIGHT: No . . .
HINDMARSH: So ready with your silken words! So glib with the phrases that roll from the tongue! I knew that sooner or later such cleverness must trip you up!
LIGHT: I said nothing . . .
HINDMARSH: Nothing! Why man . . . here in your own house you have brazenly admitted what is being whispered in every tap room in the town! And you have not even the common decency to deny your shady intrigues!

HINDMARSH *stops. There is a silence, a swollen, bursting silence tight with the quivering hatred between these two men.* LIGHT *walks straight up to the governor until they almost touch, but* HINDMARSH *stands his ground.* LIGHT *speaks with a curious repressed coldness.*

LIGHT: Even a tongue loosened by liquor can go too far! I must ask you to apologize for that last remark!
HINDMARSH: So . . . it would seem I have touched a very tender spot!

LIGHT *raises his arm and points to the door.*

LIGHT: Get out of this house!
HINDMARSH: Do you realize who I am?
LIGHT: Go! Go before I forget!
HINDMARSH: I shall go when I'm finished. I've come here . . .
LIGHT: Save your breath, Hindmarsh! I fully realize why you came here . . .
HINDMARSH: So?
LIGHT: It was not, as I first believed, to make me a target for your twisted satisfaction! In that I flattered you! Only now do I see the real depths of your infamy . . .
HINDMARSH: Words . . . !
LIGHT: You mean to take back to the commissioners this

lying tale, as proof of the shabby reputation of your accuser! And this you hope to do before the shaky mantle of authority slips from your shoulders!

HINDMARSH: Then you deny these rumours?

LIGHT *measures* HINDMARSH *with a look, then turns away in contempt.*

LIGHT: I would not even waste the breath!

HINDMARSH *looks at him for a long moment, then he crosses to the door, speaking as he goes.*

HINDMARSH: I think you may change your mind about that, sir!

He flings open the door and calls to someone outside.

Come in here!

HENRY MANNERS *enters. He carries something behind him and there is hostility in the set of his shoulders.* LIGHT *stares at him in surprise.*

LIGHT: Sir . . . ?

HINDMARSH: We arrived together. I requested the first interview.

LIGHT *turns to* MANNERS *and gestures to a chair.*

LIGHT: This is an unexpected pleasure, sir . . .

MANNERS *(still standing):* I should rather term it an unpleasant duty.

LIGHT: Unpleasant?

MANNERS: No other term can be applied to the rising tide of gossip within this colony, linking my daughter's name with your own!

LIGHT: His Excellency brought you here on this matter?

MANNERS *(coldly):* Like myself, His Excellency is deeply concerned!

LIGHT *turns away.*

LIGHT *(with irony):* Naturally!

MANNERS: Is that all you have to say?

LIGHT *turns – he speaks quietly.*

LIGHT: Only this, sir! You do your daughter a grave injustice listening to such idle gossip!

MANNERS: Were it but gossip . . . yes!

From behind his back he thrusts out the two pieces of the torn sketch.

MANNERS: This evening, His Excellency showed these to me! They were found by Mr. Orchard on the river bank!

LIGHT: Well?

MANNERS: Do you deny this is your work?

LIGHT: I have no reason to deny anything, sir. It is true I met Miss Linda there . . .

HINDMARSH: You see? He admits it!

LIGHT *(turning on* HINDMARSH *like steel):* Of course I admit it, sir. Why not? *(He quietens, bows to* MANNERS.) I have the privilege of your daughter's friendship.

MANNERS: And is that all?

There is a pause. MANNERS *adds sharply.*

Well?

LIGHT: I would prefer to answer that question . . . in private!

HINDMARSH *(sneering):* No doubt, colonel! Dirty linen washes best behind the closed door!

LIGHT: Sir . . . I beg you not to listen to this man!

MANNERS: Then answer my question!

LIGHT *draws a deep breath.*

LIGHT: Very well! It was not until a week ago that I told Miss Linda of my deep affection for her. But she refused even to listen to me . . .

MANNERS: I should think not!

LIGHT: Miss Linda warned me that, if ever I spoke so, she would never see me again. I gave her my solemn promise!

MANNERS: You have kept it?

LIGHT: On my word as a gentleman!

There is a pause. MANNERS, *uncertain how to continue in the face of* LIGHT*'s sincere avowal, hesitates and looks at the governor.*

HINDMARSH *(thinly):* Have a care, Manners . . .

MANNERS: Sir, I must accept this gentleman's word.

HINDMARSH: Does that mean so very much? What is your precious gentleman these days but a foppish product of the royal courts? Can you accept the word of one who has spent his days in petty intrigue and his nights posturing in a ballroom?

LIGHT, *smarting at the jibe, addresses* MANNERS.

LIGHT: I take it His Excellency speaks from his own wide experience of royal courts?

HINDMARSH *(wheeling on him, goaded):* No, by God! I speak from my experience with you, sir!

LIGHT: Rather you speak from rank jealousy!

HINDMARSH *(sneering):* Of what, may I ask?

LIGHT: Of me!

HINDMARSH *almost spits the words in his rage.*

HINDMARSH: Of you? Should I be jealous of a self-confessed libertine? A smooth-tongued lecherer!

The left-hand door opens. LINDA *stands in the entrance with* FINNIS. *It is obvious that she has heard the governor's last words.* MANNERS *swings round.*

MANNERS: Linda!

LINDA *(calmly):* Yes, papa.

MANNERS: What are you doing here?

LINDA: I was anxious about the colonel! He is in no state for such a scene . . .

MANNERS: But how could you have known . . . unless . . .

He stops. LINDA *nods very calmly. She speaks quietly.*

LINDA: Yes, papa. I was here with the colonel . . . earlier this evening.

MANNERS *stares at* LINDA *in shocked incredulity.* HINDMARSH *addresses him, gesturing to* LIGHT.

HINDMARSH: So much for this man who prates so glibly of honour and virtue! Carrying on an intrigue as sordid as any between potman and scullery wench!

LINDA *stiffens in cold anger. She turns to her father.*

LINDA: Papa, you must ask His Excellency to remember our position here!

MANNERS *looks at her with set face. He speaks slowly.*

MANNERS: Position? How can you talk of position . . . now?

LINDA *(piteously):* But I have done nothing wrong.

MANNERS: Nothing wrong? In God's name, child . . . are

you bereft of all shame . . . all decency?

LINDA: Papa, listen . . .

MANNERS: To a fresh tissue of lies? Stand aside . . .

He strides to the door. FINNIS, *who has not moved from his position at the door, speaks quietly.*

FINNIS: One moment, sir . . .

MANNERS: Not another word!

FINNIS: I think we talk at cross-purposes, sir. It is true that Miss Linda was here tonight. But I was with her.

MANNERS: You?

FINNIS: Mr. Kingston brought instructions from London — instructions which made it impossible for the colonel to continue in his appointment as surveyor-general. It was no easy decision. If ever friends were needed, it was tonight. I asked Miss Linda to accompany me here.

MANNERS *turns to* LIGHT.

MANNERS: Is this true?

LIGHT: Yes.

FINNIS: I have asked the colonel to join me in a private survey company, since I, too, have resigned!

There is a pause. MANNERS *turns to* HINDMARSH.

MANNERS: Excellency . . .

HINDMARSH: Well?

MANNERS: Surely you must have known of this?

HINDMARSH, *cornered, glowers around the room.*

HINDMARSH: Are you to be taken in by a cheap fiction, fabricated on the spur of the moment?

LINDA: Perhaps His Excellency would prefer that we brought Mr. Kingston here?

HINDMARSH: I'll see Kingston in my own time! I've enough enemies here already . . .

MANNERS *(shocked):* Enemies . . . ?

HINDMARSH, *cornered and beaten, stands with head thrust forward, malevolence in his eyes, in his voice.*

HINDMARSH: Yes, enemies! All of you — arraigned against your governor in a pretty conspiracy! Rats — gnawing at the very vitals of authority! But this isn't the first time I've faced rebellious scum! Aye . . . and whipped them to their knees . . . and spat in their faces when they've begged for mercy!

He turns and strides to the door. Then he wheels and addresses LIGHT.

On the quarter-deck, men still talk of my long memory, colonel! You'll live to regret this moment just as surely as you're born! And when I make MY report to the commissioners, your very name will stink through the length and breadth of England! Stink, do you hear me? STINK!

He spits the last words, then wheels through the door and exits. The bitter enmity of his words hangs in the air for a second then FINNIS *turns to* LIGHT.

FINNIS: Where is he going?

LIGHT: No doubt to Kingston!

FINNIS: But he's beside himself! He may do bodily harm . . .

LIGHT: Yes. I bear no great love for Kingston, but he must be warned.

FINNIS: I'll go at once.

He exits quickly after HINDMARSH. MANNERS, *genuinely shocked at the governor's outburst, turns to* LIGHT.

MANNERS: Colonel . . .

LIGHT: You must excuse His Excellency. He had been drinking.

MANNERS: Fine behaviour for the governor of a colony!

LIGHT: He holds that title but little longer, sir . . .

MANNERS: Hindmarsh?

LIGHT: Today Kingston brought news of his recall. Now, in his malice, he has no thought but retaliation.

MANNERS *hesitates a moment, then puts out his hand, which* LIGHT *takes.*

MANNERS: Forgive me, colonel.

LIGHT: I do not blame you, sir.

MANNERS: Your resignation will be a severe blow to the colony. I only trust your new career will be as successful. But take care! You have made a bitter enemy!

LIGHT: The governor's threats do not worry me. I have only one regret . . .

MANNERS: Yes?

LIGHT: It is that Miss Linda should have been involved in this unhappy scene. I can only pray it will never occur again.

MANNERS *(grimly):* I can promise you that much!

LIGHT: Such gossip, no matter how false, is not easily stifled.

MANNERS: There will be no further gossip.

LIGHT: How can you be so sure?

MANNERS *(slowly):* Because my daughter is leaving this colony.

LIGHT: Leaving?

MANNERS: She sails on the next vessel returning to England!

LINDA, *who has been listening quietly, suddenly cries out in surprise and anguish.*

LINDA: Papa . . . no!

LIGHT: Sir, I beg of you! Anything but that! It is harsh . . . unjust!

MANNERS: It is inevitable!

LIGHT: There must be some other course . . .

MANNERS: There is none. And I have made it plain to Linda, time and time again, that this state of affairs cannot continue . . .

LINDA: Papa . . .

MANNERS *turns to* LINDA, *who stares back at him, stony-faced and pale. She speaks very slowly.*

If you do this to me, I shall hate you just as long as I live!

MANNERS: Don't talk like that!

LINDA: This is no idle talk, papa! Surely you know me better than that!

MANNERS: But we do this for your own good!

LINDA: You think it good to break my heart! To make me suffer?

She turns away. MANNERS, *his face grave, his voice*

gentle, goes to her.

MANNERS: Linda . . . Linda, look at me . . .

Slowly, she raises her head.

Do you think this means nothing to us – to your mama – to me? When our very lives have been built around your happiness . . . is it so easy to send you away?

LINDA: Yet you would do this . . . willingly!

MANNERS: Not willingly, Linda. It takes courage to send away part of one's heart . . .

His voice slows . . . shadowed.

And . . . we shall be so very lonely . . .

LINDA: Then why must you do it?

MANNERS: There is no other way!

LINDA *turns away with a little moan of despair.* LIGHT, *who has been following this exchange, speaks suddenly.*

LIGHT: I think there is.

As they turn to him, he continues steadily.

There is no need to involve four lives in a decision which concerns only two . . .

He pauses and takes a breath.

Sir, I give you my solemn promise never to see or speak with Miss Linda again . . . so long as I am in this colony!

Sharply, LINDA *cries out.*

LINDA: Will . . . no!

MANNERS: Linda!

LINDA *(steadily):* I will never keep to that decision – never! It is asking too much!

MANNERS *(angrily):* I ask you to consider your future!

LINDA: If I give up this happiness, there can be no future for me . . . ever . . . anywhere!

MANNERS: But this man has a wife . . . children . . .

LINDA *(in a bitter cry, wrenched from her heart):* Do you imagine I have forgotten that?

MANNERS: And you would continue this hopeless alliance?

LINDA *looks at him with gentle compassion. She speaks quietly.*

LINDA: Not hopeless, papa . . .

But MANNERS *brushes this aside.*

MANNERS: You talk like a child!

LINDA: No, papa. I am a grown woman. And my life is my own . . . I do not choose to see it grow sour and bitter. Then why not take what life offers . . . take it with both hands . . . and live fully . . . joyously . . .

MANNERS *(bitterly):* And shamefully?

LINDA *looks at him. She speaks very gently, but with infinite wisdom. For this is the whole vindication of her change of front.*

LINDA: The years pass so swiftly. And . . . when I am old . . . who will remember such a little shame?

MANNERS *looks at her for a long moment, then he walks to the door and pauses.*

MANNERS *(very quietly):* Linda . . . I want you to come home with me.

LINDA *shakes her head.*

LINDA *(gently):* My place is here. This is my home.

MANNERS: And . . . that is your last word?

LINDA: Yes.

MANNERS, *bowed and defeated, turns to* LIGHT.

MANNERS: I can do no more, sir. The outcome is in your hands . . .

He pauses and draws a deep breath.

I ask you to remember one thing. We, also, love her very dearly.

He exits. LINDA *watches him go. Then she turns to* LIGHT. *Slowly, with infinite pity, he shakes his head.*

LIGHT: Dearest Linda . . . this is not the way.

LINDA: But, Will . . .

LIGHT: We cannot build a happiness on dishonour . . . on broken lives! You saw what this means to your father. There is your mother . . .

LINDA *(slowly):* Mama . . .

LIGHT: Oh, Linda . . . love raised upon such suffering can never endure! And have you thought about yourself? When we have forfeited all respect – all reputation – what can shield us from the cruelty of the world?

LINDA: Our love . . .

LIGHT: In a world of contempt and derision? No, dearest. Love is a gentle and precious thing. It needs contentment and happiness to flourish! Like this, it can only wither and die . . .

LINDA *(in anguish):* No . . . no . . .

She turns away with bowed head. LIGHT *picks up the shawl and places it gently across her shoulders.*

LIGHT: Go home, Linda.

LINDA: Papa will send me away . . .

LIGHT: No.

LINDA: You heard what he said . . .

LIGHT: I will speak to your father.

LINDA: He will not listen.

LIGHT: I think he will. I shall explain to him that my first survey with the new company will be private land near Morphett Vale. With so many miles between us, not even the most ill-natured rumour can flourish.

Suddenly LINDA *buries her face in her hands.* LIGHT, *his expression one of tender pain, says gently.*

Linda . . . dearest heart . . .

Then he reaches out and takes her wet hands from her face.

Dearest one – only a few precious moments are left to us. Do not waste them so.

LINDA *does not raise her head. She says brokenly, hopelessly.*

LINDA: What is left but waste?

LIGHT: Are you so blind?

LINDA: Would that I were.

She raises her head. Her eyes tragic with grief.

What can I see ahead of me? Only the bleak, barren years! Dawns without sunrise – nights without end . . .

LIGHT: And . . . I have brought you to this?

LINDA: Not you, Will! I chose my own path! My love was like some consuming fire, breaking all boundaries – reckless –

Her voice slows.

And now . . . what is left but despair?

LIGHT: No, Linda.

LINDA: This love of ours . . . what else has it given us?

LIGHT: Something so great that I feel humble even to name it, Linda. It is called Achievement.

LINDA: Your work?

LIGHT: Our work, dearest heart! Ours! Everything I am or hope to be! Everything I have done or will do! My future . . . aye, my very life itself – these things are yours!

LINDA *cannot hide the tears which flood to her eyes. As she turns her head away,* LIGHT *speaks, almost in pain.*

Don't Linda. You can be so strong . . . so brave.

LINDA: Not now! It is I who need you.

LIGHT *puts out his arms, an instinctive gesture of comforting. Head up, eyes shining,* LINDA *goes to him. Her arms slip around him. He holds her, hungrily, yet tender, and whispers.*

LIGHT: Dear God! How I dreamed to hold you like this . . .

LINDA *raises her head, looking into his eyes. With the same hungry tenderness,* LIGHT *kisses her passionately His arms tighten around her. Then slowly* LINDA*'s arms slip away from him. She gives a little sob, turns, and groping blindly feels her way to the door. There she turns, and gives* LIGHT *a last long look. Then with a short, sobbing cry, she exits.* LIGHT *stands looking after her. He speaks slowly, and with infinite feeling.*

LIGHT: God take care of you, sweet Linda . . .

The curtain falls slowly.

Act Three

SCENE 1

Living room of the Manners home, evening, January 1839. Before the curtain rises, we hear the music of a Strauss waltz. It continues to play. Then the curtain on the same scene as in act one, scene 1. The room is empty and the windows, closed, have the curtains drawn over them. The music is louder now. There is the sound of laughter and chatter offstage, and beyond the double doors we see waltzing couples, some of the men in dress uniform. The couples dance past the double doors, some even come through, twirl once or twice, then pass out again. The whole atmosphere is gay and youthful.

The waltz continues. It comes to an end with a clapping and a rustle of gowns. Presently, AMELIA ORCHARD, *prettily demure in her ball dress, trips daintily into the room. She looks around for a moment then, running across to the left window, slips behind the long curtains and adjusts them to conceal herself. But she is careful to allow one tiny foot to peep out . . .*

Two young men, in resplendent uniform of the new governor's aides-de-camp, enter, right. They stare around the room, surprised at finding it empty. Both are good looking, young, fresh-faced Englishmen.

HERBERT: Well! I'll swear the wench came in here!
ALGERNON: Bertie . . .
HERBERT: Yes?
ALGERNON: Don't you ever think of anything besides women?
HERBERT: Don't you?
ALGERNON: No!

They both chuckle and settle themselves down.

HERBERT: Times like this, I realize that our appointment has its brighter side . . .
ALGERNON: Still on the petticoats?

HERBERT: Drat you, no! Though, to be sure, an angel like the Orchard wench was the last thing I expected to find here!

ALGERNON: That's true. When I told the boys at the club I'd been appointed to Gawler's staff, they said there was nothing but black bread in the colony!

There is a pause, then . . .

What do you think of the Manners woman, Bertie?

HERBERT: Mama?

ALGERNON: No. The daughter – Linda.

HERBERT: Not interested.

ALGERNON: No?

HERBERT: I don't like these frozen beauties with their "hands-off-me, sirrah" attitude! Like trying to kiss an iceberg!

ALGERNON: They do say that the most dangerous part of an iceberg is always kept concealed! And from what I hear, Miss Linda's "hands-off-me" attitude doesn't apply to everyone!

HERBERT: No?

ALGERNON: She was mixed up in a pretty scandal some months ago – with a married man, too! Papa had to put his foot down very firmly!

HERBERT *(languidly):* Who was the chap?

ALGERNON: Used to be head of the survey department. Rowed with Hindmarsh and resigned. Does private work now.

HERBERT: Not William Light?

ALGERNON: That's the man!

HERBERT *waves the suggestion away.*

HERBERT: Algy, old boy . . . someone's been pulling your leg!

ALGERNON: Why?

HERBERT: The pater knew Light in London! He's one of the upper ten! Friend of the Duke of Wellington – guest of the Prince Regent.

ALGERNON: What of it? He's still a man, isn't he?

HERBERT: But he's married to one of the Duke of Richmond's daughters . . .

ALGERNON: She's twelve thousand miles away! Miss Linda is right here on the spot!

HERBERT *rises.*

HERBERT: I don't believe a single word of it!

ALGERNON: All right! Ask Charles Orchard!

HERBERT *turns.*

HERBERT: Orchard?

ALGERNON: He told me.

HERBERT: God spare me, Algy! Surely you haven't been listening to him! That fellow has the most venomous tongue in the entire colony!

The curtain twitches, reminiscent of an angry kitten's tail.

ALGERNON *(shrugging):* Oh, I admit he's a malicious old windbag! But there's no smoke without fire, you know!

HERBERT: Orchard would make smoke, for the sheer joy of causing trouble! Personally, I can't stand the fellow's loud-mouth arrogance . . .

AMELIA *(outraged):* Oh . . . !

She flings aside the curtain and stands rigid with anger. The two young men wheel, see her and stand petrified with horror. It is HERBERT *who recovers first. He gasps, swallows . . .*

HERBERT: Miss Amelia . . .

AMELIA: How dare you address me, sir! How dare you?

ALGERNON: Dear, sweet creature . . .

AMELIA: So . . . ! My kind, noble papa is a malicious old windbag? Oh, shame . . . shame . . . !

HERBERT: My companion spoke in haste! I tried to restrain him . . .

AMELIA: By naming my papa with the most veomous tongue in the colony!

HERBERT *gulps.*

Do not deny it, sir! I heard you!

HERBERT: How were we to know you were behind that curtain?

ALGERNON: And what were you doing there?

AMELIA *looks at them frigidly. And frigid is her tone when she replies.*

AMELIA: When two young gentlemen seek a lady's company, they should at least make an effort to find her!

And now HERBERT *is seized with a sudden inspiration. He smiles charmingly.*

HERBERT: But we did!

AMELIA: What do you mean, sir?

HERBERT: Sweet Miss Amelia – surely you don't imagine those unkind remarks about your dear papa were to be taken seriously?

AMELIA: Then why were they made?

HERBERT: To bring you from your hiding place, puss!

He turns to ALGERNON *and bestows on that gentleman a broad wink.*

Isn't that so, Algy?

ALGERNON: Of course – of course!

HERBERT *turns back to* AMELIA.

HERBERT: We craved your company! Yet you had hidden yourself so securely! What could we do?

ALGERNON: We propounded this simple ruse, knowing well it could be explained!

AMELIA *looks from one to the other, knowing them well for charming plausible liars. But they are so handsome and they promise such fun . . . A demure smile hovers about her lips. She drops her head demurely.*

AMELIA: It was a cruel trick . . .

ALGERNON: We apologize!

HERBERT: From the bottom of our hearts!

AMELIA *(coyly):* I am such a simple child, unused to the clever wiles of London society. You must not confuse me with one of your grand ladies . . .

ALGERNON: That would be impossible!

AMELIA: Oh?

HERBERT: For you are ever so much prettier, graceful, and more charming!

AMELIA *(smiling):* Flatterer!

MRS. ORCHARD *and her husband with* GEORGE

STEVENSON *come into the room from right.* MRS. ORCHARD *sees her daughter.*

MRS. ORCHARD: So there you are!

AMELIA *(without enthusiasm):* Yes, mama.

MRS. ORCHARD: Whatever are you doing in here?

AMELIA: The waltz fatigued me. I came in here to rest . . .

MRS. ORCHARD *allows her gaze to rest on the young men for a brief moment.*

MRS. ORCHARD: I don't think I know your friends, child . . .

ORCHARD *comes forward, strutting with importance.*

ORCHARD: These young men are attached to Gawler's staff, Emily. Captain Herbert Fyffe-Lomax. Captain Algernon D'Crepney.

HERBERT *(bowing):* Your servant, mam . . .

ALGERNON *(bowing):* An honour, mam . . .

MRS. ORCHARD *smiles at their gallantry. Then, offstage, the music of a waltz begins.* HERBERT *turns to* AMELIA.

HERBERT: May I have the honour?

ALGERNON: Please! I insist!

AMELIA: Two strings to my bow! Mama – what shall I do?

MRS. ORCHARD: Select the young gentleman who asked you first.

AMELIA: But Captain Algernon . . .

MRS. ORCHARD: He shall have the next dance with you.

ORCHARD: Now now, young people . . . run along . . .

HERBERT *makes a bow to* AMELIA, *who drops him a curtsy. He puts out his arms. Together they swing into the waltz, circle the room, and dance out through the right-hand door.* ALGERNON, *following them out, closes the doors behind him, muting the music.* MRS. ORCHARD *drops into a chair.*

MRS. ORCHARD: The ball seems quite a success.

STEVENSON *(with a sneer):* Dear lady, could you expect otherwise? With the new governor as guest of honour?

ORCHARD: What time is the governor due to arrive?

STEVENSON: Very soon, I should say.

ORCHARD, *in the act of lighting a cigar, looks up.*

ORCHARD: Shrewd move on Manners' part setting himself cosily in Gawler's pocket!

STEVENSON: Talking of Gawler's pocket . . .

ORCHARD: Yes?

STEVENSON: I happen to know that it's almost empty! He's almost spent the £12,000 allowed to restore this colony . . .

MRS. ORCHARD: But he's only been here three months!

STEVENSON: That's right.

MRS. ORCHARD: Whatever will he do?

STEVENSON: He's talking about getting a crowd of emancipists from Tasmania to do the work of the labourers . . .

ORCHARD *wheels round abruptly, his cigar truculent.*

ORCHARD: Good God! The man's mad!

MRS. ORCHARD: Charles!

ORCHARD: What does Gawler aim to do? Turn this colony into a convict settlement like New South Wales?

MRS. ORCHARD *(timidly)*: It isn't quite the same . . .

ORCHARD *turns on her belligerently, pointing with his finger.*

ORCHARD: You just wait and see! Once a criminal — always a criminal, I say!

MRS. ORCHARD: But Governor Macquarie . . .

ORCHARD: A sentimental fool! And we want none of his dangerous experiments over here. Emancipists! Good God! Next thing he'll be bringing the Russians!

STEVENSON: I agree with you, Orchard. But in this scheme, Gawler has Captain Sturt behind him.

ORCHARD: The New South Welshman? What's he doing over here?

STEVENSON: Running a newspaper keeps your ear pretty close to the ground! Don't be at all surprised if Gawler offers Sturt the post of surveyor-general!

MRS. ORCHARD: But what about Mr. Kingston?

ORCHARD: Kingston! Since he took over, there isn't a survey department worth speaking of! Look what he did after Light's resignation! Disregarded the commissioners' orders and continued Light's trigonometrical survey . . . with all its costly delays! Just going from bad to worse!

MRS. ORCHARD: I believe the colonel is away on a country survey . . . ?

ORCHARD: He made it his business to be!

MRS. ORCHARD: Why?

ORCHARD: To save these people the embarrassment of refusing him an invitation tonight.

MRS. ORCHARD: That old scandal?

ORCHARD: Yes . . . they're beginning to hope it's forgotten . . .

MRS. ORCHARD *(sharply):* Sssh!

LINDA *has entered left. She pauses in the doorway, a little disconcerted to find the room occupied. She is beautifully gowned, but thinner – and there are the faintest of shadows under her eyes. She is calm, poised, elegant as ever, but all the warmth and animation have drained from her. She speaks very quietly.*

LINDA: I beg your pardon . . .

MRS. ORCHARD *rises.*

MRS. ORCHARD: Come in, my dear. We are just going.

LINDA: Do not let me disturb you . . .

MRS. ORCHARD: We have been very rude staying away so long . . . Come, Charles . . .

STEVENSON *has advanced to the right-hand doors. He throws them open. The three people exit.* LINDA *crosses and closes the doors behind them. She comes down centre and stands, pressing her hands to her temples. Then, crossing to the window, she stands looking out into the night. Her attitude is of anticipation, tinged with highly strung weariness. She turns away and, with hands clasped, begins to pace the room.* FINNIS *enters left.* LINDA *wheels and comes down to him.*

LINDA: I thought you were never coming!

FINNIS: I arrived back only a few hours ago . . .

LINDA: How is he?
FINNIS: Sit down, Miss Linda.
She gives an impatient shake of her head.
LINDA: Never mind about me, Travers. How is he?
FINNIS *(slowly):* Not at all well . . .
LINDA: Oh . . .
It is little more than a breath. She sinks into a chair and clasps her hands together.
How does he look?
FINNIS: The months have made little difference. He is thinner – greyer – a trifle more bowed! But his fire is not yet quenched. He is still courageous – resolute!
LINDA: I must go to him!
FINNIS: It would be useless . . .
LINDA: No! He needs me!
FINNIS: He has given his solemn word never to see you again. And it would be cruel! He suffers enough . . .
LINDA *(piteously):* Think you I know not how he suffers!
She rises and, hands clasped, begins to pace the floor. Suddenly she turns.
Why did you let him go away this time?
FINNIS: He insisted on going.
LINDA: But if he is so sick . . .
FINNIS: Had he been here, his absence from the ball would have revived the old gossip.
LINDA: But papa has long forgiven him . . .
FINNIS *goes to her.*
FINNIS *(very gently):* Miss Linda – it is not of your father he thinks, but of you . . .
LINDA: Yes?
FINNIS: Never for one instant are you out of his thoughts! Each time I go back, he hungers after every crumb! The words you spoke – the gown you wore – the way you look . . . and as I talk I can see the old light flood back into his face!
LINDA: What would I give to see it, too!
She moves restlessly to the chair and sits down.
Tell me more about him! How does he spend his time?

FINNIS: Every spare minute he has is taken up with writing.

LINDA: His defence?

FINNIS: Yes . . . for the commissioners. Another few weeks should see its conclusion.

LINDA: But he is not working too hard?

FINNIS: How can we stop him? He lives for nothing save the clearing of his name! It is his final goal – his burning ambition! And he writes furiously – frantically – far into the night, almost as though . . .

LINDA: As though what?

FINNIS *(quietly):* As though he realizes he is working against time . . .

LINDA *(pitifully anxious):* He will burn out what little strength he has!

FINNIS: So we tell him. But it is useless! He has even taken some of this manuscript on the survey journey with him . . .

LINDA: But the rest of it?

FINNIS: Locked in a sea-chest in the colonel's cottage. He feels it is safest there.

LINDA: I suppose so . . .

FINNIS *(smiling):* Do not worry, Miss Linda . . .

LINDA: But if anything were to happen to it . . .

FINNIS: He would never survive the blow. For that very reason I visit the cottage every morning.

LINDA: The chest is sealed?

FINNIS: With one of the strongest locks in the colony! Not that I fear thieves . . . the contents are valueless to anyone save the colonel.

LINDA *rises and begins to pace the floor again. Suddenly she turns.*

LINDA: Travers . . .

FINNIS: Yes?

LINDA: Will you do something for me?

FINNIS: Of course.

LINDA: This chest – is it heavy?

FINNIS *(puzzled):* No . . .

LINDA: Then you could carry it . . . alone?

FINNIS: Quite easily.

LINDA: I want you to bring it up here tonight!

FINNIS: The chest?

LINDA: Yes! To leave it in an unprotected cottage is madness! It is like risking the colonel's own life!

FINNIS: But surely . . .

LINDA: Had I known of this before, I would never have left it there a single night! We must get it here, where it is safe!

FINNIS: And your parents . . . ?

LINDA: I will get mama's consent.

FINNIS *hesitates a second, then nods.*

FINNIS: Very well. I'll bring it from the cottage myself. And now I must go back. Keep up your courage, Miss Linda . . .

LINDA *(taking his hand):* You're a very good friend, Travers . . .

He exits through left-hand door. LINDA *stands watching him go. Then she smiles a little, a gentle smile as though recalling a part of their conversation.* MRS. MANNERS *enters right. She is fashionably dressed, but about her manner is a certain anxiety that she strives to cover with a smile.*

MRS. MANNERS: Linda, dear . . .

LINDA: His Excellency has arrived?

MRS. MANNERS: Not yet. But he is on his way . . .

LINDA: Isn't it rather late?

MRS. MANNERS: It seems he was delayed . . . there was some small disturbance. They had to call out the militia.

LINDA: What was it?

MRS. MANNERS *(evasively):* We'll know soon enough. *(Abruptly, she changes the conversation.)* Come, child, your father is waiting in the ballroom . . .

She begins to walk out of the room, but LINDA *restrains her.*

LINDA: Mama . . . before we go . . .

MRS. MANNERS *(turning):* Yes?

LINDA: Would you mind if I kept a chest in my bedroom?

MRS. MANNERS: A chest?

LINDA: It belongs to Colonel Light, mama. It contains property so valuable that it is reckless to leave it unprotected in his cottage . . .

MRS. MANNERS: Linda!

She stares at her daughter for a moment, her face reflecting her dismay. Then she recovers herself.

We will talk about it later! Come now . . .

But LINDA *blocks her way.*

LINDA: Mama! What is it?

MRS. MANNERS: Come, child . . .

LINDA: Why did you cry out like that? What has happened?

MRS. MANNERS: Nothing . . .

LINDA *takes hold of her mother and almost shakes her in her impatience.*

LINDA: Mama – what are you keeping from me? Tell me! Mama – look at me! What is it?

MRS. MANNERS *(slowly):* We wanted to spare you . . . tonight . . .

LINDA: Spare me? Why?

MRS. MANNERS: Nothing can ever be recovered from the colonel's cottage . . .

LINDA *stares at her mother in horror.*

It was burnt to the ground . . . Every stick within its walls destroyed, not ten minutes ago . . .

LINDA *gives a soft wailing cry of despair.*

They called out the militia in an attempt to save it. But it was too late.

She breaks as LINDA *sways, half fainting, against her.* LINDA *moans brokenly.*

LINDA: No, mama . . . not his manuscript . . .

MRS. MANNERS: Linda . . .

LINDA: It would be too cruel! He has borne more than his share of misfortune . . .

MRS. MANNERS *(gently):* These things are God's will, Linda . . .

LINDA: No . . . God is merciful . . . kind . . . He does not punish unjustly . . . He would not do this thing . . .

Suddenly she fights to free herself from her mother's arm.
Let me go! I must go down there . . . I must see . . .
MRS. MANNERS: No, Linda . . . it is too late . . .
LINDA *(struggling hysterically):* The chest WAS saved . . . I know it was! It must be! Let me go, mama . . . let me go!
She tears herself away from her mother and half falls into a chair, burying her face in her hands. At that moment, MANNERS *enters quickly and importantly right, speaking as he comes.*
MANNERS: Gawler has arrived at last and . . .
He stops, then . . .
Linda! In heaven's name . . . !
His eyes fly to his wife's face.
You told her?
MRS. MANNERS: I had to. Now she wants to run down there . . .
LINDA: Papa . . . I must!
MANNERS: Linda . . . child . . . control yourself! The governor is here! We want to present you . . .
LINDA: No, papa . . . please . . . not now! Ask His Excellency to excuse . . .
VOICE *(offstage – loud):* His Excellency Sir George Gawler!
Immediately the strains of the National Anthem are heard. MANNERS *and his wife stiffen to attention.* LINDA *huddles miserably in her chair, oblivious to everything but her grief. She looks up and becomes aware for the first time of the anthem and rises unsteadily to her feet. She stands there fighting to control herself. Then suddenly she gives a strangled little cry, she turns, and runs through the double doors and out into the ballroom . . .*MANNERS, *scandalized, cries sharply.*
MANNERS: Linda! Linda – come back . . . Linda!

But the National Anthem swells to a triumphant finale as the curtain falls quickly.

Act Three

SCENE 2

Living room of the Manners home, some months later. It is about eight-thirty on a mild night. A fire is burning in the fireplace. A chair is placed some little distance away, with a warm rug set over the back. The room is lit only by the glow of the fire and the light of the two candelabra on the mantelpiece.

When the curtain rises, TRAVERS FINNIS *is standing near the fireplace, poking the blazing embers. The right door opens and* MRS. MANNERS *enters. She looks strained, tired; but she smiles at* FINNIS *as she comes in.*

MRS. MANNERS: I am so glad you could come over.

FINNIS: Nothing would have kept me away. Your housekeeper said it was about the colonel.

MRS. MANNERS: Yes . . .

Something in her tone causes FINNIS *to glance at her quickly.*

FINNIS: Worse?

MRS. MANNERS: I'm afraid so. Doctor Woodeford has been with him most of the afternoon.

FINNIS: Is there much pain?

MRS. MANNERS: No. But his cough is much worse. Woodeford is worried because the heart is so weak . . .

She shakes her head sadly.

It's cruel to see him now.

FINNIS *(gently):* You've both been wonderful! Heaven knows what the colonel would have done if you hadn't taken him in here!

MRS. MANNERS *(simply):* With the cottage burnt over his head, where else could he go?

FINNIS: That was the tragedy that hastened his illness! To finish those records was Light's one ambition.

MRS. MANNERS: I'm surprised he's lingered so long . . .

FINNIS: What does Woodeford say?

MRS. MANNERS *(shrugging):* He admits he's helpless. The cleverest doctor in the world can do nothing for a man who has lost all desire to live!

She sinks into a chair and, leaning back, closes her eyes.

FINNIS: You must get some rest.

MRS. MANNERS: I'm all right . . .

FINNIS: Remember what Mr. Manners said before he left . . .

MRS. MANNERS: Yes.

FINNIS: We promised to look after you. And night after night, you've been sitting up with the colonel.

MRS. MANNERS: It's Linda who has nursed him these past months.

FINNIS: I suppose Miss Linda is with him now?

MRS. MANNERS *(nodding):* She dare not leave him in case anything should happen. When I left, Linda was sitting by the bed. Will had fallen asleep, holding her hand. She wouldn't move in case it disturbed him.

FINNIS: He still knows her?

MRS. MANNERS: Oh, yes! He knows us all. Except . . .

FINNIS: Except what?

MRS. MANNERS: Just before he went to sleep, he made the strangest request.

FINNIS: To Miss Linda?

MRS. MANNERS *nods.*

MRS. MANNERS: Do you remember that night — a wild night almost two years ago when you came to dinner . . . ?

FINNIS: With the Orchard couple? Yes, I remember.

MRS. MANNERS: Tonight, the colonel asked Linda if she would wear the same gown.

FINNIS: Why?

MRS. MANNERS: I don't know.

There is a sombre pause. Then FINNIS *says hesitantly.*

FINNIS: You don't think he's . . . wandering . . . ?

MRS. MANNERS: Indeed, no! Today he seemed more alert and cheerful than he's been for weeks!

There is a tap on the right door. It opens to admit the housekeeper.

What is it, Dixon?

DIXON: If you please, ma'am, the colonel is awake.

MRS. MANNERS: Oh . . .

DIXON: He's dressed, and he said he would like to come in and sit by the fire.

MRS. MANNERS *rises, but* FINNIS *speaks quickly.*

FINNIS: No, no. I'll bring him in.

He exits with the housekeeper. MRS. MANNERS *pulls the chair nearer the fireplace and sets the rug preparatory to wrapping it round* LIGHT*'s knees. She takes one set of candelabra from the mantel and places it on the piano. Then* FINNIS*'s voice is heard offstage.*

FINNIS: Just a few more steps, old man . . .

He appears, supporting the invalid, LIGHT. *The colonel, weak and tottering, is marked with the final stages of consumption. His cheeks have fallen away and dark shadows emphasize his too-bright eyes. They reach the chair.* LIGHT, *clad in dressing gown and slippers, is lowered into it, while* MRS. MANNERS *adjusts the rug about his knees.* LIGHT *relaxes, leans back with a sigh, then he smiles weakly at his friends.*

LIGHT: Thank you, Finnis. I am beginning to realize how good it is to have a friendly arm to lean upon . . .

FINNIS: Are you comfortable?

LIGHT: Quite.

FINNIS: Then I have some good news for you . . .

He takes from his pocket a folded document.

Governor Gawler sends you his kindest regards. He also sends you this.

LIGHT: Another dispatch?

FINNIS: Not this time. It is a copy of a letter His Excellency is sending on to the commissioners in London.

LIGHT: Then Gawler may save himself the trouble! I am finished with the commissioners . . .

FINNIS: But, Will –

LIGHT: I never want to hear their names mentioned!

FINNIS *(gently):* Yet I think you should listen to this . . .

He unfolds the document and reads quietly.

. . . and there is one circumstance in Colonel Light's official conduct which is becoming more and more apparent to his honour. That is the wisdom of his choice in regard to the site of the capital . . .

MRS. MANNERS: Splendid!

FINNIS: . . . For the influence which that choice has made toward the rapid progress of the prosperity of the province, his memory claims the warmest gratitude from every lover of South Australia.

He folds the letter and, crossing to the mantel, puts it down. LIGHT *is staring into the fire.*

LIGHT: So . . . at last they begin to realize my worth . . . when I am so near the end . . .

FINNIS: What nonsense you talk, Will!

LIGHT: You think so?

FINNIS: I'll wager that a few months will see you squinting through a theodolite, chirpy as a junior surveyor!

LIGHT *raises his head, speaks gently.*

LIGHT: You have an excellent bedside manner, Travers.

FINNIS: No . . .

LIGHT: Please! It was wrong of me to say that. But I never lacked the courage to face . . . the truth . . .

FINNIS *is silent, not knowing what to say.* MRS. MANNERS *comes forward cheerfully.*

MRS. MANNERS: Now, what shall it be tonight, Will? Would you like me to read to you? Or we can go on with your dictation . . .

LIGHT: I think I should prefer to sit quietly . . . to talk . . .

FINNIS: By the way, Will – I wish you could see your garden. The wattle trees have never looked more beautiful! Just a mass of bloom! And the perfume . . . it makes your head swim . . .

LIGHT: Travers . . .

His quiet voice cuts through his friend's artificial chatter. He has been staring into the fire. At his name. FINNIS *stops abruptly.* LIGHT *looks up.*

You don't honestly think I'm ever going to get well again?

FINNIS: But you must . . .

MRS. MANNERS: And we have all kinds of things planned for your recovery!

LIGHT: No . . . Tonight I am going to ask you to make other plans. There is so little time left . . .

FINNIS: Will . . .

LIGHT: Please . . . *(He speaks with gentle impatience.)* Surely I can talk over these matters with you? Talk truthfully – without foolish pretence?

FINNIS: But you must never give up hope . . .

LIGHT: I have done with hope. Therefore, I ask you one small thing.

FINNIS *nods.*

When I am gone, will you have placed under my hands a bronze tablet? And on that tablet the words engraved . . . "The Founder of Adelaide" . . . ?

FINNIS: I give you my word.

MRS. MANNERS: Anything you ask, Will . . .

LIGHT: There is . . . one more favour.

MRS. MANNERS: Yes?

LIGHT: Linda will be coming to me soon. Could I see her . . . alone?

MRS. MANNERS: Of course.

LIGHT: Then . . . would you tell her . . . ?

MRS. MANNERS: You will be quite all right?

LIGHT: Yes . . . yes . . .

MRS. MANNERS *rises, takes one set of candelabra, and moves to right-hand door.* FINNIS *puts a comforting hand on his friend's shoulder then crosses with her. The pair exit. The room is now lit only by the glow of the fire and the light of the candles on the piano.* LIGHT, *left alone, turns his head and looks around the room, a long searching slow look almost as though he knows he sees it for the last time. Then he smiles, relaxes, his head drops back, his eyes close . . .*LINDA *enters. She stands just inside the right-hand door, and, dressed as we saw her in the opening act, she has never looked more beautiful. All the warmth and radiance have flooded* *back into her face, but it is a warmth made gentle by tender pity. And as she stands there,* LIGHT, *without moving, speaks softly.*

LIGHT: Linda . . .

She comes down and stands in front of him.

LINDA: I thought you were sleeping.

LIGHT: Even so, I would know if you were near . . .

Then he raises his head, opens his eyes. He whispers softly.

Dear God . . .

LINDA *spreads her dress and curtseys.*

LINDA: You like me, sir?

LIGHT: Let me look at you . . . standing there as I saw you on that night . . .

LINDA: You remember so well.

LIGHT: I have never forgotten an instant of it! Come closer, Linda . . .

She comes round behind his chair, laying her hands across his eyes. He relaxes with a sigh of comfort. His voice is soothed . . . drowsy . . .

How cool your hands are . . . cool and soft . . . They set me to dreaming, Linda . . .

LINDA: Yes?

LIGHT: The dew on the lilacs in Maida Vale . . . and the wet purple bluebells in St. John's Wood . . .

LINDA: All so far away now . . .

LIGHT: Are they? Dreams and memories and reality . . . all so confused and yet . . . so clear. The girls crying sweet lavendar . . . and the crossing sweepers by the little miniature shop near Leicester Square . . . Do you know it, Linda?

LINDA: No . . .

LIGHT: It was there I first met her . . . she was having a miniature of herself painted . . . She looked so lovely . . . her bonnet had pink ribbons . . . and her eyes were blue . . .

LINDA *(softly):* Your wife . . . ?

LIGHT: Where did we go wrong? Why was it suddenly all

so . . . ugly? It was in Paris I first noticed the difference . . . we didn't laugh so much . . .

Suddenly the fever grips him. His voice rises, high-pitched, rambling.

Mary . . . what have I done? Only tell me! But she would never answer. She turned her face away. I thought . . . if there were children . . . but it made no difference . . .

His voice trails away. In the silence, LINDA *smooths his burning forehead. Then she speaks quietly.*

LINDA: Try to rest, Will . . .

LIGHT: One time we were happy . . . so radiantly happy . . .

LINDA: Yes?

LIGHT: It was in Sicily, I think. I remember the sunshine . . . the blue skies . . . I wrote a little sonnet. Mary set it to music. It was late and the children were in bed. Mary and I were alone. She sat down at the piano and played it for me . . . It was Mary as I had never known her before . . .

LINDA, *suddenly realizing, tightens her face in pain. She drops her hands from his eyes and turns away.* LIGHT *cries out suddenly like a frightened child.*

Mary . . . oh, my darling . . . where are you?

LINDA *drops on to the hassock at his feet and, reaching up, takes his thin hands in her own.*

LINDA *(very gently):* I am here, Will.

His fingers tighten around her own. Then he opens his eyes, sees her, and smiles weakly.

LIGHT: What have I been saying?

LINDA: Nothing, dearest.

LIGHT: It seems so strange to come back to this room. I was so far away. In the Palace Yetrionni. Remember the little statue in the pool, Linda?

LINDA *(very gently):* No . . .

LIGHT: Yes . . . we used to place garlands around it.

LINDA: I was never in Sicily, Will..

LIGHT *(like a child):* No?

LINDA: It was someone else.

LIGHT *looks at her for a long second, then he turns his head away.*

LIGHT: Yes . . . I remember now.

LINDA: You must try to rest . . .

LIGHT: I had a long sleep this afternoon. I dreamt I was a child again, back in the wide fields near Theberton Hall. It was a Sunday and far down in the valley I heard the bells of a little church ringing . . .

LINDA: Yes?

LIGHT: And I could still hear those bells ringing after I had awakened. Soft they were, of exceeding sweetness. But I could hear them, Linda . . . clearly . . . for some seconds . . .

LINDA: It was nothing but a dream . . .

LIGHT: No, Linda . . .

He speaks with intense simplicity.

I know now. It was the bells of heaven I heard ringing for me.

LINDA *turns her head away, moved by his simple faith.* LIGHT *speaks very gently.*

Linda . . . sweet Linda. Don't grieve for me . . . I am going to be so happy . . .

LINDA: Yes . . .

LIGHT: For me there is peace . . .

LINDA: And for me?

LIGHT: Memories . . . Look around this room . . .

LINDA: So many memories here . . .

LIGHT: Of a night wild with storm, when the rain splashed the window . . . and a tired man drank a glass of wine before the fire . . .

LINDA: So long ago . . .

LIGHT: You remember our song, Linda?

LINDA: Every word!

LIGHT: Sing it for me.

Then, as she hesitates, he says gently.

I will not go away until you've finished . . .

She rises and, crossing to the piano, opens it and sits down. LIGHT, *watching her, whispers.*

LIGHT: Now the pain and anguish are forgotten. This is what I have prayed for, Linda . . .

He lies back, relaxed, quiet. LINDA *puts her hands to the piano and the sad little air steals gently through the silent room.*

LINDA: I saw you on a blue Spring day
At dawn.
The little birds a-flutter at your
Feet.
You smiled; and then the blue was turned
To gold . . .
Because you smiled on me . . .

Abruptly LINDA*'s voice ceases and the piano notes jumble in a sharp dissonance. She wheels, tense with a sudden premonition, and looks at* LIGHT, *who lies back in his chair, limp, relaxed, eyes closed, a faint smile about his lips.* LINDA *speaks softly, fearfully.*

LINDA: Will . . .

Then sharply she cries.

Will!

But he makes no move. She rises swiftly from the piano and moves across to the chair. Almost fearfully, she reaches out her hand and touches his face. Then she gives a sharp gasp of realization and her hand drops away. Slowly, she sinks to her knees. With bowed head, she whispers brokenly, but with infinite tenderness.

LINDA: I charge you, O daughters of Jerusalem, that ye stir not up, nor awake my love . . . until he pleases . . .

The curtain falls slowly.

Lady in Danger

(A comedy-thriller)

Characters and Original Cast

The play was first presented at the Independent Theatre, Sydney, by Doris Fitton in February 1942 with the following cast in order of appearance:

BILL SEFTON	James Pratt
MONICA, his wife	Gwen Plumb
MRS. IDAMAE LAMPREY,* their landlady	Dorothy Whiteley
DR. GILBERT NORTON,* a neighbour	Norman Haire
SYLVIA MEADE	Hazel Hollander
ANDREW MEADE, a crime reporter	Kenneth Fowles
DETECTIVE DENNIS MARSH	Desmond Rolfe
CONSTABLE POGSON	Sydney Chambers
CHIEF INSPECTOR WILLIAM BURKE	David Rattner

Also a corpse

The play was then presented by J. C. Williamson Ltd. at the Theatre Royal, Sydney, in 1944, and by the Lee Sherbert management at the Broadhurst Theatre, Broadway, New York, in 1945. It was televised by the Australian Broadcasting Commission in September 1959.

* In the original stage version of this play, these characters were named MRS. BRIGID FLANNAGAN and DR. FRANCIS GRESHAM. Max Afford revised the play in 1953, changing the names of the landlady and doctor. The text of *Lady in Danger* in this collection follows the 1953 version.

Act One

SCENE 1

The entire action of the play takes place in the living room of the flat of BILL *and* MONICA SEFTON *in South Kensington, London. This is a comfortable and well-furnished room on the ground floor. The rear wall has two windows, curtained in chintzes and overlooking a small back garden. Under the left-hand window is a dining room table and chairs. Under the right window, a small desk on which stands a portable typewriter and reference books. Centre stage, between the windows, a tall built-in cupboard. Entrance to the flat is in the right-hand corner. Curtains screen a small entrance hall. Down right stands a TV cabinet and top a telephone. Up left an entrance to the bedroom. Up right the entrance to the kitchen. Other necessary furnishings are an old-fashioned sideboard with drawers, a divan, and several chairs. On the walls are a number of good prints.*

When the curtain rises, the room is empty. It is about nine o'clock of a warm summer's evening. Both windows are partly open and a breeze flutters the curtains. At the desk, a piece of paper has been placed in the typewriter and the chair is pushed back as though someone has risen hurriedly. After a pause, the hall door opens. BILL SEFTON, *a stocky athletic young man in his mid-twenties enters the living room. He is carrying a number of small parcels, some in brown paper, some in tissue. He crosses to the table and puts them down.*

BILL *(calling):* I couldn't get any milk!

No answer. He begins to unwrap the parcels, revealing a loaf of bread, half-pound of butter, a jar of fish-paste, and a packet of paper serviettes. Then, realizing he has not been answered, he calls:

Monica . . .

No reply. He looks puzzled, then crosses into the kitchen, taking the groceries with him. Returning, he looks around, frowns, and crosses, peering into the bedroom.

Monica – are you in the bathroom?

Still no reply. BILL *stands irresolute for a moment, then he notices the chair pulled back from the desk. He starts toward it and stumbles over something on the floor. Muttering, he bends down and picks up a broom. He calls to the empty room:*

Can't you put things back in their place!

He moves to the built-in cupboard and swings open the right hand door. The figure of a young woman is revealed . . . it falls forward into his arms. BILL *gives a yelp of mingled dismay, horror, and surprise.*

Monica! Darling, for God's sake –!

He glances frenziedly left and right then carries the limp figure to the divan. Kneeling beside it, he begins to massage the girl's hands, helplessly and almost incoherent with alarm.

Monica . . . ! Darling . . . ! What happened? Monica – speak to me! Monica . . . !

He gives another helpless, frenzied glance around the room.

She's still breathing, thank God! Brandy! Brandy's the thing –

He rises and starts for the sideboard. MONICA SEFTON *on the divan suddenly sits upright, revealing herself as an attractive and vivacious young woman.*

MONICA: Bill darling . . .

As he wheels, staring wide-eyed at her.

What's the matter?

BILL: Monica! You're all right?

MONICA: Of course I'm all right. Did I frighten you?

BILL *(almost shrilly):* Did you . . . ? *(His voice deepens.)* Look here, what the hell's your game!

MONICA: Darling, it's no game. It's a deadly serious business. But tell me – what was your reaction? Ringing the police or calling a doctor? What flashed through your mind – suicide, murder, accident –

She stops abruptly at the expression on his face and jumps from the divan.

Easy now, old boy . . . easy . . . !

BILL: Easy be damned! You hid in the cupboard to scare the living daylights out of me!

MONICA: Bill darling – if I'd known you were going to be so upset, I'd never have done it! Honest! But I just had to know –

BILL: Know what?

MONICA: The emotions of a husband who stumbles on a situation like that! You see, I'm on the wretched third act . . . where Henry Maltravers finds the body of his third wife stuffed in the linen basket –

BILL: Of all the utter drivel!

MONICA: It's only by personal observation I can get Henry's true emotions down on paper! That's why I have to know how you feel –

BILL: Like turning you over my knee and spanking some sound commonsense into you!

MONICA: That's fine encouragement when I'm trying to write the crime play of the ages . . .

BILL: Sure! The ages between four and six!

MONICA *(shortly):* Sell those bright quips to the Light Entertainment Programme!

BILL: I'll stick to honest newspaper reporting Honest, Monica – I can't think what's come over you! Three weeks ago, you were a sane normal woman.

MONICA: Three weeks ago you had a job, my pet. Through no fault of your own, you lost it.

BILL: So what!

MONICA: Now it's up to me to do something!

BILL: By taking nose dives out of cupboards? The only writing you'll do is on a free medicine form! Anyhow, what happened to your mystery novel?

MONICA: I've decided to try the drama.

BILL: Why?

MONICA: Some plays make a lot of money . . .

BILL: So do some poker machines! But always for the next chap!

MONICA *(warmly):* You can't say my writing interferes with your comfort. You still get three good meals a day.

BILL: After what happened this afternoon, we mightn't have those much longer.

MONICA: Oh, Bill . . . ! Bad as that?

BILL: Worse!

MONICA: I thought you seemed mighty quiet over dinner this evening.

BILL: I felt too rotten even to talk about it. Mops, I've had one hell of a day! It didn't take Digby-Smith long to start spreading his poison – there wasn't an editor who'd even see me!

MONICA *(gently):* Never mind . . .

BILL: We've got to mind! Thirty quid in the bank and we're three weeks behind with the rent!

MONICA: Mrs. Lamprey will just have to wait.

BILL: I hate owing money – rent particularly. Kind of shabby pride, I suppose.

MONICA: Perhaps I could get a job somewhere . . .

BILL: I'll earn the salary in this family! You stick to play-writing!

MONICA: Bill! I might even sell something to television!

BILL: Not even when they sell soap on it!

MONICA: Darling, I'm serious. Goodness knows they need new stuff – instead of filling out their programmes with ten-year-old films.

BILL: So that's where you got the idea for the cupboard stunt! That old Gracie Allan film we saw! And it wasn't funny even then!

MONICA: I've told you I'm sorry. It's just that I didn't think . . .

BILL: That's the trouble with you – you're always leaping head first into things!

MONICA: Such as?

BILL: Well – this nonsense about wanting a Kensington address – and signing a long lease for this apartment!

MONICA: When I signed the lease we could afford a Kensington address!

BILL: Not any longer!

He prowls the room, a restless unhappy young man.

Of course, there's one way out of this mess . . .

MONICA: Tell me.

BILL: I could always pocket my pride and apologize to Digby-Smith.

MONICA: You couldn't possibly do that! It would be admitting his charges were right!

BILL: I see all that.

MONICA: And you'd let yourself be humiliated?

BILL: Damn it all, Monica, do you think I'd enjoy crawling to that clot? But if we don't earn some money very soon, we'll have no more home than a banshee.

MONICA *(after a worried pause):* What makes you think you'd get back the job?

BILL: Coming out of the bank today I met Andy Meade. He says Marden felt pretty rotten about being ordered to fire me. Marden hinted to Andy that if I made a statement, saying I'd misreported Digby-Smith, the paper would take me back like a shot!

MONICA: You musn't do anything so foolish! Besides, everyone knows how unreliable Andy is!

BILL: You've got a stupid prejudice against him . . . and all because he happened to take a few drinks at our wedding!

MONICA: He was too tight to stand! And look at the life he leads poor Sylvia . . . disappearing for days on end!

BILL: Andy Meade's a crime reporter. You can't expect him to lead office hours! What's more, he's the best friend we've got!

MONICA: Speak for yourself!

BILL: If that's the way you feel, you'd better take yourself to a movie tomorrow evening . . .

MONICA: Why?

BILL: I've asked Andy and Sylvia to dinner.

MONICA: I like Sylvia, but Andy . . . ! Really, Bill, you are the limit! This morning you make a ridiculous scene because I'd asked Dr. Norton in for supper – yet without even mentioning it you ask people for dinner!

BILL: I'm mentioning it now, aren't I?

MONICA: Anyhow, what's the idea?

BILL: Andy's coming around to discuss what's to be done about an out-of-work reporter! They're trying to help me because they're friends . . . which is more than I can say for that pill juggler next door!

MONICA: Now Bill . . .

BILL: How did we ever come to get on his visiting list?

MONICA: A few days ago I cut my hand opening a tin of soup. I was on my way to the chemist's for some sticking plaster when I met Dr. Norton in the hall. He took me into his flat and dressed the wound.

BILL: Touting for business in the corridor, eh?

MONICA: Don't be ridiculous!

BILL: Your hand's all right now?

MONICA: Quite.

BILL: Then why is he coming here this evening?

MONICA: I want some information from him.

BILL: What about?

MONICA: Poisons.

BILL: Poisons? Good Grief, we're not back on the play again?

MONICA: We are.

BILL: But when you were fooling around with that detective novel, you collected enough drivel on poisons to fill several garbage bins!

MONICA: But this is a completely new plot. Now I've got to have expert medical advice. I want to know just how long a certain poison takes to work.

BILL: For Pete's sake . . .

MONICA: All right – you can sneer! But I've worked out what looks to be the perfect murder. And for two pins, I wouldn't mind trying it out on Mr. Digby-Smith . . .

BILL *(shortly):* And finish up with a rope around your neck!

MONICA: Not this girl! You just wait till you read my third act! It's all a matter of finding the right kind of poison – something that the police would never suspect as being –

She stops abruptly as BILL *makes a warning gesture and glances out into the hall. He crosses and pulls aside the curtains.*

BILL: Mrs. Lamprey!

MRS. IDAMAE LAMPREY *enters. She is in her late sixties, an untidy grey-haired woman exuding an air of gone-to-seed gentility. She has the dreamy, vaguely resentful expression of one completely out of her generation and her pinched, refined speech is studded with archaic phrases. She stands blinking just inside the curtains as* BILL *says:*

What is it?

MRS. LAMPREY: Dear Mr. Sefton . . . I'm afraid little Susie has been saucy again . . .

BILL: Oh, for Pete's sake!

MRS. LAMPREY: Now now, you musn't scold the thoughtless fribble –

MONICA: But after what she did yesterday . . .

MRS. LAMPREY *(quickly)*: That was very, very brazen of the little romp and I gave her a serious talking-to! But on this occasion, it is but a very minor indiscretion and I've wiped it up . . . every tiny trace of it!

BILL: Why can't that dog stay upstairs where it belongs?

MRS. LAMPREY *(plaintively)*: No matter how many times I rebuke her, the minx simply cannot comprehend. In the times past, before my husband was taken, all this residence was hers . . . I've tried to explain to Susie that we have fallen upon evil times . . .

BILL: And you've had to convert your ground floor into two flats. Yes – we know all about that!

MRS. LAMPREY *(vaguely)*: So difficult to make Susie comprehend that we've had to take in . . . lodgers. So very, very humiliating, you understand? When I was a gel, papa would not let us even walk past a lodging house –

BILL *(interrupting)*: Times have changed, Mrs. Lamprey! And now, if you will excuse us . . .

MRS. LAMPREY *(hesitating)*: To be sure. But there is one

small, distasteful circumstance . . .

MONICA *(bluntly):* If it's the rent . . .

MRS. LAMPREY: It does so distress me to mention money . . . so very, very vulgar, don't you think? Oswald always attended to such gross necessities . . . Papa brought us up never to acknowledge that coinage even existed . . .

MONICA: Very handy! But we'll settle our account at the end of the week, won't we Bill?

BILL: Sure thing!

MRS. LAMPREY *(who has been staring vaguely at* BILL, *says to* MONICA): He's got a vastly fine head, hasn't he? Papa always impressed us that you could tell a gentleman by the way he held his head. It's just . . . something! *(She nods to herself.)* Dogs have it, too, mark my words . . .

BILL: We'll do that!

MONICA: And sometime later, we'd love to have a talk about it. But right now, we're expecting Dr. Norton . . .

MRS. LAMPREY *leans toward them, hand to mouth. She speaks in a confiding whisper.*

MRS. LAMPREY: HE hasn't got it! He may call himself a professional gentleman, but I take leave to disagree. Papa would have conned him at a glance . . . a nondescript leech . . . a quack . . . *(She pauses and gives an ingratiating little smile.)* Could either of you young people obleege me with a cigarette?

MONICA: Of course.

She produces a packet and hands over a cigarette. MRS. LAMPREY *takes it, saying:*

MRS. LAMPREY: I trust it isn't one of your poisoned variety, my dear . . .

MONICA *(startled):* Poisoned?

MRS. LAMPREY *(archly):* I could not help but overhear your conversation . . . Such strange and wild romancing! I do trust it was merely some odd kind of jesting . . .

She gives them a meaning look and exits, leaving BILL *and* MONICA *staring at each other. As the outer door shuts . . .*

MONICA: Now just what did she mean by that crack?
BILL: Listening, eh?
MONICA: I hope she doesn't go around spreading that kind of talk!
BILL *(uneasily):* Don't worry – no one would take her seriously. Poor old duck's halfway round the bend, anyhow. It's my fault for not closing the door when I came in.
MONICA: You can't. The lock's on the blink.
BILL: Since when?
MONICA: This morning. It's jammed or something.
BILL: You know, I'm getting heartily sick of this place. We've had nothing but bad luck ever since we moved in here!
MONICA: So what do we do?
BILL: Look around for something else.
MONICA: But there's the lease . . .
BILL: We might get someone to take it over. How about phoning Sylvia – she might know – *(A tap on the outer door interrupts him.* MONICA *glances quickly at her wrist-watch.)*
MONICA: Dr. Norton!

She glances around the flat, sees a broom propped against the wall. She moves across and puts this in the tall cupboard centre. She returns and begins to punch and shake out the cushions. Her eye falls on BILL.

Darling, straighten your tie! And just look at your hair!

BILL *grunts something uncomplimentary and goes into the bedroom. The tap on the door sounds again.* MONICA *gives a last glance into the sideboard mirror and then goes into the hallway. We hear her open the door and then her voice offstage.*

This is very kind of you, doctor . . .

NORTON *(offstage):* Pleasure, Mrs. Sefton – downright pleasure!

He enters with MONICA. DR. GILBERT NORTON *is a plump, pink-faced, genial little man in his mid-fifties who peers through rimless glasses. While he is neatly dressed there is somehow a suggestion of soiled linen underneath. His manner has a kind of professional heartiness that would be frowned on in Harley Street. He pauses and peers short-sightedly around the flat.*

Nice . . . very nice. But the pictures are yours, am I right?

MONICA: Yes. Mrs. Lamprey's taste rather ran to Holman Hunt and the *Stag at Bay.* You should have seen the examples that were here!

NORTON: I have. She shifted 'em into my flat!

There is a slight awkward pause. MONICA *says quickly:*

MONICA: Doctor, I hope you won't think it's like my cheek, but . . . well . . . this is a kind of professional visit.

NORTON: Oh?

MONICA: Please sit down. My husband will be here in a minute.

NORTON *(sits):* Your husband's not feeling up to scratch?

MONICA: Bill? Oh, no – he's got a constitution like a horse! Never a day's illness in the twelve months we've been married. No . . . you see . . . I'm the one who wants your advice.

NORTON *(his eyes twinkling):* Something on your mind, am I right?

MONICA: And only a doctor can help me.

NORTON: Generally a worrying time – the first twelve months. But it might be better if you came into my flat . . .

MONICA: Oh, no, I don't want to put you to any trouble –

She stops as BILL *enters from bedroom.*

Bill – this is Dr. Norton.

NORTON *(rising and shaking* BILL*'s hand):* How d'you do, Mr. Sefton. Your good lady's just been telling me –

BILL *(interrupting):* I know. It's ridiculous taking up your time like this.

NORTON: Ridiculous? But that's what we're here for, you know. But you'd both better just pop next door . . .

BILL: What for?

NORTON: The examination.

BILL: What examination?

NORTON: My dear fellow, you both want an end to your worries, am I right? So –

He stops, sensing the embarrassment and seeing the rising dismay in their faces.

I say, I'm NOT right!

BILL: By God you're not!

MONICA *(quickly):* Oh, no, doctor. It's nothing like that!

BILL: I'd better explain before this business gets more complicated. You see, doctor, my wife's trying to write a play.

NORTON: Really now?

MONICA: It's a play all about murder and crime. That's what I meant by professional advice, doctor. I want some help on poisons and their effects on the body.

NORTON: What kind of poisons?

MONICA: Well, aren't there certain kinds that leave no trace?

NORTON *stares from one to the other. It is plain he can't quite make up his mind whether* MONICA *is serious. He takes off his glasses and polishes them with a handkerchief as he speaks.*

NORTON: Now look here, Mrs. Sefton – you're a pretty intelligent young woman. But you ought to know better than to ask a question like that.

BILL *(to* MONICA): I told you so!

MONICA: Darling, go and put the kettle on . . .

BILL: But it's –

MONICA *(firmly):* Bill – please!

BILL *turns to* NORTON, *gives a helpless half-shrug and goes into the kitchen.* MONICA *says rather awkwardly.*

I'm sorry if I've been – what do you call it – unethical.

NORTON *(replacing glasses):* Ethics have nothing to do with it. It's plain commonsense. If we doctors went around broadcasting that kind of information, we'd find ourselves in Queer Street! Now, don't take me up the wrong way when I say this, but after all . . . we're more or less strangers now, am I right?

MONICA: I suppose so.

NORTON: Except that you cut your hand on a tin-opener, I don't know a thing about you.

MONICA *(impetuously):* I'm an only child, doctor – my

parents were killed in the blitz. I'm all alone except for Bill –

NORTON *(interrupting):* Hold on there – hold on! I don't want your personal history. But what about this writing you're doing?

MONICA: WHAT about it?

NORTON: If you'd said it was some kind of lovey-dovey romantic thing, I could understand it. But murder! What's put that idea into your head?

MONICA *hesitates and gives a side-glance at the half-open kitchen door before she goes on.*

MONICA: Do you know Alistair Digby-Smith?

NORTON: The politician married to Lord Cookhaven's daughter?

MONICA: That's the man!

NORTON *(frowning):* Something in the press recently . . . he stood for Democratic Independent but was licked by the Liberals . . . am I right?

MONICA *(nodding):* Bill worked on the *Echo* – about a month ago, he went around to interview Digby-Smith. The old boy was half-tight although Bill didn't realize it until he came out with some pretty dangerous statements.

NORTON: How dangerous?

MONICA: Well, among other things he said that Britain's only hope of avoiding total bankruptcy was to ally herself with Red China. In that way, the nation could salvage some of its investments in that country.

NORTON *(impressed):* Digby-Smith said that?

MONICA: That was mild compared with other nonsense. Anyhow, when Bill got back to the office he showed his notes to Marden, the sub-editor. Marden got such a shock he rang Digby-Smith who'd had time to sober down . . .

NORTON: And he denied the whole thing, I suppose?

MONICA: Worse than that!

NORTON: Indeed?

MONICA: He accused Bill of a deliberate frame-up. So that

when I tell you Lord Cookhaven owns the *Echo* –

From the kitchen comes a warning call.

BILL: Monica!

MONICA *(calling back):* There in a minute, darling! *(To* NORTON.) Now Digby-Smith has fixed it so Bill can't get another job on a newspaper in London.

NORTON: Victimization, eh?

MONICA: But it gave me the idea for my murder play. If only you knew the slow, lingering deaths I'd planned for that precious politician –

From the kitchen, BILL *calls in growing alarm.*

BILL: MONICA!

MONICA *(calling):* If it's boiling dear, make the tea! *(To* NORTON.) That's why I need medical advice.

NORTON *(after slight pause – fatherly):* Mrs. Sefton, you surprise me – bless me if you don't! But surely you need a lot of other knowledge to write a crime play?

MONICA: Oh, I've got that!

She moves to the sideboard, opens drawer, and takes out a large book. Brings it across and opens it before NORTON.

Months ago I started a detective novel. So I began collecting cuttings on famous crimes. A reporter friend of ours helped me. He spent some time in the States.

NORTON *(shaking his head):* I'd never have believed it, honestly! And I suppose your husband helps you?

MONICA: Bill? Oh, no – he'd like me to chuck the whole thing! Only this morning he complained you couldn't pick up a piece of paper without finding a formula for poison scribbled on it.

NORTON *closes the book as* BILL *enters from kitchen with crockery on a tray.*

NORTON: Your wife's a very interesting young woman, Mr. Sefton.

BILL: She talks too much!

NORTON: I'd no idea I had such a bloodthirsty young neighbour . . .

BILL: Bloodthirsty? Don't make me laugh! One peep at a

real corpse and Monica'd pass out like a light!

MONICA: Oh, you know everything!

BILL *(cheerfully)*: I know that you've been handing the doctor a lot of mouldy cock in here. You and your perfect murders! You can't even see a stray dog in the street without practically bursting into tears and –

He stops as from somewhere in the room a distinct tapping sounds.

What's that?

MONICA: Someone at the door?

BILL: I thought it came from the window . . .

They turn and look.

. . . might be the wind . . .

MONICA: There isn't even a breeze tonight . . . *(She stops as the curtains move slightly.)* Bill! Someone's out there!

BILL: I'll find out!

MONICA: Darling, be careful . . .

He puts her gently aside and crosses to the window. He jerks back the curtains. A large black cat sits on the sill, staring into the room.

BILL: Good Grief, it's a moggie! Scat . . . ! Get away, you black brute! Shoo!

MONICA: Bill – don't you dare!

She runs to the window and gathers the cat in her arms, crooning to it as she returns.

Poor pussy – poor, poor darling. Bill, how could you? You've almost scared the life out of it!

BILL: That makes it mutual! He damn near scared the daylights out of me!

MONICA: He didn't mean to – he's just terribly, terribly sweet.

BILL: Don't put your face near him – he's probably mangy!

MONICA: He isn't – is he, doctor?

NORTON: Looks in the pink to me!

BILL: Healthy or not, he doesn't stay here.

MONICA: Why not?

BILL: Because it's in the lease! Mrs. Lamprey won't have a cat about the place because of that menace Susie!

MONICA: Mrs. Lamprey just isn't going to know! I wonder if he's hungry?

She moves into the kitchen and we hear her voice offstage.

I want a saucer . . . ah, yes . . . now, my precious, down you go. And drink that!

She emerges, watching through the door.

Bill, do come and look at him. You never saw such an expression of pure bliss!

BILL: Monica! Once and for all –

MONICA: Darling, don't be difficult. You know I've wanted a pet ever since Master died.

BILL: Master was a dog! And this ugly brute doesn't even belong to us. What's more, we'll be kicked out of this flat if –

MONICA *(interrupting):* But we were going to give notice in any case!

She turns to NORTON.

Doctor, don't you think the cat should stay?

NORTON: I say, Mrs. Sefton – that's the second curly one you've asked me this evening.

BILL *(to* MONICA): You ought to have more sense than to ask a thing like that!

MONICA: You don't want the doctor to give his opinion because you know he'll agree with me!

BILL: I've got too much regard for his commonsense!

NORTON: Tell you what I'll do. Let's have pussy and I'll turn him loose out in the street.

BILL: By all means! Take the brute now!

MONICA: Bill! That's downright dishonest! How can we possibly give something away which doesn't belong to us in the first place! Why, that's close to larceny!

BILL: Oh, my God!

NORTON: You've made up your mind to keep the cat, am I right?

MONICA: Yes!

NORTON: Then that seems all there is to it.

MONICA: There now, see? Everybody's happy!

BILL: Not if I bed down with fleas tonight! Oh, let's forget the brute and have supper.

He turns to NORTON.

Er . . . do you have milk in your tea, doctor?

NORTON: Never touch it! Supper, I mean. Eat three regular meals a day and you'll sleep your seven hours at night. That's a bit of free medical advice for you!

He holds out his hand to them.

It's been quite a treat to meet you, I must say.

BILL *(as they shake hands):* Sure we can't offer you anything? What about a sherry?

NORTON: Wouldn't dare risk it – not with my stomach. Got to pamper it, you know. All right for you young bloods – eat and drink what you want. But you wait till you're my age . . . Now, don't come out . . . I'm only next door, you know. Good evening to you . . . good evening . . .

He exits and the door closes in the hallway.

MONICA: Well! I hope you're satisfied!

BILL: Now what have I done?

MONICA: Ruined the entire evening . . .

BILL: If you're beefing about your cock-eyed play, he never intended giving you any information!

MONICA: I could have talked him round. But you had to place him in such an embarrassing domestic situation that he left at the first opportunity!

BILL: It'd have been a damn sight more embarrassing if he HAD stayed!

MONICA: Why?

BILL *picks up the milk jug and inverts it.*

BILL: Empty!

MONICA: But I told you to buy some . . .

BILL: And I told you I couldn't get any. But you were too busy nose diving out of cupboards to listen to me!

MONICA: But there's half a pint in the fridge.

BILL: And it's staying there! I've got to be up bright and early looking for a job. I need some breakfast before . . .

But MONICA *has suddenly clapped a dismayed hand over her mouth.*

What's the matter?

MONICA: Bill darling, you're going to be absolutely livid

. . . You see, I was certain you'd bought some milk. And that poor lost creature looked so hungry . . .

BILL: Monica! Oh, no . . . no . . . You haven't given my breakfast milk to that mangy horror . . . ?

MONICA, *staring wordlessly, just nods.*

That settles it!

He strides for the kitchen.

That bag of fleas goes out of the window on his ear – right this moment!

MONICA: Bill! Are you crazy! Touch that cat and you're tempting fate! Don't you ever want to get another job?

BILL: What's that got to do with it?

MONICA: Everything! It's a black cat, isn't it? And everyone knows how lucky it is for a black cat to cross your path!

BILL: Not when it takes the milk out of my tea!

MONICA *goes to him and slips her arms around him.*

MONICA: Bill darling – let me keep him, please. I'll promise I'll never ask you for anything else . . . ever!

BILL *(weakening):* Hang it all, Monica – you can't want a pet as much as that!

MONICA: It's not so much a pet as . . . a kind of omen. A lucky omen. And we do need luck, Bill, so very badly! You, especially, darling! I want you to have all the luck in the world! Please, Bill . . . let me keep him . . . may I?

BILL: I knew you'd load the dice somehow. All right. You win.

MONICA *(happily):* And you'll see how right I am, darling. You'll never regret it. Bill, I've got the strangest hunch about that cat. Something seems to tell me things are going to be quite different –

There is a loud crash of crockery from the kitchen. MONICA *and* BILL *spring apart in alarm.* MONICA *rushes to the kitchen door and looks in. She stands appalled.*

My dinner set! Your mother's wedding present . . . ! Oh, Bill . . .

The cat scuttles through the open kitchen door and darts across the stage as the curtain falls quickly.

Act One

SCENE 2

The scene is the same. It is about six o'clock on the following evening. The flat is lit by the dying light of the afternoon sun which fades as the action proceeds. The hall door opens and there is the sound of voices offstage.

MONICA: Go through, Sylvia.

SYLVIA MEADE *enters followed by* MONICA. SYLVIA *is a smartly dressed young woman, brittle and sophisticated in manner and speech. As* MONICA *switches on the light, she stands looking around the room.*

What do you think of it?

SYLVIA: Looks all right from here.

MONICA: Of course it's in a perfect mess . . .

SYLVIA: Darling, don't apologize. I know nothing disconcerts a woman more than having her friends drop in and find the place looking as it usually does! Is it clean?

MONICA: We haven't scratched yet.

SYLVIA: Where's the kitchen?

MONICA *(gesturing):* Through there. Bedroom there and bathroom beyond. Sylvia, do you think your friend will take over the lease?

SYLVIA: It's possible. The rent seems reasonable . . .

MONICA: Not to us!

SYLVIA: Any pests? It's not haunted or anything?

MONICA: Only by Mrs. Lamprey – she's the old duck who owns the place. She lives upstairs.

SYLVIA: Aren't you nervous living on the ground floor?

MONICA: Oh, no . . .

SYLVIA: I'd be scared some of Andy's thick-ear gangster friends might come around peeping in my teepee!

MONICA: Darling, the way we are at the moment a burglar wouldn't make his bus fare! Slip into the bedroom and take off your hat while I look to the dinner.

SYLVIA *starts for the bedroom and enters, switching on light.* MONICA *takes off her hat and gloves and is moving to the kitchen when her friend's voice halts her.*

SYLVIA *(coming from bedroom):* What's this – animal week?

MONICA: Why?

SYLVIA: There's a cat the size of a Landseer lion curled up on your bed!

MONICA: That's Rameses. But I shut him in the kitchen . . .

SYLVIA: Then it is yours?

MONICA: Well, it is and it isn't. The poor darling wandered in here last night and I gave him some milk. Bill was furious, particularly as he wreaked havoc with our dinner set.

SYLVIA: Bill?

MONICA: No, no – the cat! That's why I christened him Rameses – the Wrecker, you know. Ever study Egyptology?

SYLVIA: Good heavens no. I never got beyond recognizing Cleopatra's Needle on a foggy afternoon . . .

A knock sounds at the door.

Is this Bill?

MONICA: He wouldn't knock – Pull that door shut.

SYLVIA *closes the bedroom door and* MONICA *goes out into the hall.*

Oh, hello Mrs. Lamprey . . .

MRS. LAMPREY *(offstage):* Could I have a few minutes civil conversation with you, Mrs. Sefton?

MONICA: Of course . . . come in.

MRS. LAMPREY *enters, obviously ill at ease but stiff backed and tight lipped.*

MRS. LAMPREY: I am rather nonplussed as to how to handle this situation. It is times like this I greatly miss Oswald. Papa always brought us up to avoid any suggestion of a SCENE . . . so very undignified and common . . .

MONICA: But . . . what's wrong?

MRS. LAMPREY *(bracing herself):* I . . . I really must ask

you to vacate these premises at the end of the week! One of the circumstances made most plain in our agreement was that we could not have a pussy-cat in this dwelling.

MONICA *(wide-eyed):* But whatever makes you think we're keeping a cat in here?

MRS. LAMPREY: Aren't you?

MONICA: Of course not! How ridiculous!

MRS. LAMPREY: Then, pray, how do you explain the extraordinary event that happened this afternoon? I was lying down with Susie at my side when all unexpectedly, the minx became vastly discomposed. Such sniffing and growling and scratching – la, it was most alarming! Then I had a notion that perhaps she wished to pay a wee visit, so I let her free. She ran helter-skelter down the stairs to your door where she began her fantastic motions all over again . . .

MONICA: I hope you jolly well stopped her in time!

MRS. LAMPREY: I was too dismayed! For within this very room, it was as though bedlam had broken loose! Such commotion as to be near indescribable . . . and a hissing and spitting and caterwauling fit to raise the very hair upon your head! And there was Susie, acting like something demented! There were sudden heavy footsteps and then an outburst of words in some outlandish foreign tongue . . .

MONICA *(amazed):* Oh, no . . .

MRS. LAMPREY: Yes, indeed! I was trembling from head to foot. But I took my courage in both hands and knocked a loud summons on the door . . . and abruptly, like a miracle, every sound in here ceased! It was so silent I could hear my fluttering heart . . .

MONICA *(firmly):* I'm sorry, Mrs. Lamprey, but you must have dreamed it . . .

MRS. LAMPREY *(stiffly):* I assure you –

MONICA: And I assure you this apartment's been empty all the afternoon. My husband's out and I've just come in from a matinee with my friend. Could the noise have been out in the alleyway? Sounds carry, you know . . .

BILL *(entering with two wrapped bottles):* What's the trouble?

MONICA: Hello darling. The funniest thing. Mrs. Lamprey thought she heard a cat in here. You haven't noticed one around, have you?

BILL *(shortly):* No.

MONICA *(begins shepherding her out):* You see, you must have been mistaken. Now, as we have guests for dinner, I must get busy . . .

MRS. LAMPREY: But there is Susie . . . SHE knows there's something strangely amiss. This evening, she wouldn't even look at the fine serving of plaice I'd bought especially for her . . . And DOGS KNOW . . . they have a sixth sense . . .

She exits, bewildered. BILL *waits until* MONICA *returns.*

BILL: I told you something like this would happen!

MONICA: You haven't said hello to Sylvia.

SYLVIA: Let's skip that. I want to know why you publicly disown a cat . . . when it's in there larger than life and blissfully fleaing itself on your bed!

BILL: Is it, by God!

He leaps into the bedroom and we hear his angry voice offstage.

Scat, you brute! Get off – get away – shoo!

A door slams offstage and he appears somewhat dishevelled.

I've shut the brute in the bathroom and I hope it drowns itself in the cistern!

He proceeds to unwrap the bottles of sherry and place them on the sideboard as MONICA *says:*

MONICA: Does Andy carry on like this?

SYLVIA: Does he? My dear, I had a canary once – for company while Andy was away! The rows we had over that poor bird! Andy did everything except sue it for alienating my affections.

MONICA: Bill – weren't you calling for Andy?

BILL: I missed him at the office. They said he'd gone out on a story.

SYLVIA: Don't be at all surprised if he forgets about the whole arrangement.

BILL: Not Andy!

SYLVIA: You haven't seen him since he stopped drinking!

MONICA: Andy has?

SYLVIA: Doctor's orders! He came home one night last week, sat down in a chair and couldn't get up again. I don't know who was scared most – Andy or me. It was some kind of alcoholic paralysis.

MONICA: Whatever did you do?

SYLVIA: Phoned the doctor. He called another and they took Andy off to hospital. Did all kinds of odd things to him. Now he's on some ghastly diet of grated carrots and orange juice.

As MONICA *moves into the kitchen.*

Can I help, dear?

MONICA *(exiting to kitchen):* No. But I'll leave the door open so I won't miss anything.

BILL *(grinning):* Poor old Andy! How is he now?

SYLVIA: Never looked better – except that the paralysis seems to have worked upward! At the most inconvenient moments, his mind goes blank . . .

BILL: No kidding?

SYLVIA: Cross my heart! He gets bushed on the silliest things. Last night he went to introduce me to some people and couldn't think of my name!

BILL: You'd better look after him. It's probably over-work.

SYLVIA: Over-work my eye! It's his boozing. A system that's been hardened to double whiskies for a decade can't be expected to adjust itself to pure orange juice without complications.

BILL: But what if he gets one of these temporary amnesia attacks while he's away from home?

SYLVIA: He's got his name and address on all his underwear.

BILL: Now, Sylvia – what kind of situation would have him rambling around in his underwear?

SYLVIA: The kind of situation he's always in . . . when he doesn't come home to me!

MONICA *enters from kitchen carrying a cloth.*

MONICA: Bill, if Andy isn't drinking, you might as well serve some sherry now.

BILL *takes a bottle from the sideboard and goes into kitchen while* MONICA *lays the cloth.*

SYLVIA: Doing anything interesting lately?

MONICA: Didn't you know? I'm writing a play.

SYLVIA: Why?

MONICA: We hope to make some money.

SYLVIA: Darling, I hate to disillusion you. But the only certain means of making money out of a play is to do it in a double bed in a Brighton hotel!

BILL *enters with decanter and glasses on a tray.*

BILL: That's what I tell her.

MONICA: I'm still going on with it.

SYLVIA: Watch your step, Monica. This writing business is like the love urge. You decide to dabble, just for fun's sake. Before you know where you are, you're up to your eyes in it. I know! I've been keeping a diary for years!

BILL: True confessions?

SYLVIA: Four blushes to the page!

BILL: Monica's effort is much less exciting. A child's essay on murder.

MONICA: How do you know! You've never seen it.

BILL: I'm psychic!

SYLVIA: Now now, you two! (*To* MONICA.) How much have you done?

MONICA: Finished the first two acts. I'll show you . . .

She crosses to the desk as SYLVIA *says quickly:*

SYLVIA: I'll take your word for it, darling. I'm sure it's frightfully good because –

She stops as MONICA, *after opening a drawer, turns a puzzled face to them.*

What's the matter?

MONICA: That's funny. It isn't here.

BILL: So what?
MONICA: You haven't taken my manuscript, have you?
BILL: Of course not.
MONICA: Then where is it?
BILL: Maybe the cat ate it!
MONICA: Very funny, I'm sure!
She resumes her search of the desk, getting more flustered and angry.
SYLVIA: When did you have it last?
MONICA: I was working on it this morning. I'll swear I put it away in this drawer.
BILL: No one ever goes to that drawer except you.
MONICA: I'm not so sure! It would be like you to hide it . . . just to be funny!
BILL: That's not my idea of being funny!
MONICA: Then where is it?
BILL: Just where you put it!
MONICA *gives him a "look" and, turning, rummages through the drawer a third time. Then she turns to him.*
MONICA: Bill – a joke's a joke but this is carrying things too far! I've spent valuable time on that play! Think of all the trouble I've gone to on research . . .
BILL: Like falling out of cupboards and giving me heart failure! I'd like to know how you'd carry on if I did a thing like that!
MONICA: You wouldn't! Because you've neither the wit nor the imagination to think of it!
BILL: Is that so! Well, two can play at that game!
As they stand glowering at each other, SYLVIA *crosses to the sideboard.*
SYLVIA: In between rounds, can I help myself to a sherry?
MONICA: Oh, Sylvia, I'm sorry . . .
SYLVIA: Don't worry about me. It's all so nice and homely . . .
MONICA: Now, Bill, for the last time –
BILL: For the last time I haven't touched your infantile play because I haven't seen it! If you say you put it in the drawer it must BE there!

A knock is heard at the hall door but the angry contestants do not hear it. SYLVIA *cocks an ear as she sips her sherry.*

MONICA: But I've searched –

BILL: Then you've probably left it lying around and it's been thrown out with the rest of the rubbish. In which case it serves you right!

MONICA: SERVES ME RIGHT?

BILL: You need a sharp lesson. Look at the way you scribble those notes on poisons on anything that comes to hand! God knows what anyone would say if they found them!

MONICA: They'd say that there was at least one person in this family with intelligence!

BILL: Ha-ha-ha!

The knock is repeated. SYLVIA, *unnoticed, moves into the hall.*

MONICA: All right, my boy! You'll laugh on the other side of your face when my play's produced!

BILL: When your play's produced, I won't be here to laugh! Nor will any other members of this present generation!

MONICA: You'll eat those words, my boy! I swear to you that one day I'll be famous! I'll be written up in every newspaper in this city! I'll be interviewed – and photographed – and pointed out as a Personality! I'll be NEWS – and you'll be darned proud to be my husband!

MEADE *(entering):* SO THERE!

BILL: Andy!

ANDY MEADE *is a thin, untidy man in his mid-thirties. He has a tired, experienced, rather droll face lightened by a pair of sharp intelligent eyes. A highly strung person, he moves quickly and illustrates his speech with quick nervous gestures.*

SYLVIA: I just let him in – does anybody mind?

BILL: Could you hear us out there?

MEADE: Hear you? You were coming at me from all sides – like Cinerama!

MONICA: Oh Gosh – what will Mrs. Lamprey think?

BILL: Bit late to worry about that now! Andy, let's have your hat.

MEADE: No dice, Bill. I can't stay.

SYLVIA: Why not?

MEADE: I've just run up against the juiciest assignment since the Christie murders. Supposed to be on the job right now, but I grabbed a taxi and came around here to let you all in on the Stop Press news . . .

BILL: Something big broken?

MEADE: I'll say it's big! Your buddy, Alistair Digby-Smith just handed in his pail . . .

BILL: Andy . . . !

SYLVIA: Not dead?

MEADE: Stiff as mutton! In a private hospital at four o'clock this morning.

MONICA: Oh . . . .

Distressed, she turns away. BILL *slips his arm about her and there is a short awkward silence.*

BILL: This wouldn't be another of your cock-eyed jokes . . . ?

MEADE: I don't pull faces over a corpse. I'm giving it to you straight.

BILL: Four o'clock this morning?

MEADE: Sure!

BILL: But how did the afternoon papers come to miss it?

MEADE: There's an elaborate game of hush-hush going on, my boy! Don't ask me why. But if one of the ambulance men hadn't hit the hops and blabbed, it'd still be a secret. Forced into a corner, the hospital guys are hinting about a heart attack.

SYLVIA: What's the truth?

MEADE: I've been a newspaper man for so long I wouldn't know the truth if it slapped me on the back! But my guess is that someone's put the finger on this Digby-Smith character – and pressed hard!

SYLVIA: Oh, you've got murders on the brain!

BILL: You know something, Andy?

MEADE: Just this. The C.I.D. are swarming all over Digby-Smith's house. And the top brass at the hospital won't let anyone see the body – gentlemen of the press are especially taboo!

SYLVIA: You don't seem actually in the dark!

MEADE: Trouble with me, I'm no gentleman! Mind you, I played square with that little nurse – boy, was she curvacious! Even told her I was married. But not until she came across with the information that Digby-Smith was wearing pyjamas when he was brought in. And his face and body were covered in scratches.

SYLVIA: What kind of scratches?

MEADE: Take a look at those talons you're wearing on the ends of your fingers, sugar!

He sees the sherry decanter and begins to casually veer toward it.

BILL: But that doesn't even start to make sense, Andy! Digby-Smith was a husky six-footer. A fingernail scratch couldn't cause the death of that big ox!

MEADE: Agreed . . .

He has casually reached for the decanter, but SYLVIA *slaps his hand.*

. . . and to cock it up still more, the chauffeur's missing.

BILL: Who's he?

MEADE: His name's Frederick Smith and I figure he's something they work with mirrors. Been with Digby-Smith only two weeks. No one knows anything about him.

BILL *(after a pause):* Any ideas yourself, Andy?

MEADE *(shrugging):* Just guess-work, laddie. But Digby-Smith's got a dirty record. I think he's been horsing around with some woman. When he ticks her off the list, she gets sore and lets him have it.

SYLVIA: And the chauffeur?

MEADE: Could be in the know and gets out before the cops start taking him apart.

He takes a photograph from his pocket and passes it around.

This is a street snap I hoisted from the chauffeur's room while the master minds were sampling the old port. It's Smith out of uniform. Take a good look. If you see anyone like that, ring me first and then the police.

SYLVIA: You think this is the killer?

MEADE: I think he's a red herring. Scratches – fingernails – cherchez la femme!

He glances at his wrist-watch and starts for the hall.

Holy bells! As for me, cherchez la taxi! Not a syllable of this to a soul, remember!

BILL: All right. I'll come out with you.

MEADE: Sorry about the chow, Monica . . . some other time . . .

SYLVIA: I've got the car outside. Can I drive you?

MEADE: Not on your life, sugar. When the road turns the same way as you do, it's sheer coincidence!

He exits with BILL. SYLVIA *turns and looks at* MONICA. *She is sitting on the divan, rather white and shaken.*

SYLVIA: So it caught up with him at last! How do you feel about it?

MONICA: Quite sick in the stomach!

SYLVIA: But I thought you'd be dancing in the street –

MONICA: Sylvia . . . don't!

SYLVIA: But it's turned out just as you planned . . .

MONICA: That's the horrible part. It's one thing to wish but it's different when it actually happens. It's almost as though I . . . I had something to do with it . . .

SYLVIA: But that's crazy!

MONICA: I know. But it doesn't make me feel any better.

BILL *enters from hallway and he, too, is looking rather subdued.*

SYLVIA: Anything new?

BILL: Only that Andy's impressed on me again that we hold our tongues. It might mean his job.

SYLVIA *(tapping her chest):* Meet the sphinx!

BILL: Before this mess is cleaned up, he's got a hunch there's a pile of dirty linen to be washed –

MONICA: Don't let's talk about it any more, Bill. Do you mind?

BILL: Suits me. How about a sherry?

SYLVIA: Do us all good!

BILL *pours and hands three glasses around. He sits on the divan with* MONICA. SYLVIA, *sensing that they would prefer to be alone, says:*

Anything I can do in the kitchen?

MONICA: You might take a look at the meat. It's probably black by now.

SYLVIA *takes her drink into the kitchen. There is a pause.* BILL, *watching* MONICA, *gives a half smile and raises his glass.*

BILL: Bung-ho, darling.

MONICA *forces a worried smile but makes no attempt to drink.* BILL *reaches out and takes her free hand.*

Sorry I blew my top about that manuscript, moppet. After dinner, we'll all look for it.

MONICA: No, Bill. I never want to see it again.

BILL: What about all the work you've put into it?

MONICA: I don't care. After this, I do all my creating over the stove. I've learned my lesson.

BILL *(gently):* No more thinking out complicated murder plots?

MONICA: Never again!

BILL: Or scribbling down formulas for poisons?

MONICA: After dinner, I'm going to find all those silly pieces of paper and burn them.

BILL: But don't you want to be a famous playwright – written up in every newspaper?

MONICA: I must have been very angry to say such a stupid thing!

BILL *(smiling and raising his glass):* Bung-ho?

MONICA: Bung-ho, darling.

She smiles and they drink. BILL *gives her fingers a squeeze as they rise.*

I'll go on with the table. Would you give Sylvia a hand in the kitchen?

BILL *exits to kitchen.* MONICA *picks up her hat, together with* SYLVIA*'s hat and gloves. She goes into the bedroom. The stage is empty for half a minute.*

MONICA *returns and crosses to the table. On the way, she brushes against an ashtray on the arm of the divan and scatters the ashes to the floor. She gives a little gasp of irritation.*

Where's the dustpan . . . ?

She crosses to the tall cupboard and swings open the door. The figure of a man is revealed inside, standing rigid with his back to MONICA. *She says irritably:*

Now listen, Bill. I'm in no mood for this kind of nonsense . . . Come out of there!

She grabs impatiently at his shoulder. The figure crumples at his knees and begins to fall outward as BILL *enters from the kitchen.*

BILL: Were you talking to me —?

He sees the falling figure and yelps.

Monica!

MONICA: Bill! Oh, Bill . . . !

She runs to him. They both stare transfixed at the figure on the floor.

BILL: How the blazes . . . ?

MONICA: I don't know . . . he was in the cupboard . . . I thought it was you, Bill . . . I touched him . . .

SYLVIA *comes from the kitchen.* BILL *gives the half-fainting* MONICA *to her then he moves to the body and turns it over on its back.*

SYLVIA: It's that chauffeur!

MONICA: What's wrong with his face?

BILL: Covered in deep scratches! We'd better get a doctor.

MONICA: Next door! Dr. Norton . . .

SYLVIA: Will you be all right?

BILL: I'll look after her.

SYLVIA *exits quickly.* BILL *helps* MONICA *to the divan.*

Better sit down, old girl. Take it easy. You don't want to go passing out or anything.

MONICA: I . . . I'm all right now.

BILL: Good!

MONICA: But . . . the man in our cupboard . . . his face so scratched . . .

BILL: Easy, darling. He can't hurt you. Besides, I'm here.

MONICA: Yes . . . *(She glances at the figure and shudders.)* Hadn't we better . . . cover him up . . .

BILL: I'll get a sheet from the bedroom. Sure you're all right to be left alone for a minute?

MONICA: Yes . . .

BILL *(going toward bedroom):* If you feel like going off, take deep breaths and put . . . put . . .

Suddenly he gulps and grasps the back of a chair.

Funny . . . but I feel kinda . . . swimmy . . . myself . . .

MONICA *(realizing):* Oh, no . . . Bill . . . no . . . don't . . .

But BILL *turns, looks at her glassily for a moment, and then slides down to the carpet.* MONICA *runs to him, is bending over him when* MRS. LAMPREY *enters – a very dignified, angry* MRS. LAMPREY *who talks as she enters . . .*

MRS. LAMPREY: Oh, la, miss . . . and what a deceit! What a gross romancer! To say you had no pussy-cat here when the animal itself just leapt headlong from the bathroom window! And to terrify poor Susie so she let out one wild scream of surprise and . . .

Her voice trails off, taking in the extraordinary tableau of the room. MRS. LAMPREY *blinks, focusses, and says vaguely:*

But surely that's your husband?

MONICA *(almost overcome):* Yes . . .

MRS. LAMPREY: Bless me now . . . what ails the lad? Is he sick?

MONICA: No . . . he . . . he just fainted.

MRS. LAMPREY: Sal Volatile! I have a special potion of my own . . . And what of the other gentleman? Is he swooning, too?

MONICA *(gulping):* No, Mrs. Lamprey . . . he . . . he's dead . . .

MRS. LAMPREY *(a weak smile):* Another of your foolish, idle jokes –?

MONICA *(nerves tight with hysteria):* Listen, you stupid old woman! Get yourself down to earth for a minute! This chap's dead . . . what's more, we think he's been murdered! Murder, do you understand – here, in your house . . . That's going to mean police . . . and reporters . . . and newspaper headlines and . . .

But MRS. LAMPREY, *staring at her with dropping jaw, has in turn started to sway dangerously. She rolls up her eyes and pitches forward into* MONICA*'s arms . . . and* MONICA *calls wildly . . .*

Bill . . . Sylvia . . . doctor . . . someone come and help me . . . help . . . help . . . help . . .

The curtain falls rapidly.

Act Two

SCENE 1

The scene is the same. It is about seven-thirty on the following evening. The setting is unchanged, except that on the floor before the linen cupboard pieces of stamp paper are seen roughly marking the position occupied by the mysterious body. At the table, DETECTIVE DENNIS MARSH *sits writing in a note book. He is a fresh-faced, worried looking young man in his mid-twenties.*

Presently the telephone on the sideboard rings. MARSH *jumps to his feet as though galvanized and crosses to the instrument, jerking the receiver from the hook.*

MARSH *(eagerly):* Hello . . . yes, yes, this is Marsh speaking! Who . . . ? *(His face falls.)* Oh, all right . . . let him come up . . .

He replaces the receiver, pulls out a handkerchief, and mops his face. Then he heaves a worried sigh and looks at his wrist-watch. Resignedly, he returns to the table and picks up his notebook as, offstage, MEADE*'s voice is heard.*

MEADE *(offstage):* Evening, Pogson!

POGSON *(offstage):* Evening, Mr. Meade . . . I say, sir, you can't go in there!

MEADE *(offstage):* Relax, Poggie. You know I never go where I'm not invited . . .

He enters, cigarette in mouth, as untidy as ever. By this time, MARSH *has crossed and is poking through* MONICA*'s desk.* MEADE *pauses just inside the door.*

Have you got a warrant to do that?

MARSH *(turning):* All right, Andy, what is it?

MEADE: What's what?

MARSH: You told the constable on guard outside that you had an urgent message for me. Is it about the wife?

MEADE: Your wife or mine?

MARSH: Mine!

MEADE: Denny boy, you surprise me! I always believed you bedded down with the *Manual of Balistics!*

MARSH *(hotly):* So that's it! Just a cheap trick to get your nose inside here? *(He jerks a thumb at the door.)* BLOW!

MEADE *(soothingly):* Now now, Denny . . .

MARSH *(hunching his shoulders):* Listen, smart guy . . . get out of here before I – *(He stops abruptly as the phone makes a ghostly tingling.)*

MEADE: What's the matter?

MARSH: Sssh! *(He continues to stare at the now silent phone.)* I thought that was going to ring . . .

MEADE *(curiously):* What's got you so strung up?

MARSH: Never mind!

MEADE: If it's something new on this case . . .

MARSH: Now, get this, Andy! You don't worm as much as a syllable out of me. All information comes from the chief inspector.

MEADE: But I thought old trout-face was up to his ears in the Digby-Smith case . . .

MARSH: This IS the Digby-Smith case!

MEADE *(triumphant):* So there IS a connection! *(He drops his facetiousness, glances quickly around the room and his eye lights on the bedroom door.)* Do me a favour, will you? Let me move in there and listen.

MARSH: Not on your life! If they ever found out, next week I'd be back pounding the pavement!

MEADE: Just what's the big conspiracy around here? On other murders, I'm welcome as pay day! But mention the Digby-Smith affair and the iron curtain comes down with a clang!

MARSH: Look here, Andy – I'm worried enough as it is . . .

MEADE: That makes it unanimous! Open the book!

MARSH: I've told you – we've got orders from way up top! As far as you vultures are concerned, Digby-Smith died of a heart attack following a stroke.

MEADE *(gesturing to cupboard):* And the boyfriend fell dead in sympathy?

MARSH: Have it any way you like!

He turns back to the desk. MEADE *crosses to the divan. Lighting a cigarette, he lolls back on the cushions. Hands behind head, he addresses the ceiling.*

MEADE: Jesus, it's been a lousy day! Eighty-nine at three o'clock and hotter tomorrow! I pity those poor bastards on the beat . . . Just think of it . . . some of them might be detectives with cushy inside jobs . . . if they'd had a pal in the reporters' room . . .

MARSH *(short):* Get going, will you?

MEADE *(reminiscently):* What was the line I used in the report on the Colchester snatch? Oh, yes . . . "The initiative and resource shown by Constable Dennis Marsh . . . " Then there was that cat burglary when we ran your photograph on the front page . . .

MARSH: I know all about that, Andy.

MEADE: And when I heard about your promotion, I must have been one of the first people to ring you. Funny how certain phrases stick in your mind! "Andy," you said, "this is your work and if ever I have a chance to put a favour your way . . . "

MARSH: Damn it all, man! I can't do it! It's too big – too risky!

MEADE *(on his feet – dynamic):* Let me stay in that bedroom and so help me Caesar, if newspaper influence can do it, they'll be painting Inspector on your door!

MARSH: But if they find you!

MEADE: I'll stay so quiet you'll hear my dandruff drop!

MARSH *(after slight hesitation):* All right, but on one condition.

MEADE: Name it!

MARSH: You print nothing until it's been sieved by Security!

MEADE *(impressed):* Security, eh?

MARSH: You heard me . . .

He crosses and throws open the bedroom door.

God help us both if they find you in here!

MEADE: Security can't hurt me . . .

MARSH *(doubling his fist):* No! But I can!

He slams the door shut behind MEADE *and moves back to the table as* POGSON*'s voice, very respectful, is heard offstage.*

POGSON: Good evening, sir.

BURKE *(offstage):* Evening, my man. Marsh inside?

POGSON: Yes, sir.

CHIEF INSPECTOR WILLIAM BURKE *enters. He is a heavily built man in his mid-fifties. He carries a small attache case and his manner is curt, brisk, and official. His deep voice has a slightly adenoidal edge.*

BURKE: Evening, Marsh.

MARSH: Evening, sir.

BURKE: Everything in hand?

MARSH: Yes, sir.

BURKE *(crossing to table):* Glad to hear it. So far, the only thing I've caught is a cold! That mausoleum of Digby-Smith's has more draughts than a monkey house!

MARSH: Bad show, sir. You tried eucalyptus?

BURKE: Eh?

MARSH: Old-fashioned, sir, but my wife swears by it. Few drops in boiling water – wrap your head and inhale the fumes.

BURKE: Messy, too. I'll stick to the antibiotics. *(He looks keenly at* MARSH.) You don't look too chipper yourself, my boy. Anything wrong?

MARSH: Not with me, sir. It's the wife. She's in hospital.

BURKE: Too bad. Anything serious?

MARSH: Yes . . . no . . . that is . . . it's her first, sir.

BURKE: Well, well! Congratulations!

MARSH: Yes, sir – thank you, sir. But it hasn't arrived yet.

BURKE: Oh!

MARSH: I know there's no danger, sir, not with all these modern aids. But all the same, a chap can't help worrying . . .

BURKE: Fine way to start a murder investigation! I'm going to have the flu and you're going to have a baby!

MARSH: Er . . . the wife, sir.

BURKE: Amounts to the same thing! Look here, you'd better cut off to the hospital. I can phone through to the Yard and –

MARSH: I'd rather you didn't, sir. I'd rather be doing something to keep my mind off it.

BURKE: Please yourself. They know where to get you?

MARSH: I've given them this number. They'll ring here. That's another reason I'd like to stick around.

BURKE: All right! *(He takes a small phial from his pocket and shakes out two tablets.)* Where's the kitchen?

MARSH: There.

BURKE: Find a glass and bring me some water. I've got to get these things down.

MARSH *exits to kitchen.* BURKE *stands looking around the apartment.* MARSH *re-enters.* BURKE *takes water, swallows tablets, and drinks.*

That's over for another hour! Now, how long have you been here?

MARSH: Since four o'clock.

BURKE: Got your report?

MARSH: Yes.

BURKE: Let's have it boiled down small!

MARSH: How much do you know, sir?

BURKE *(consults notebook):* At seven-forty-five last night, constables Timmins and Hart were summoned to this apartment by the owner, a Mrs. Lamprey. They found a man paralysed on the floor. There was a doctor already in attendance . . .

MARSH: Name of Norton. G.P. Lives next door.

BURKE: He's standing by?

MARSH: Ready whenever we want him!

BURKE: Good! *(Glances at notes again.)* Taken to hospital, the dead man was subsequently identified as Frederick John Smith, chauffeur to Alistair Digby-Smith. Later, Smith died of curare poisoning introduced through scratches on his skin. That was at ten o'clock this morning. He was moved to the morgue where one of our men noticed the injuries and commented on their similarity to Digby-Smith's . . . *(Shuts his notebook.)* You carry on.

MARSH: I came here with Donlin and Armstrong. We made enquiries and discovered such evidence as to enable us to return with a warrant to search this apartment.

BURKE: Find anything?

MARSH: In the dustbin were several pieces of charred paper – recently burnt. They're down at headquarters being photographed under the infra-red camera.

BURKE: Anything else?

MARSH: No, sir.

BURKE: Nothing resembling a weapon?

MARSH: Well . . . *(He hesitates a moment and crosses to the sideboard, opening a drawer and producing an object.)* Only this, sir.

BURKE: An automatic!

MARSH: No, sir. Fooled me in the beginning. You watch . . . *(He presses the trigger and a cigarette pops out of the barrel.)* Trick cigarette case . . .

BURKE: Huh!

MARSH: Several gadgets about like this. *(He returns the object to the drawer.)* Property of the young lady here. I believe she used to work for a toy manufacturer.

BURKE: Young woman occupant of this flat?

MARSH: Mrs. Monica Sefton.

BURKE: Where is she now?

MARSH: With her husband under guard. We've put them in the owner's living room while –

The telephone shrills abruptly and MARSH *leaps toward it.* BURKE *watches with a sardonic eye.*

Hello . . . yes, speaking . . . *(Deflated.)* Oh, yes, he's here. Hold the line. It's for you, sir.

BURKE: And they say the mother has the worse time! *(Takes receiver.)* Burke here. Yes. *(Sharply.)* All of them? Good . . . good . . . *(Hangs up and turns to* MARSH.) That was the lab report on your charred paper.

MARSH: What was it?

BURKE: Data on a number of well-known poisons. Curare among them. *(As* MARSH *reacts, he delves inside his attache case and turns with a framed photograph in his hand.)*

When you searched this place, find anything connected with this chap?

MARSH *(surprised):* That's Oscar Sneddon!

BURKE *(grimly):* One of the most dangerous subversive agents this country ever spawned! He's the man behind the attempted sabotage of the naval base and that disastrous fire at the docks six months ago!

MARSH: But he was never caught . . .

BURKE: Security has the answer to that! They swear that Sneddon was planning his biggest coup – something that made those other acts look like child's play! They were giving him rope . . . hoping they would step in at the right moment and grab the whole gang! But somehow, Sneddon must have got wise! Almost overnight, he vanished!

MARSH: McLean and Burgess all over again, eh?

BURKE: Just like that!

MARSH: Where did you get this photograph, sir?

BURKE *(heavily):* From a drawer in Alistair Digby-Smith's private study . . . Now, take a look at the inscription at the bottom.

He hands the photograph to MARSH, *who squints at it then looks up in amazement.*

MARSH: This is dynamite!

BURKE: Security thinks the same. That's why they've clamped down on this dirty business. They realize that if the newspapers got as much as a breath of the truth, it could mean another election!

MARSH: Y . . . yes, sir.

BURKE: We're sitting right on the edge of a volcano, my boy. And this is no time to be having babies!

MARSH *gives a wild, despairing glance at the closed bedroom door.* BURKE, *returning the picture to his case, does not notice it. He looks up as* MARSH *speaks again.*

MARSH: Where does the girl fit into this?

BURKE: Girl?

MARSH: Mrs. Sefton.

BURKE: That's what we're here to find out! Any proof she knew Digby-Smith?

MARSH: She knew him all right. Hated his guts!

BURKE *(sharply):* Eh?

MARSH: Pretty expert at this poison business, too.

BURKE *(staring at him):* What are you talking about?

MARSH: It's true, sir! What's more, she was heard to boast about it!

BURKE: Heard by whom?

MARSH: The owner of this place – Mrs. Ida Lamprey.

BURKE *(slowly):* You know, I think we might start with this woman . . . Get her in here.

MARSH *(crossing to hallway – calling):* Pogson! Ask Mrs. Lamprey to come here.

He returns as BURKE *closes the attache case. Suddenly he wrinkles his nose, stiffens. His head goes back and he draws a deep breath to sneeze. Then he relaxes and grunts.*

BURKE: No . . . dammit!

MARSH: Looking at a bright light is supposed to help, sir . . .

BURKE: Pshaw!

POGSON *(at door):* Mrs. Lamprey, sir.

MRS. LAMPREY *enters, looking even more vague and out-of-touch than before. She stands looking from one official to the other with a little frown of perplexity.*

BURKE: Mrs. Ida Lamprey?

MRS. LAMPREY *(correcting):* Ida MAE. *(She quotes dreamily:)*

"Ida Mae,
Blithe and gay,
Spreading joy the livelong day . . . " I can still
hear dear sweet nanny telling the other children –

BURKE *(interrupting):* Yes yes, of course! Now, about this tragedy that occurred here . . .

MRS. LAMPREY: So very, very vexatious!

BURKE: We'd like to know something about your tenants – this Mr. and Mrs. Sefton.

MRS. LAMPREY *(vaguely):* Oh, there were others before them, sir. I had a coloured gentleman here, but he made the most distressing smells in the kitchen. He said he was in the diplomatic service, but his head was quite the wrong shape . . .

BURKE *(patiently):* We're only interested in Mrs. Sefton.

MRS. LAMPREY: Such a sweet, sweet face . . . but you never can tell. Although Susie knew! Dogs do, you know! Susie never took to her, not from the very beginning. I shouldn't be surprised if she'd KICKED Susie . . .

BURKE: Yes, but –

MRS. LAMPREY: Mind you, she could be so very kind! She gave me a cigarette last night . . . not that I dared smoke it after all that outlandish talk about poisoning people . . .

BURKE: That's what we want to know! What exactly did this girl say?

MRS. LAMPREY: Such odd talk! I tried to put it right out of my head . . .

BURKE: It's very important that we know, Mrs. Lamprey. Try to remember!

MRS. LAMPREY: Now . . . let me think . . . *(She places her hand on her forehead and closes her eyes.)* I remember. She said that she knew all about poisons and that she could commit a crime no one would suspect.

BURKE *(grimly):* She did, eh?

MRS. LAMPREY: Then she mentioned a name . . . some person she appeared to dislike. Oh dear, I'm such a dunce at remembering names . . .

BURKE: Was it . . . Digby-Smith?

MRS. LAMPREY: I don't know . . .

BURKE: But if you heard the other part of her conversation . . . ?

MRS. LAMPREY *(with faded dignity):* I trust you don't think I was eavesdropping, sir! If so, I find the suggestion most distasteful! All my life –

BURKE *(quickly):* Nothing like that was meant at all, Mrs. Lamprey! But how did you feel about this girl's remarks?

MRS. LAMPREY: I thought she was just being a tease. Because she didn't always speak the truth. She had a pussy-cat in here yesterday and if it hadn't been for Susie, I would never have known –

The telephone rings abruptly. MARSH *half-rises from the chair where he is taking notes but* BURKE *is before him. He lifts the receiver.*

BURKE: Hello . . . yes speaking. But hold on for a moment, would you? (*To* MARSH.) Would you take Mrs. Lamprey back and ask Mr. Sefton to come here?

MARSH: Thank you, Mrs. Lamprey.

MRS. LAMPREY: It was a black pussy-cat and it jumped out of the bathroom window. Susie was DEMENTED – it terrified the poor, wee romp . . .

MARSH *(as they exit):* Very interesting, Mrs. Lamprey, I'm sure . . .

BURKE *(turning to phone):* Right. Let's have it! *(His tone sharpens.)* Actually inviting him to the apartment? Of course I want to see it! Send a man over with it at once!

He hangs up as MARSH *re-enters.*

Better luck next time!

MARSH *(worried):* If anything went wrong, I suppose they'd let me know?

BURKE: Nothing's gone wrong!

MARSH: They're taking a devil of a time . . .

BURKE: Might mean a double issue! What's Mrs. Sefton's first name?

MARSH: Monica.

BURKE: Got a specimen of her handwriting?

MARSH: There's a grocery list in the kitchen . . .

BURKE: Get it.

MARSH *enters and emerges from kitchen with a scribbling pad.* BURKE *glances at it, tears off the top slip, and is putting it in his notebook as* BILL, *far from amiable, enters from hallway.*

Ah, Mr. Sefton?

BILL: Look here, what's the idea of locking us up like this? We're not criminals!

BURKE: Just a formality. Sit down . . . *(As* BILL *obeys reluctantly.)* You told Detective Marsh that the man found in the cupboard was a complete stranger to you?

BILL: That's right.

BURKE: And to your wife?

BILL: Naturally!

BURKE: Naturally. Mr. Digby-Smith . . . was he also a stranger?

BILL: No.

BURKE: A friend?

BILL: Far from it. The blighter was responsible for me losing my job on the newspaper. Said I'd misreported him.

BURKE: In what way?

BILL: He gave out some dangerous political statements . . . not that he meant them – he was drunk as an owl at the time!

BURKE: What did your wife think of your dismissal?

BILL: She took it pretty much to heart.

BURKE: She . . . disliked Digby-Smith?

BILL: We both did. Heartily!

BURKE: But your wife's dislike was scarcely strong enough to inspire . . . personal injury?

BILL *(on his feet – incredulously):* Monica? Injure Digby-Smith? Are you crazy?

BURKE: We have a witness, Mr. Sefton, who alleges over-hearing your wife make certain curious statements. The young lady was heard to say that she was an expert on poisons and could commit a perfect murder that could baffle –

BILL *has been listening incredulously. Now he sits back with a broad, relieved chuckle.*

You find this amusing, Mr. Sefton?

BILL: For Pete's sake, inspector! You surely haven't been wasting time taking down that tripe?

BURKE: Wasting time?

BILL: Yes . . . because it's all about Monica's play! You see, my wife's got a maggot in her mind she can write a detective play for television.

BURKE: Indeed?

BILL: We used to talk over the plot together. Sometimes she'd come out with the craziest things!

BURKE *(after slight pause):* This work . . . is it finished?

BILL: I don't think it ever will be. Monica gets a kick out of playing with these ideas. That's why she borrowed that scrapbook of unusual crimes.

BURKE: Scrapbook?

BILL: It's in the sideboard . . .

BURKE *crosses, opens sideboard drawers till he finds a large book. He returns with it as* BILL *continues.*

It belongs to a friend of mine – a crime reporter. He's been collecting those cuttings for years.

BURKE *(flicking through pages):* Curious hobby, I must say. *(He closes the book and asks almost casually:)* Has Mrs. Sefton ever been out of England?

BILL: Oh, yes!

BURKE: Where?

BILL: To the Continent.

BURKE: What part?

BILL: West Berlin. She went there on business.

BURKE: What kind of business?

BILL: She was private secretary to a Swiss importer of toys and novelties. Chap named Vogel.

BURKE: Where is Mr. Vogel now?

BILL: I haven't a clue. Some months ago, the import restrictions knocked him out of business and Monica found herself without a job. But I say, what's all this leading up to?

BURKE: We have to ask all kinds of questions. Sometimes they don't lead anywhere.

BILL: Can I go back to my wife now? She's still a bit upset . . .

BURKE: We'd prefer you didn't worry her just now –

He breaks as CONSTABLE POGSON *enters with an envelope.*

POGSON: Just arrived from headquarters, sir.
BURKE: Thank you.

He slits the envelope and extracts a sheet of paper. Glances at it then slips the paper into his notebook. Nods to POGSON.

No answer. Would you take Mr. Sefton back and ask his wife to come here? Keep the young lady with you until we call.

POGSON: Yes sir. (*To* BILL.) This way, sir.
BILL (*to* BURKE): I don't understand the half of this!
BURKE *(gravely):* Neither do we, son. Get along now.

BILL *gives him an angry puzzled glance and exits with* POGSON.

How do you feel about him?

MARSH: Sorry!
BURKE: Because he happens to be in love with his wife?
MARSH *(nodding):* And because he's got a nasty shock coming to him!
BURKE: Then he's in the clear?
MARSH: Why else would he give us the motive for Digby-Smith's murder so pat?
BURKE: Talking too much . . . yes! *(Slight pause.)* You know Marsh, if we could establish a link between the chauffeur and this girl, we might almost say they were chosen to shut Digby-Smith's mouth between them.
MARSH: But why this particular girl, sir?
BURKE: This particular girl had connections in West Berlin, remember!
MARSH *(doubtfully):* Yes, but –
BURKE: Remember what Hastings told us this morning? These agents no longer go around in false beards and pockets bulging with bombs! They're ordinary bluff workmen like that foreman at the Darlington Steel Mills or short-sighted clerks or servant girls . . .
MARSH: Or nice little housewives like Mrs. Monica Sefton, eh?
BURKE: Who knows all about crimes and poisons because she happens to be writing a play! Funny you didn't run

across the manuscript when you searched the apartment.

MARSH: Nothing like that here, sir.

BURKE: So . . . if it doesn't exist, we might assume that it was just a smokescreen to cover her researches into obscure methods of murder! Any idea how she might have committed the crime?

MARSH: Well . . . if it wasn't too far-fetched, I'd say she might have painted her fingernails with curare and just let both those men have it!

BURKE *(grunting):* Before this case is finished, that might be the least fantastic thing about it. Did you check up on the estimated time Digby-Smith was attacked?

MARSH: Approximately ten o'clock on the night before he died.

BURKE: I wonder if Mrs. Sefton has an alibi for that time?

MARSH: Ready for her now, sir?

BURKE: Yes.

MARSH *exits.* BURKE *reaches into his vest pocket and takes out a small thermometer. He thrusts this into his mouth. Then he takes out his notebook, extracts the folded piece of paper and compares it with the grocery list. Then he takes the thermometer from his mouth, holds it up to the light, and grimaces.*

BURKE: I'm practically a dead man myself!

He returns the thermometer to his pocket as MARSH *enters with* MONICA. *She is not yet aware of the danger in which she stands and, although her manner is worried, it is still fairly self-possessed.*

MONICA: Inspector Burke?

BURKE *(nodding):* Sit down, Mrs. Sefton. We're sorry to trouble you after your nasty experience yesterday, but there are a few points we'd like straightened out . . .

MONICA: What is it you want to know?

BURKE: What made you go to the linen cupboard at that particular time?

MONICA: I wanted some serviettes . . . we use part of the cupboard as a linen press.

BURKE: The man concealed inside – you'd no idea how he came to be there?
MONICA: None whatever.
BURKE: Did you recognize the man?
MONICA *(she hesitates a moment):* Well . . . just how do you mean?
BURKE: Come, come, Mrs. Sefton – surely the question is simple enough! Had you met this man before?
MONICA *(promptly):* Oh, no!
BURKE *(pressing the point):* The fellow, then, was a complete and utter stranger to you?
MONICA: Y . . . Yes . . .
BURKE *(watching her closely):* You don't seem exactly certain on that point . . .
MONICA: But I can assure you, inspector, I have never met nor spoken with that man in my life – never!
BURKE: I see. *(He pauses.)* There is, of course, an alternative . . .
MONICA: I don't understand.
BURKE: You might have known this man through some . . . correspondence?
MONICA: If by that you mean I might have written to this stranger – the answer is no, never!
BURKE: You're perfectly certain of that, Mrs. Sefton?
MONICA *(half amused, half angry):* Of course I'm certain!

BURKE *gives her a long, searching look. Deliberately he takes out his notebook and extracts the folded paper. Keeping one part folded back, he shows her the other.*

BURKE: Is that your hand writing?
MONICA *(after slight pause, nods):* Yes, it looks like mine. What is it?
BURKE: You don't know? (MONICA *puts out her hand to take the paper but* BURKE *withdraws it swiftly.*) I want you to listen to this note . . . (*He reads slowly.*) "I must see you at once. Something HAS GONE WRONG. The same address. Urgent – don't fail me!" (*He looks up.*) It's signed with the initial M.

He pauses and watches MONICA'*s puzzled expression.*

Well, Mrs. Sefton?

MONICA: Well what?

BURKE: Did you write those words?

MONICA: Of course I didn't!

BURKE: Yet you admit they are in your handwriting!

MONICA: It . . . it looks like mine, but . . . Inspector, where did you get that note?

BURKE: It was found in the pocket of the man hidden in your cupboard!

MONICA *(she stares at him, utterly bewildered):* But that's quite impossible . . .

BURKE: Nevertheless, it's true, Mrs. Sefton.

MONICA: But how could it possibly . . . ? May I see the note?

BURKE *hesitates a moment and then passes it over.* MONICA *frowns over the words for a few seconds then her face clears.*

But this is part of my play!

BURKE *(glancing at* MARSH): Indeed?

MONICA: That's how it comes to be in my handwriting. I'm writing a detective play. In it a man called Henry Maltravers murders his wife for her insurance money, hoping to make it look like an accident . . . .

She pauses, catches an expression of open incredulity on BURKE*'s face, and hurries on nervously.*

Suspicion is aroused when Maltravers bungles the job. He writes to his accomplice – his mistress. That's why it's signed like that . . . M. for Maltravers . . . *(She stops and hands the paper back to* BURKE *who receives it in stolid silence.)* You . . . you believe me, don't you, Inspector?

BURKE: I think you've overlooked the circumstances under which this note was found.

MONICA: I haven't overlooked them. It's just that I can't understand them.

BURKE: Neither can we, Mrs. Sefton!

He turns away. Relieved, MONICA *rises.*

MONICA: Is that all?

BURKE *(turning):* Not quite. This . . . er . . . play you were writing.
MONICA: Yes?
BURKE: Could we see it?
MONICA: Of course! I keep it in –
BURKE *(as she stops):* Yes?
MONICA: Do you want to see it at this moment?
BURKE *(steadily):* If you please.
MONICA: I've just remembered. It's been . . . mislaid . . .
BURKE *(with a glance at* MARSH): Mislaid?
MONICA: Last night I wanted to show it to . . . to somebody. When I went to get it, it wasn't where I'd put it. But I'm certain it will turn up.
BURKE *(drily):* No doubt. Was it a large manuscript?
MONICA: Fairly. I'd already finished the first two acts.
BURKE: Not a very easy thing to . . . mislay, Mrs. Sefton?
MONICA: No – that's why it must be around here somewhere.
BURKE: Mrs. Sefton, before you say anything more, I should tell you that three detectives have searched this apartment very thoroughly. So that, if any manuscript such as you describe existed, it could not have possibly been overlooked.
MONICA: Inspector . . .
BURKE: I suggest my men didn't find the manuscript because it doesn't exist and never has existed!

For the first time, MONICA *begins to sense the net closing about her and from now on her manner becomes more desperate.*

MONICA: But that's ridiculous, inspector! Of course I was writing the play. That's why I collected all that data on poisons!
BURKE: Oh, yes – your data on poisons . . . We're rather interested in that. How long did it take you to gather that material?
MONICA: About six months.
BURKE: A difficult task, I should say?
MONICA: I had to wade through all kinds of medical books

and encyclopaedias – I certainly wouldn't care to do it all over again.

BURKE: Had you used this data?

MONICA: Oh, no. I didn't need the information until the last act.

BURKE *(abruptly):* Then why burn the notes?

MONICA *(caught off guard):* Burn . . . ? How did you know I'd burnt them?

BURKE *(snapping):* Answer the question! You admit you went to considerable trouble to collect the information – yet without waiting to use it, you burn the papers! WHY?

MONICA: Because – *(She is about to say something else but obviously changes her mind.)* Because I'd finished with them!

BURKE: Meaning that it had served its purpose? A purpose quite unconnected with the writing of this so far purely hypothetical play?

MONICA: Yes – no – *(She looks around desperately.)* Why are you asking me all these questions?

BURKE *does not answer. He walks across to the desk and begins to tap idly on the space bar of the typewriter.*

BURKE: Is this your machine?

MONICA: It belongs to my husband, but I use it.

BURKE: What for?

MONICA: Typing what you call my hypothetical play!

BURKE *(almost casually):* Don't you find that long fingernails interfere with your typing?

MONICA: I don't wear my fingernails long.

BURKE: Do you mind if I see them?

He puts out his hand. MONICA *is about to extend her fingers – indeed, is in the act of doing so when abruptly she pulls them back, staring at him.*

MONICA: So that's it! You think I'm the mysterious woman who scratched Digby-Smith's face – *(realizing she has been told this in confidence, she stops. There is a moment's pause, then* BURKE *speaks very quietly.)*

BURKE: How did you know that the face was scratched?
MONICA *(cornered):* I – I –
BURKE: Go on, Mrs. Sefton.
MONICA: I – must have read it in the newspapers . . .
BURKE: No newspaper printed that information and you know it! Isn't it time you stopped lying? You were lying, weren't you?
MONICA: Y–Yes . . .
BURKE: Then how did you know?
MONICA: A . . . friend told me.
BURKE: Why not say so in the first place?
MONICA: Because it was told to me – in confidence. If it ever came out, he might lose his job.
BURKE: And what's the name of this obliging friend?
MONICA: You've no right to ask me!
BURKE *(disgusted):* So . . . you're still lying?
MONICA: No!
BURKE: I say you are, young woman! I say that the friend who told you how Digby-Smith died was the man to whom you wrote that note – the man hidden in your cupboard and whom you discovered only when he was as good as dead!

MONICA, *almost speechless, stares at him in terror. Then she whispers.*

MONICA: You can't believe that – you can't!
BURKE: Mrs. Sefton . . .
MONICA: I've told you over and over again! I didn't write that note! I never knew the man! I didn't dream he was in the cupboard . . . *(Her voice breaks and she is very near tears.)* Oh, what's the use? I can see you don't believe me . . .

She sinks back into her chair, very white and shaken. BURKE *watches her for a few moments before continuing.*

BURKE: On the evening before last, where were you?
MONICA: Here.
BURKE: ALL the evening?
MONICA *(wearily):* Yes . . . yes . . .

BURKE: You didn't leave for an interval of say . . . half an hour between ten and half-past?

MONICA: No, no. I was here – all the time!

BURKE: Alone?

MONICA: No. Bill – my husband was with me.

BURKE: Anyone else?

MONICA: No . . . yes, yes! Dr. Norton was here. He lives next door and he came in for supper.

BURKE: I see . . . *(He calls.)* Pogson!

POGSON *enters.*

I'll want to talk with you again, Mrs. Sefton. Meanwhile, I must ask you to wait with the constable.

MONICA: But I've told you all I know . . .

BURKE *(coldly):* Please!

MONICA *gives him a despairing look and exits with* POGSON. BURKE *stands looking after her. He takes out his handkerchief, blows his nose, and wipes his eyes. Turns to* MARSH.

This is one hell of a business!

MARSH: Your cold or Mrs. Sefton?

BURKE: Both! But she's giving me the worst headache!

MARSH: Seems pretty straightforward to me, sir . . .

BURKE *(grunting):* Really?

MARSH: Notice how she sidestepped producing the play manuscript?

BURKE: True.

MARSH: And she gave herself away properly over Digby-Smith's injuries . . .

BURKE: Yes. If it wasn't for two things, Marsh, you could pack up and go off to the hospital and leave me to finish the case.

MARSH: Two things, sir?

BURKE: There's the chauffeur . . . why did she want him so urgently? Why kill him? And having killed him, why reveal the body in that way?

MARSH: As the note said, something went wrong. Mrs. Sefton bundled the body into the cupboard since it was the only thing to do!

BURKE: And I suppose she couldn't hope to keep it hidden indefinitely . . . Then there's the actual METHOD of murder . . .

MARSH: Those scratches surely mean personal contact with Digby-Smith?

BURKE: Then the woman's lying when she says she never left this apartment?

MARSH: The husband would know . . .

BURKE: I'm afraid we can't place much weight on his testimony. But there's this doctor fellow . . .

MARSH: Norton?

BURKE: Yes. Ask him if he'd mind giving us a few minutes. Don't send Pogson. Go yourself.

MARSH *nods and exits.* BURKE *stands irresolute for a moment, then takes a phial from his pocket. He empties two more tablets into his hand. He goes into kitchen and emerges with a glass of water. Is about to swallow the tablets when* DR. NORTON *enters with* MARSH.

Dr. Norton?

NORTON: That's right.

BURKE: I suppose Detective Marsh told you . . . ?

NORTON: Oh, yes, inspector.

BURKE: Sorry to bother you, doctor, but I think you can help me.

NORTON: In a professional capacity?

BURKE *(seeing his eye on the glass and tablets):* Oh, no. This is rather more serious than a flu attack. Excuse me . . .

He takes the tablets with the water.

I've got to do that to stop my head falling off.

NORTON: Bad as that, eh? Better let me prescribe something for you.

BURKE: Later perhaps. *(He gestures to a chair and* NORTON *sits.)* You know, of course, what happened in here last night?

NORTON: Extraordinary business!

BURKE: You attended the man found in here?

NORTON: Well – attended is hardly the word . . . You see, a young woman burst into my apartment to say there was a dead man in this place. My first thought was that something had happened to Mr. Sefton. I hurried in here but the fellow was a complete stranger to me.

BURKE: You examined the body?

NORTON: The fellow was rigid with some organic paralysis. His condition was so serious I ordered him to hospital straight away.

BURKE: Do you know the Sefton couple very well?

NORTON: We're just neighbours.

BURKE: And before you were called in last evening, had you visited this apartment before?

NORTON: Once.

BURKE: When was that?

NORTON: Mrs. Sefton asked me in for supper on the evening before last. She . . . wanted some medical information.

BURKE: On what branch?

NORTON *(after slight hesitation):* Poisons . . . *(He adds quickly.)* It was for some kind of play she was writing.

BURKE: Oh? You saw the manuscript?

NORTON: No. But –

BURKE *(as he stops):* But what, doctor?

NORTON: Nothing – nothing.

BURKE *(watching him closely):* Doctor, while you were in this room, did you hear Mrs. Sefton mention either directly or indirectly a man named Digby-Smith?

NORTON: Why?

BURKE: Because Digby-Smith was murdered, doctor – in a manner identical with the man found in Mrs. Sefton's cupboard!

NORTON *(obviously shocked):* Oh Lord no – she wasn't serious! I'm certain she wasn't . . .

BURKE: Serious? Serious about what?

NORTON *(uncomfortably):* Look here, inspector, I don't know that I want to be mixed up in all this . . .

BURKE: Doctor . . .

NORTON: Well?

BURKE: Your reluctance is understandable. On the other hand, we have a difficult job to do.

NORTON: But surely this girl's childish threats –
BURKE *(interrupting sharply):* Then she DID make threats? Threats against whom?
NORTON *(uncomfortably):* Look here –
BURKE: Was it Digby-Smith?
NORTON *(after a pause):* Yes.
BURKE: Why?
NORTON: She appeared to think the man was responsible for her husband's dismissal.
BURKE *(watching him):* I believe you said you were just a casual acquaintance, doctor?
NORTON: True.
BURKE: Surely this was rather a . . . personal subject to discuss with a comparative stranger?
NORTON: It came out in connection with her play . . .
BURKE: Yes?
NORTON: I'd asked the young lady why she chose a crime motif. She said she'd got the idea after brooding on . . . on punishing Digby-Smith for his persecution of her husband.
BURKE *(softly):* Great Scott!
NORTON: But I'm certain it was just a lot of silly nonsense! You've only got to look at Mrs. Sefton to realize she wouldn't harm a living soul!
BURKE *(aside):* That's why they chose her . . .
NORTON: Beg pardon?
BURKE: I was just thinking aloud.
NORTON: Is that all, inspector?
BURKE: Bear with me just a little longer . . . *(He takes his notebook from his pocket and flicks through it.)* What time did you come into this apartment?
NORTON: Sometime after nine o'clock.
BURKE: And you left?
NORTON: Possibly fifteen minutes later.
BURKE: Then you weren't here around ten o'clock?
NORTON: Oh, no.
BURKE: But I was under the impression Mrs. Sefton had asked you for supper?

NORTON: That's right. What's more, I might have stayed if it hadn't been for that wretched cat.

BURKE: Cat?

NORTON: Mrs. Sefton brought it in. Her husband told her to get rid of the animal, but she refused. So I decided it was time for me to leave.

BURKE: You don't like cats?

NORTON: I loathe them!

BURKE: They affect some people that way – something to do with an allergy . . .

NORTON: Not in my case! It's just pure funk. I had a nasty experience in Edinburgh just after the war.

BURKE *(politely):* Really?

NORTON: I was house surgeon at a hospital and pretty ragged from overwork. I'd been yarning with some of the other doctors and the talk turned to murders. One chap told a particularly ghastly story about a cat – I think some of the students overheard what we were saying. That night, after I'd dropped off to sleep, one of them dropped a cat through my bedroom window. It landed smack on my chest. I awoke with a yell, thinking I'd been scratched by its poisoned claws –

BURKE *(sharply):* Poisoned claws?

NORTON *(a little surprised at the bark):* That's right. I suppose I must have been dreaming about the crime . . .

BURKE *(slowly):* What crime, doctor?

NORTON: It happened in Rouen – a woman took a cat, painted its claws with poison and dropped it on a sleeping man suspected of being a collaborator . . . *(He shudders.)* Now, the very sight of a cat gives me the creeps!

BURKE *has recovered his poise. Behind* NORTON*'s back, he makes a warning gesture to the excited* MARSH.

BURKE *(smoothly):* Quite understandable, doctor. Now, you've been extremely patient with us. I don't think we need keep you any longer.

NORTON *(shaking his head):* You know, it's extraordinary how we're made . . .

BURKE: After your experience in Edinburgh –

NORTON *(interrupting):* I wasn't thinking of myself, inspector. It's the young woman. I judged her as . . . well . . . rather scatterbrained. I never dreamt –

He breaks as BURKE *buries his face in his handkerchief to check an abortive sneeze.*

Look here, are quite sure I can't help about that cold?

BURKE *(shakes his head):* Don't worry about me, doctor. I'll soon be home in bed.

NORTON *(grunting):* Best place for you!

He nods and exits. MARSH *watches him go then rises excitedly.*

MARSH: That would be the cat the landlady saw jumping from the bathroom window!

BURKE: Of course!

MARSH: Certainly something new in weapons, sir!

BURKE: That's why she used it.

MARSH: And the chauffeur?

BURKE: Came here to get the cat. Either by accident or design, he got himself scratched.

MARSH: What's the next move, sir?

BURKE: I'm going to talk to Security. Give me three minutes and then bring Mrs. Sefton back in here.

MARSH *(starts to exit):* Very good, sir.

BURKE: And close the hall door after you!

MARSH *exits and the hall door closes.* BURKE *stands thinking for a moment then he crosses to the telephone. Dials a number, waits, and when he speaks his voice is lowered.*

Section Eight-O. One-four-one, please. *(Pause.)* Yes, sir – reporting from South Kensington. We've struck a very broad lead on the Digby-Smith affair. Young married woman – Mrs. Monica Sefton. You'd better have someone check, sir. *(Pause.)* Too involved to tell you over the phone, but I suggest you talk to the woman yourself. *(Pause.)* Oh, no sir – just a minnow, I'm afraid. The big fish are still at the bottom of the pool. *(Pause.)* I'd say in about twenty minutes . . . yes, sir . . . thank you, sir . . .

He hangs up and stands looking around the room. Then he picks up MONICA*'s scrap book. Opening it he begins to check each item carefully. Suddenly he stiffens, nods, marks a page in the book, and is closing it when a tap sounds at the door.*

Come in!

MARSH *enters with a pale and worried* MONICA. BURKE *addresses her abruptly, his manner much more official than before.*

Mrs. Sefton . . .

MONICA: Yes?

BURKE: We've been talking with Dr. Norton. He said that while he was in here the other evening, you brought a cat into the room.

MONICA *(wearily)*: I didn't bring it. I found it curled up on the window sill.

BURKE: Weren't you afraid?

MONICA: Afraid?

BURKE: Afraid the creature might have scratched you?

MONICA: It never entered my head!

BURKE *(smoothly):* Strange . . . ! Have you any idea what happened to your cat?

MONICA: It wasn't MY cat! It strayed in here. Because it was half-starved, I gave it some milk.

BURKE: Yet you denied any knowledge of the animal to your landlady!

MONICA: Only because I was afraid she'd send it away!

BURKE: And naturally you wouldn't want this particular creature falling into strange hands . . .

As MONICA *stares at him, he picks up the cutting book and begins to turn the pages.*

Quite an amount of dangerous information here, Mrs. Sefton . . .

MONICA: I . . . I suppose so.

BURKE: Information like this, for example!

He stabs a finger at a cutting. MONICA *looks at his tight, stern face and then at the cutting. Her own face is a study in bewilderment.*

MONICA: Where did that come from?

BURKE: Are you trying to tell us you've never seen this before?

MONICA: Never – never! What is it?

BURKE *(heavily):* An account of a murder committed at Rouen . . . a woman painted the claws of a cat with poison. She used it as a murder weapon . . . just as you murdered Alistair Digby Smith!

MONICA *is staring at him in horror. She says huskily*:

MONICA: You're making a dreadful mistake . . .

BURKE: No, Mrs. Sefton! You're the one making the mistake! In fact, you made two! You didn't imagine the cat would find its way back here . . . and you should have destroyed this press cutting along with your notes on curare poisoning!

MONICA: Inspector . . .

BURKE *(interrupting quietly):* Who's the top man in your group?

MONICA: What are you saying?

BURKE *(stern):* Mrs. Sefton, you've made two mistakes! Don't make a third! We're asking you to cooperate with us . . . giving you your last chance!

MONICA: But I've done nothing wrong . . .

BURKE: Mrs. Sefton –

MONICA: This is just crazy, inspector . . . I've never harmed anyone! I took the cat in because it was homeless and hungry . . . because I wanted a pet more than anything . . . I . . . I . . .

She sees BURKE*'s rigid face and her voice trails away helplessly.* BURKE *stares at her fixedly for a moment.*

BURKE: That's your answer?

MONICA: There's no other answer . . .

BURKE: Very well! I must ask you to come with me.

MONICA: What for?

BURKE: We have reason to believe that you're deeply involved in murder and treason against Her Majesty's Government. On these charges, you're to be questioned by an agent of Security Intelligence!

MONICA *gives a shuddering sigh and drops back into her chair, looking from right to left, a little trapped movement.*

MONICA: I . . . I want my husband . . .

BURKE: Sorry!

MONICA *(cracking):* I want my husband . . . *(She screams hysterically.)* Bill . . . Bill, where are you? Bill . . . !

BURKE: Now, Mrs. Sefton . . .

MONICA: Bill . . . ! Help me . . . help me . . . !

She collapses sobbing. There is a sudden scuffle in the hallway and BILL *enters, pushing past* POGSON *doing his best to restrain him.*

BILL: Monica . . .

MONICA: Bill . . . oh Bill . . .

He runs to MONICA, *who slips into his arms.* BILL *soothes her, glaring over his shoulder at* BURKE.

BILL: What the hell are you doing to her? *(He touches* MONICA*'s hair gently.)* Darling, for God's sake . . .

MONICA: They've been saying terrible things to me . . . They want to take me away . . .

BILL: Just let 'em try!

BURKE: We're taking your wife along for further questioning, Mr. Sefton.

BILL: Does this mean she's under arrest?

BURKE: Not yet.

BILL: Then she doesn't have to go!

BURKE: There's no compulsion, sir. It's merely a question of cooperation. If your wife has nothing to hide . . .

BILL: Nothing at all!

BURKE: . . . then there's no reason why she should refuse to come with us, is there?

BILL, *plainly nonplussed by this, turns to his wife.*

BILL: Monica . . .

MONICA: I'll have to go, darling. It's just too silly . . . they can't hold me for anything. I'm sorry I went to pieces just now . . . But I'm all right now . . . really I am.

BILL: You look anything but all right to me!

MONICA: The sooner this thing's straightened out, the better for everyone. Would you get me a hat from the bedroom . . . oh . . . and my bag . . .

BILL *gives her a helpless look, then pushes rudely past* BURKE.

BILL: EXCUSE ME!

He exits into the bedroom. The telephone rings. BURKE *answers it.*

BURKE: Hold the line, please. (*To* MARSH.) Your call, I think.

MARSH *leaps for the phone.*

MARSH: Hello . . . yes . . . speaking . . . *(His face falls.)* Another HOUR? Oh well . . . thanks . . . thanks . . . .

He replaces the receiver as BILL *re-enters carrying a hat and handbag. Hands these to* MONICA *and wheels on* BURKE.

BILL: I'm coming, too!

BURKE: We'd rather you didn't, sir. You'll have plenty of time to talk with your wife later on.

MONICA (*to* BILL): Yes, darling. I'll be back soon.

BILL: You bet your sweet life you will!

He takes her in his arms and kisses her. MONICA *clings to him for an instant, then she walks steadily from the room.* MARSH, *who has been gathering the scrapbook and other evidence, exits behind her.* BURKE *picks up his case and moves toward the door. There he turns.*

BURKE: Believe me, I'm very sorry about this.

BILL: You can go to hell!

BURKE *shrugs and walks through into hallway. We hear him sneeze loudly.* BILL, *a picture of bewildered misery, stands looking after him. The bedroom door opens and* MEADE *enters.*

MEADE: Bill . . .

BILL *(wheeling):* Where did you come from?

MEADE: The bedroom.

BILL: But I was in there!

MEADE: Ever heard of a bathroom? But never mind the whys and wherefores! Monica's up to her bridge-work in trouble . . .

BILL: I know. But they can't DO anything to her.

MEADE: Stop kidding yourself, Bill. I was in that room for the whole show. Digby-Smith's a member of a commo cell. The rest of the red noses rubbed him out because he talked out of turn. But those cops think Monica did the job!

BILL: But Monica only has to explain . . .

MEADE: Get the wax out of your ears – they've framed her prettier than an old master! If I didn't know Monica . . . if I was on a jury and presented with the evidence I've been hearing –

BILL: Circumstantial evidence!

MEADE: Sure – sure! But 90 per cent of murderers are hanged on circumstantial evidence!

BILL, *horrified as much by the futile anger in his voice as by* MEADE*'s words, stares at him, then drops into a chair.*

BILL: Andy . . . I'm lost . . . Monica, why Monica . . . of all people?

MEADE: That's the nut and kernel of the mess! Why Monica? Tens of thousands of people packed into this corner of the city – yet they choose her! Why? Then there's the chauffeur . . .

BILL: The blighter in our cupboard?

MEADE: I've a feeling he's the key to the whole puzzle. What's more, I could prove it, if only –

BILL: If only what?

MEADE: I could remember his name!

BILL: His name's Smith!

MEADE: And mine's Danny Kaye! I'm not clowning, Bill – you know I never forget a face! Somewhere during the past year I've seen that ugly pan – and it didn't come under the heading of the Smith family!

BILL: Smith – Brown – Jones! Does it matter WHAT he called himself?

MEADE: Does it matter if you ever see Monica free again? It makes just that subtle difference!

BILL: Then think, man . . . think!

MEADE: I can't!
BILL: And you're the master mind! What's got into you?
MEADE: Orange juice! I've got acidity of the brain!
BILL: Can't you be serious?
MEADE: This is serious! I can't think because I'm too sober!
BILL: Then get drunk!
MEADE: Eh?
BILL: Get drunk! Roaring, stinking drunk!
MEADE: You know, you've got something there . . . What's in the house?
BILL: Sherry.
MEADE *(shuddering):* Holy bells! I couldn't think of my own name on that!
BILL: I'll slip down to the local . . .
MEADE: No, wait!

He crosses to the telephone and dials a number.

I want you here, Bill – you've got to be wise to the whole affair. It's much deeper than we think, because . . .

Breaks – curtly into phone.

Hello honey . . . yes . . . I'm ringing from Bill's apartment, so don't ask any questions but just do as you're told for once. Get the car out, call in at the club, and pick up a quart of scotch – yes – you heard! And listen, Syl . . . bring along that diary of yours . . . Why? Because I want to read it! I'll tell you why? A pack of treasonous rats have tossed a noose around Monica's neck and unless we're smart, they're going to pull it tight . . . What's that? Am I drunk? No . . . BUT I BLOODY SOON WILL BE!

Black out. Quick curtain.

Act Two

SCENE 2

The curtain rises almost immediately on the same scene. MEADE, *in his shirt-sleeves, lies full length on the divan, an empty glass in his hand. A pint of scotch has been emptied, the second is half full.* BILL *is pacing restlessly backstage.* SYLVIA *sits in one of the chairs reading from a small leather bound book.*

SYLVIA: June 25th: Andy and I had a row because he swore I hadn't given him the money to pay the telephone account. Had hair set in morning. In afternoon went to charity matinee *Uncle Tom's Cabin.* The bloodhounds were poorly supported by the rest of the cast . . .
She turns a page.
June 26th . . .
BILL *(shaking* MEADE): Here . . . listen! Don't go to sleep!
MEADE: Not sleepin' . . . just thinking with my eyes closed. Go on, Syl.
SYLVIA: Do you want everything read out?
MEADE: Everythin'!
SYLVIA *(sighs – reads):* June 26th – still not speaking. Ella Perkins rang me all in a flap. Was it true Cecily Rankin was having a baby in December? Rang Cecily, who was so vague about dates I'm certain it must be true. Rang Ella but she'd gone. Felt awfully miserable. Went to Abbott and Costello film and had a good cry. Felt better.
Turns page.
How am I doing?
MEADE: Lousy!
BILL: Oh, this is hopeless! We've been messing around like this for more than an hour!
MEADE: Patience, laddie. You can't hurry nature.
BILL: But I want to be doing something!
MEADE *holds out his empty glass.* BILL *glares at it then, during the next reading, fills and hands it back.*

SYLVIA: June 27th: Last night, Lover Boy didn't even arrive home. Tried to ring Ella this morning re Rankin scandal but phone was dead. Found to my horror it had been cut off . . . Andy still hasn't paid that account! Had lunch with mother who was deeply sympathetic – said she warned me at the altar that Andy was a complete mess . . .

MEADE *(muttering)*: The old battle-axe!

SYLVIA *(turning page)*: June 28th: All is forgiven! The beast that walks like a man not only came home sober but brought a present for me. The sweetest little canary he'd bought at a pet shop –

She stops as MEADE *sits upright with a sudden ejaculation.*

Have I struck uranium?

MEADE: Quiet!

He rises and begins to pace the floor, muttering to himself.

Canary . . . canary . . . a pet shop . . . that's right . . . the pet shop in St. Saviour's Lane . . . it had a glass door with gilt lettering . . .

Suddenly he wheels, his face alight.

That's the Joe! The proprietor! Peter . . . Peter . . . Peter something . . . Peter Rose . . . no . . . Ross . . . Ross . . . Rostov . . . *(Snaps his fingers.)* Got it, by cracky! That's the name he was using! Peter Rostov! Well . . . congratulate me!

BILL: What for? Smith's real name was Rostov and he once kept a pet shop! Good! But how did he get into our cupboard?

MEADE: He came to get the cat!

SYLVIA: But Andy –

MEADE: Back to bed, Mrs. Pepys!

SYLVIA: No, listen Andy – how did Rostov know the cat was here?

BILL: Yes! Answer that one!

But MEADE *is staring at them, a curious expression dawning on his face. Suddenly he beats his forehead with his fist and speaks slowly.*

MEADE: Holy bells! Just how dumb can you get . . . *(He wheels on* BILL.) This doctor from next door . . .

BILL: Norton?

MEADE: What d'you know about him?

BILL: Nothing . . . except he's a neighbour Monica got friendly with. Why?

MEADE: There's a fish-like smell about good neighbour Norton! Tell me, when Monica found the cat on the window-sill, you and the doctor were the only other two people in this room?

BILL: That's right!

MEADE: So you didn't tell Rostov the cat was here . . . nor did Monica . . . Two from three leaves one, Bill!

BILL: Norton! Oh, no – it couldn't have been Norton! He made a voluntary statement that the dead man was a complete stranger to him!

MEADE: Yes . . . that's why it looks all lopsided to me!

SYLVIA: From where I sit, it looks even worse! Why should Rostov leave the cat here in the first place?

MEADE: Norton lives next door, doesn't he? In the darkness – particularly if one was jittery and in a hurry to get rid of dangerous evidence – it would be easy to confuse the two windows. Particularly when Norton was actually IN this room!

BILL: But . . . that would mean Norton was hand in glove with Rostov?

MEADE: So the puppy's opening its eyes at last! Don't you see, Bill – when Norton realized what had happened, Rostov got orders to rectify the mistake – before pussy got to prowling . . .

SYLVIA *(on her feet):* Objection!

MEADE *(growling):* Sit down!

SYLVIA: If this gang wanted to frame Monica, why not leave the cat as additional evidence?

MEADE: Because the plot wasn't hatched then! Listen . . . Norton orders Rostov to get the cat from this apartment. Peter makes an entrance through the window, gets himself scratched and starts to stiffen up. Norton, waiting for him, decides to investigate. But the damage is done . . .

BILL: Then Norton hides the body in our cupboard?

MEADE: Sure! After which, it must have occurred to him that with a little dirty juggling, Monica could take the rap for the whole thing! To remove her play manuscript and plant that French news cutting in my scrapbook could be done in a few minutes.

SYLVIA: But what about the note found in Rostov's pocket – he couldn't have had that prepared!

MEADE: Oh, no! He had several hours to select that from the manuscript! And you played slap into his hands by asking him in to examine the body!

BILL *(with slow angry realization):* Doctor Bloody Norton!

MEADE: It's the only answer to the question . . . why Monica! Because she was the one person in this city with a ready made motive and a set of circumstances that stank to high heaven!

BILL: Well? What are we waiting for?

MEADE: Relax, laddie . . .

BILL: Relax? With Monica getting the works at headquarters?

MEADE: Sure! And if you take my advice – that's where you'll leave her! Before this case is finished, the most important witness is going to be Monica herself. Backed by this fresh evidence, her statements could bust this Red group sky-high. But remember this – those babies aren't exactly shy when it comes to shutting people's mouths . . .

SYLVIA: And what do we do in the meantime? Sit in a corner and sew a fine seam?

MEADE: No . . . we three are going to have a quiet little pow-wow with Dr. Norton . . .

BILL *(moving to hallway):* I'll get the swine in here now . . .

MEADE: Ah-ha! But no rough stuff. We've got to be subtle about this.

BILL *exits.* SYLVIA *picks up* MEADE*'s coat and holds*

it as he slips into it.

SYLVIA: Know something, Andy? This just about establishes a record for us.

MEADE: Eh?

SYLVIA: We've been together a whole hour without scrapping!

MEADE: I've had something else to think about.

SYLVIA: You've always had a wife, you know.

MEADE: What's this? Sentimental session?

SYLVIA: No . . . just a change.

MEADE *(after slight pause):* You think I'm a lush, don't you?

SYLVIA: They don't come any wetter – or lower. But then you do some crazy little kindness and slip right past my guard.

MEADE *(mocking):* In spite of what mamma says?

SYLVIA *(quietly):* In spite of what anyone says . . . that's the hell of it!

MEADE *presses her hand awkwardly and turns away as* BILL *runs back into the room.*

BILL: He's not there! When he didn't answer the door, I went outside. There's not a light in the whole apartment!

MEADE: We've got to get to the Yard. Tell Burke what we've nosed out and get him to round up Norton. Then we can pick up Monica . . .

BILL: But she may not be at the Yard! Burke talked about Security. Not that they'll get anything out of her . . .

MEADE: Security might release her under watch . . . in which case she might come back here. *(He pauses an instant.)* Sylvia, you'd better wait . . .

SYLVIA: In this place – alone? Oh, no!

BILL: I'll stay.

MEADE: No. I want you down at headquarters for corroboration. And it's going to need both of us to convince them. But Monica's got to know the truth about Norton . . .

SYLVIA: Surely there must be someone among us who can

write? Why not leave a note?

BILL *crosses to the desk. He takes a pen and paper from a drawer and begins to scribble a note. He looks up.*

BILL: I've given her the low-down on Norton . . . what else?

MEADE: Tell her to lock the door and keep it like that till we get back!

BILL *scribbles, then folds the paper, slips it into an envelope, and addresses it. He holds it up.*

BILL: Where's somewhere she's sure to see it?

SYLVIA: The sideboard?

As BILL *crosses and props the letter up against an ornament.*

Just to make certain Monica knows where we are, we'd better mention it to Whistler's mother as we go out!

MEADE: Right! And the sooner we get down to Scotland Yard, the quicker we wrap up this affair and cock –

He breaks as the telephone rings abruptly. They all freeze for an instant, exchanging puzzled glances.

Answer it, Bill!

BILL *crosses and takes up the receiver – speaks cautiously.*

BILL: Hello? No, she's not here. Who is –? *(Then sharply.)* Hello . . . hello . . . hello . . .

MEADE: What is it?

BILL *(slowly replacing receiver):* A man . . . asking for Monica . . .

MEADE: Recognize the voice?

BILL: Maybe I've got him on the brain . . . but I'd lay a fiver to a penny it was Norton. Probably ringing to find out the lie of the land . . .

MEADE: And we've played right into his hands by letting him know that the cops have picked up Monica! Now . . . I wonder what the blighter's next move –

BILL *(interrupting):* Never mind Norton! Let's get Monica back here safe. Come on . . .

The three start across for the hall door when the telephone shrills again. It brings them to a halt. BILL, *after a moment's hesitation, starts toward it. But*

MEADE *waves him back. He crosses to the instrument and lifts the receiver.*

MEADE *(strained):* Hello . . . yes . . . yes, this is the Sefton apartment . . . Eh? What's that?

He listens with a look of blank amazement. Then he replaces the receiver and turns slowly.

BILL: Andy . . .?

MEADE: Everything certainly happens to me! Now I'm the father of goddam twins!

Quick curtain.

Act Three

The scene is the same, between ten and fifteen minutes later. When the curtain rises, the stage is in darkness. Presently, we hear the sound of a key fitted into the lock. The door opens and a figure enters, reaching and turning on the light. MONICA *is revealed. She still holds the doorkey in her hand and then puts it back into her bag. The living room is exactly as in the last scene. The bottles are on the floor, ashtrays are filled with butts, the cushions of the couch crumpled and awry. The envelope stands propped up against an ornament on the sideboard.* MONICA *looks haggard and almost at breaking point. She stands just inside the hallway and calls.*

MONICA: Bill . . . Darling, where are you?

She waits. There is no answer. She looks wearily around the apartment then, crossing to the bedroom, opens the door and calls.

Bill . . . Bill. I've come back . . .

Still no answer. She turns and surveys the untidiness of the room and, as if this is the last straw, she sinks into a chair and buries her face in her hands. There is a knock on the outer door. MONICA *jumps to her feet, dabbing hastily at her eyes. She runs across to the curtains of the hallway, crying out . . .*

Bill! Oh, Bill . . . !

She sweeps the curtains aside and her tone drops to disappointment as NORTON *is revealed.*

Oh . . . doctor . . . !

NORTON: I saw your light come on – I naturally thought that your husband . . .

He stops as his eye takes in the litter of the apartment.

I say! Someone's been here!

MONICA *(bitterly, shredded with nerves):* Oh, yes! Quite a merry party!

She crosses and sinks into a chair.

This is all I needed to complete a perfect evening! You

think at least Bill would be here to welcome me home . . .

NORTON: But you musn't blame your husband too much.

MONICA *(deep in self-pity):* Soaking up scotch almost as though he was glad to be rid of me!

NORTON: On the other hand, he might have been drowning his troubles . . .

MONICA: But why not wait for me?

NORTON: Well, you know how it is. He could have gone on to the local. Look here, I'll see if I can find him for you . . .

He starts toward the hallway but MONICA *detains him.*

MONICA: Doctor . . .

NORTON *(turning):* Yes?

MONICA: Would you mind staying a while?

NORTON: As long as you wish. I've got a free evening – not even a local call.

MONICA: Just until Bill comes back. I don't think I could face being here alone. I . . . I've had just about as much as I can take. You don't even have to talk . . . just stay with me . . .

NORTON, *very sympathetic in manner, comes back and sits opposite her. He says gently.*

NORTON: It's been pretty sticky for you, eh?

MONICA: Yes.

NORTON: Nasty business being mixed up with the police . . .

MONICA: If only that was all!

NORTON: But surely –

MONICA *(interrupting):* Doctor, I've got the frightful feeling I'm going off my head . . .

NORTON *(soothingly):* Now now now . . .

MONICA: You've no idea what those men said to me down there! First one – then another! "Did you kill Digby-Smith?" The same question – and then, "Who gave you your instructions? Who's your head man?" Over and over and over again . . . !

NORTON: Tch tch tch!

Now wound tight with nerves, MONICA *is talking only*

for release from strain.

MONICA: The terrifying part is that after the same question has been fired at you time and time again, you begin to doubt your own mind! And they all seemed so certain I could answer their questions! It was like some awful nightmare where you know the things happening to you aren't true, yet you can't wake up to prove that they're not! *(She stops, then almost desperately.)* Doctor, I . . . I haven't done anything like they say, have I? Tell me truly!

NORTON: Of course you haven't, my dear.

MONICA: You're only saying that to be kind – because you don't really know, do you? But Bill knows! That's why I need him so much just now . . .

Her control slips and she cries again, fumbling for her handkerchief.

I . . . I'm sorry to make a fool of myself . . .

NORTON *(after a pause – gently):* Mrs. Sefton?

MONICA: Yes?

NORTON: They've let you free – free to come back here. Doesn't that prove they believe that you're innocent?

MONICA: I don't know . . .

NORTON: Try to look at things sensibly, my dear. If they thought you were guilty, they would never have let you go. You'd be arrested . . . charged . . .

MONICA: But that makes it only more confusing . . .

NORTON *(patiently):* In what way?

MONICA: Between questioning me, they said they had all the evidence they needed to convict me. I couldn't understand why they *didn't* arrest me. But I remember that the telephone in the room rang and one of the detectives answered it . . .

NORTON: Yes?

MONICA: Then the other men got together and went outside, leaving me quite alone. I thought it was some kind of trick . . . I didn't know what to do. But presently one of the detectives came in and said I was quite free to go. I couldn't understand it at all. There was a police car waiting outside . . . they drove me back here . . .

She passes her hands over her face.

One minute they were accusing me of murder and treason and all kinds of horrible things . . . Next they just turned me loose as though nothing had happened. Nothing seems to make sense any more, doctor . . .

NORTON *watches her distress for a few moments, then . . .*

NORTON: Mrs. Sefton – may I give you a little advice?

MONICA: Of course.

NORTON: Put the wretched business right out of your mind. Lie down and try to relax.

MONICA: I couldn't sleep . . .

NORTON: Don't try. Just make yourself comfortable here on the sofa . . . *(He rearranges the cushions at one end.)* I'm sure you'll feel so much better.

MONICA: All right.

She rises, picks up her handbag, and takes off her hat.

I'll just get rid of these things.

NORTON: And don't forget . . . your oldest and most comfortable pair of slippers . . .

MONICA *smiles and exits into the bedroom, leaving the door partly open.* NORTON *frowns and stands irresolute as though uncertain just what to do. He looks idly around the room and his eye encounters the envelope on the sideboard. More out of curiosity than anything he crosses, picks it up, notes the name on it, and weighs it in his hand, still frowning as a tap sounds at the hall door.* NORTON *lies the envelope flat on the sideboard. In this position it is naturally less conspicuous. He is moving toward the hallway when the curtains part and* MRS. LAMPREY *enters. She is dressed for the street and stops in surprise at seeing* NORTON.

MRS. LAMPREY: Why, Dr. Norton . . . but how very strange! I thought the young woman had come back . . .

NORTON *(quickly):* Mrs. Sefton is in the bedroom. I'm just

waiting with her until her husband returns . . .

MRS. LAMPREY: Oh . . . ! But he's gone journeying to Scotland Yard!

MONICA *(coming from bedroom):* Scotland Yard?

She has changed into smart slacks but she is still wearing her shoes.

Mrs. Lamprey . . . how do you know?

MRS. LAMPREY *(a trifle stiffly):* The young gentleman mentioned this . . .

MONICA: When?

MRS. LAMPREY: About ten minutes ago . . . it could have been longer . . . I'm so very nonplussed about time. But I was dressing when all at once there was such a wild commotion in the hallway I was certain a herd of wild blackamoors had been let loose! Then came a loud tattoo at my door and there was your husband, all agog with the news that they had discovered some fresh evidence about this wicked murder . . .

NORTON *(sharply):* What's this nonsense you're saying?

MRS. LAMPREY *(tightly):* I am passing on the communication exactly as it was given to me. Such alarms and excursions I've never seen . . . and there was poor wee Susie hiding under the bed and wailing in her terror. I don't know which of us was the most upset . . .

NORTON: Thank you, Mrs. Lamprey. And now we musn't keep you. I notice you're going out.

MRS. LAMPREY: Oh, not far . . . just across the square. A dear friend of mine has discovered the most remarkable woman . . . and we are hoping for a manifestation . . .

NORTON *(rudely):* I've got no time for that rubbish!

MRS. LAMPREY *(archly):* You're too, too worldly, doctor . . . all you medical gentlemen are the same. Now I must go and give Susie her sleeping tablet . . .

MONICA: What for?

MRS. LAMPREY: Oh, I always take Susie with me. Usually she sleeps under the table as good as gold. But last time, I forgot her tablet and the wee romp did something quite, quite outrageous to a gentleman's leg It was sheer nervousness, you understand. So, just to be on the safe side . . . now it's a sleeping pill . . .

She exits.

MONICA *(slowly):* Fresh evidence . . . ? Now, whatever can Bill have meant by that?

NORTON: We'll know very soon.

MONICA: Do you think I ought to ring Scotland Yard?

NORTON: I think you should change into your slippers and wait until your husband comes back. If this evidence is so important, he'll want you to be among the first to know.

MONICA: I'll give him another five minutes . . .

She goes into the bedroom, closing the door. NORTON *waits only until the door shuts then turns and looks at the letter on the sideboard. He crosses to it and puts out his hand to take it when the door opens and* MONICA *emerges in her slippers.* NORTON *pulls back his hand, moving away from the sideboard and saying . . .*

NORTON: Now . . . that's much better!

MONICA *curls herself up on the sofa.* NORTON *surveys her for a few moments.*

MONICA: What's the matter?

NORTON: I'm still not sure you wouldn't be much better tucked up in bed!

MONICA: I'm all right now. Besides, doctor, I want to talk to you.

NORTON: What about?

MONICA: The new evidence Bill's discovered . . . I don't suppose it could have anything to do with Mrs. Lamprey?

NORTON *(astonished):* OUR Mrs. Lamprey?

MONICA: Yes . . . I don't suppose she could possibly be mixed up in this affair?

NORTON *(staring at her):* You're joking, surely?

MONICA: No . . .

NORTON: My dear child . . . whatever put an idea like that into your head?

MONICA: Several odd things . . .

NORTON: What were they?

MONICA: You remember the scrapbook I showed you the first night you came here?

NORTON: With all those cuttings in it? Yes, I recall it very well.

MONICA: In it the police found an account of a murder that paralleled the Digby-Smith case . . .

NORTON: Good gracious!

MONICA: But I'd never set eyes on it, doctor . . it was completely strange to me. Someone had put it inside the book . . . deliberately put it there for the police to find . . . so that I'd be involved and suspected!

NORTON *(very firmly)*: Mrs. Sefton! Now, once and for all, this must stop!

MONICA: But I'm trying to work out –

NORTON: Then leave it until the morning! How do you expect to relax when you keep churning this thing round and round in your mind?

MONICA: I suppose it's all pretty useless . . .

NORTON: Not only useless but downright stupid! What you want is something to take your mind right off the business.

MONICA *(a half-smile)*: What do you suggest, doctor?

NORTON: A good old-fashioned remedy! A nice hot cup of tea!

MONICA *(doubtfully)*: Well . . .

NORTON: I assure you it'll do us both the world of good!

MONICA: I thought you didn't drink tea . . .

NORTON: There's an exception to every rule, you know. Now, do you feel up to putting on the kettle?

MONICA *(rising and smiling)*: I'm not paralysed, doctor . . . only very tired.

NORTON: Then tea's the answer!

MONICA *exits into the kitchen.* NORTON *stands stockstill for a moment then moves slowly across to the sideboard, keeping his eye on the open kitchen door. He reaches the sideboard and stretches out his fingers to take the letter when the telephone rings sharply.*

NORTON *jerks back his fingers as* MONICA *flies out of the kitchen.*

MONICA: Bill . . . it's Bill . . .

NORTON, *suddenly tense with suspicion, moves away from the sideboard.* MONICA *has picked up the receiver and is talking into it.*

Bill! Is that you, darling . . . ? *(Her elation fades.)* What? No! No, this isn't the Cumberland Hotel! No, no – it's a private apartment . . . *(Patiently.)* You're on the wrong number . . . WRONG NUMBER. *(Pause.)* I don't care how many sheep your father owns . . . No, no, I certainly will NOT have dinner with you! No, I did not call you darling! NO . . . CERTAINLY NOT!

She hangs up and turns.

Some Australian – full as a boot!

Some of her old nervous excitement has returned. She takes a packet of cigarettes from her dressing gown pocket and takes a cigarette, talking as she does so.

I hope I wasn't too hard on him, but I was so certain it was Bill. And all I get is a lot of drool about the price of wool . . .

She has picked up a matchbox and opened it but her fingers are shaking so much she spills the contents on the floor.

Oh dear . . . !

She is about to drop on her knees when NORTON *comes forward with a lighter.*

NORTON: Here . . .

MONICA: Oh, thanks . . . *(She lights her cigarette.)* I must be worse than I thought.

NORTON: The tea will help . . .

MONICA *goes back into the kitchen.* NORTON *moves to the sideboard. This time he picks up the letter. He fumbles with the flap when, abruptly, from the kitchen comes a loud crash of crockery.* NORTON, *tight with nerves, wheels and drops the letter. He bends to pick it up as* MONICA *comes out holding the fragment of china.*

MONICA: It happened again . . . this was the teapot that Bill's mother –

She stops as she sees the letter on the floor.

What's that?

NORTON *(with an effort at steadiness):* It . . . must have fallen from the sideboard . . .

MONICA: It's for me . . . from Bill! I KNEW he wouldn't go away without some explanation. And just fancy it being there all the time!

She drops the piece of china and rips open the envelope, extracting the message. As she reads it, her face tightens. She raises her eyes to NORTON *and quickly drops them again.* NORTON *stands watching her. There is a long stretching silence . . . When she can maintain it no longer without embarrassment* MONICA *slowly folds the paper and slips it into the envelope.*

NORTON *(watching her):* Bad news . . . ?

MONICA *(huskily):* Oh, no . . . no . . .

NORTON: Something good?

MONICA: Yes . . .

NORTON: You don't actually look like a person who's had good news . . .

MONICA *(stung into retaliation):* You can't always judge by outward appearances, can you, doctor?

NORTON: True enough . . .

There is another pause. Now something watchful and rather dangerous has crept into the atmosphere.

Just what does Mr. Sefton say?

MONICA: Say . . . ? Oh . . . well, it's not much more than Mrs. Lamprey told us. Bill says he's uncovered fresh evidence and gone to Scotland Yard with it . . . and . . . and he wants me to join him there.

NORTON: But why go to the trouble of leaving you a note when he'd already told our landlady?

MONICA: I suppose . . . just in case she forgot . . .

She tucks the note in her pocket.

I'm afraid I must ask you to excuse me, doctor . . .

NORTON: But surely you're not going racing across the city now?

MONICA: I must!

NORTON: In your present state of hypertension, anything might happen to you!

MONICA: I can take care of myself!

NORTON: As a medical man, I disapprove most strongly. However, if you've made up your mind . . .

MONICA: I have!

NORTON: Then I can only say that you're being very foolish. Good evening, Mrs. Sefton.

He makes a stiff-backed exit. MONICA *waits until she hears the outer door shut. Then she brings out the note and re-reads it, obviously uncertain what to do. Then she comes to a decision and, crossing to the phone, dials a number, glancing at her watch as she waits.*

MONICA: Hello . . . Scotland Yard? Would you put me through to Inspector Burke, please? My name is Mrs. Sefton . . . Monica Sefton . . . Yes, I'm sure he'll talk to me . . . but hurry . . . please . . .

She puts BILL*'s note down by the telephone and sits drumming impatient fingers until . . .*

Hello – inspector . . . ? *(From eagerness, her voice dies to disappointment.)* Not there? Oh dear . . . Do you know where I'd find him? Yes, it's so very urgent. Thank you . . . I'll try there.

She dials another number and waits, gnawing a thumb. The telephone rings and rings. Finally, she gives an impatient shake of her head and hangs up.

I could get there quicker in a taxi!

She crosses into the bedroom. In her haste, she leaves the letter by the phone. She emerges a minute later, her slippers changed for shoes and carrying a top-coat and a silk scarf. She moves to the entrance and throws back the curtains, to recoil with a gasp of dismay. NORTON, *twinkling and smiling, stands there. He holds a small glass containing some dark coloured liquid.*

NORTON: So you were serious when you said you were going out?

MONICA: How long have you been there?

NORTON: I came back to bring you this.

MONICA: What is it?

NORTON: A simple nerve draught . . . twenty grains of chloral hydrate . . . ten grains sodium bromide . . .

MONICA: What else?

NORTON *(frowning)*: I don't understand . . .

MONICA: Do you imagine I'd drink anything you gave me?

NORTON: Frankly, Mrs. Sefton, from your attitude I'd say you were very much in need of something like this.

MONICA *(shrilly)*: I don't want it! Isn't that enough?

She has been retreating slowly as NORTON *advances into the room. She drops the coat and scarf on the sofa.*

Now, will you please go away and leave me alone?

NORTON *(injured)*: Look here, you're giving a pretty poor return for what was a simple neighbourly gesture. However, if you want to run yourself ragged, that's your affair. I'll leave the mixture here and hope that you come to your senses . . .

He has reached the desk and he puts down the glass. At the same time, his eye falls on the note by the telephone. He whips this up and runs his eyes over it as MONICA *gives a gasp of dismay at her carelessness. She makes a movement toward the hallway but* NORTON *steps in front of her. He says very quietly:*

Sit down, Mrs. Sefton.

MONICA *drops back onto the sofa.*

We've got to have a little talk.

MONICA: You haven't much time, doctor . . .

NORTON: No?

MONICA: My husband's down at Scotland Yard . . .

NORTON: Probably reporting the crazy notion he's written in this note. No wonder he's finding it so hard to convince them!

MONICA: Convince them?

NORTON: Your husband and his friends have been gone almost half an hour. Do you imagine that if the authorities placed the slightest importance on his statement they wouldn't have been on my track long before this?

MONICA: But –

NORTON: The police aren't fools, Mrs. Sefton. They realize your husband would go to any lengths to save you. Can you see them accepting a fantastic theory like this without substantial proof? Because it is quite fantastic.

MONICA: If you didn't kill Digby-Smith yourself, you know who did!

NORTON *(gravely):* Scotland Yard believes you're responsible . . .

MONICA: Then why did they let me go?

NORTON: They need additional evidence . . .

MONICA: They'll never get it!

NORTON: Oh yes they will! We're going to give it to them.

MONICA: What do you mean by that?

NORTON: Rather than give up the names of the rest of the group, you're going to commit suicide. It will be a martyr's death . . . and quite painless . . .

He rubs his hands, once again the affable twinkling little man.

Oh, quite painless, I assure you. Just a prick with a needle . . . and your body found floating in the Thames. No marks . . . not a sign of violence. Only a letter bearing your signature . . . a suicide note explaining that you prefer to take this way out . . .

MONICA *(huskily):* You . . . you'd kill me . . . ?

NORTON: Don't blame me, Mrs. Sefton. Blame this state of society that demands an eye for an eye! Someone has to pay for all this and I can assure you it's not going to be me! Besides, all our plans have been made to –

He breaks suddenly as a noise sounds in the hallway. NORTON *stiffens, staring at the curtains. They part and* MRS. LAMPREY *enters. She stands blinking vaguely at the tableau before her. Before she has time to speak,* MONICA, *now on the edge of hysteria, gives a cry of relief and runs to her.*

MONICA: Mrs. Lamprey . . . thank heaven you came back! You've got to help me! This man's a murderer – he's planning to murder me! Call the police! Get help . . .

As MRS. LAMPREY *gives a helpless gasp and blinks at her . . .*

Don't you understand what I'm saying to you? We're in terrible danger! This man's responsible for everything . . . he's the murderer the police are looking for . . .

And now two things happen. NORTON *gives an amused little chuckle and turns away.* MRS. LAMPREY *brushes* MONICA*'s entreating hands from her. The vague, dreamy manner drops like a cloak; she seems suddenly to gain in stature. Her face hardens. Abruptly her hand comes up and she slaps* MONICA *who recoils with a cry.*

MRS. LAMPREY *(with slow bitterness):* You little fool . . . !

MONICA, *almost bemused with terror at this fresh revelation, backs away as* NORTON *turns to the woman.*

NORTON *(snapping):* Where the devil have you been?

MRS. LAMPREY: It took longer than we expected. You can't do a perfect forgery in a few minutes.

NORTON: But you got it?

MRS. LAMPREY: Here . . .

She opens her handbag and produces a folded sheet of paper, passing it over.

Peter copied her signature from the lease . . . it's perfect! Fool any handwriting expert in Whitehall!

NORTON *(examining it):* The confession's got just the right note of hysteria. *(He nods to typewriter.)* You did it on that machine, of course?

MRS. LAMPREY: Only a few minutes before she got back here!

NORTON: Very nice work, Ida. His nibs is going to be very pleased with this.

MRS. LAMPREY: I've got final instructions . . .

NORTON: Well?

MRS. LAMPREY: Peter brings the car around in ten minutes. After we've got rid of her, we drive on out to Harrow. There'll be a private plane waiting for us . . .

NORTON: Good!

MRS. LAMPREY: We're expected at the usual place in Montmartre at ten o'clock tomorrow morning. We'll get passports for Switzerland. Orders are to lie low for the next few months.

NORTON: Then we musn't waste any more time. You've brought the things I need?

MRS. LAMPREY *takes a tin box from her handbag.* NORTON *opens it and extracts a hypodermic syringe and a glass ampule. With careful deliberation, he breaks the ampule and begins to fill the syringe . . . as* MONICA, *sidling desperately around the room, makes a sudden break for the hallway. But* MRS. LAMPREY *leaps forward, grasps her, and pulls her back into the room.* NORTON *looks up, says sharply.*

Careful now! We don't want any brusies!

MRS. LAMPREY: I know my training, doctor!

MONICA *(struggling):* Why do you do this to me? I've never harmed you . . . How can you be so cruel! Please don't hurt me . . . please . . .

MRS. LAMPREY *claps a hand over* MONICA*'s mouth but the girl still struggles.*

NORTON *(sharply):* Hold her still! If she breaks the needle . . .

MRS. LAMPREY *pins* MONICA *across the arm of the sofa with one hand. With the other she slips back the girl's sleeve.* NORTON *bends over and lowers the syringe . . . A shot sounds from the window.* NORTON *gasps, drops the syringe, and clasps his arm with a grimace of pain.* MRS. LAMPREY *starts upright, releasing* MONICA *as the hallway curtains are swept aside and* INSPECTOR BURKE *enters with* MARSH. *The latter carries an automatic.* BILL *enters, goes to* MONICA, *and gathers her in his arms.*

MONICA: Bill . . . oh Bill . . .

BILL: It's all right, darling. Everything's all right now . . .

He leads her to the sofa as BURKE *raps to* MARSH.

BURKE: Take 'em outside and turn them over to the boys. Then come back here.

NORTON *(whimpering):* You've broken my arm . . .
BURKE: Pity!
MARSH: Get going . . .

NORTON walks through the hallway, but MRS LAMPREY *stands her ground. She addresses* BURKE.

MRS. LAMPREY: Nothing is changed. We allow this kind of . . . margin for error. But the work goes on just the same. We have so very many friends . . .

Abruptly, she turns and exits, followed by MARSH. BURKE *shrugs, then crosses to the window. Pulling back the curtains he reveals a small tape machine. From it he lifts a reel of tape.*

MONICA: How did that thing get there?
BURKE: Part of our routine. That was why we let you go. We thought we might pick up something . . . a conversation, perhaps a telephone call. But we never dreamt of uncovering a cosy communist cell.
MONICA: Then you were outside . . . all the time?
BURKE: We have to take dangerous chances like this. The hardest part was keeping your husband quiet out there. Once or twice I thought we'd have to gag him.
MONICA: Bill . . . ! You let them keep you out there – knowing what was happening in here?
BILL: We didn't get here until five minutes ago, darling . . . The rest of the time we were down at Scotland Yard, trying to sell them the truth about Norton. But they wouldn't believe us – they said no one person could ever have laid all those false clues. Now we know that Norton and Mrs. Lamprey worked it between them.

During this conversation, MARSH *has returned. He crosses to one of the pictures on the wall and removes a small microphone from behind it.* BURKE *hands him the reel of tape.*

BURKE: Take care of that! It's much more precious than your twins!

MARSH *grins sheepishly and exits.* BURKE *comes forward to* MONICA.

Mrs. Sefton . . .

MONICA: Yes?

BURKE: If it's any consolation, the government's going to be very grateful over what's happened this evening. And I'm going to suggest they show their appreciation in something more useful than words. *(He pats her shoulder and smiles.)* And incidentally, I think you've quite cured my cold . . .

He nods to BILL *and, turning, makes for the hallway. On point of exit, he stops, screws up his face, and sneezes violently. Grunts . . .*

Hmm . . . spoke too soon!

He exits. MONICA *and* BILL *look at each other. Then they smile and* BILL *laughs and holds* MONICA *closer.*

BILL: All right now?

MONICA: Yes, darling.

BILL: Tough day ahead, you know.

MONICA: Why?

BILL: When this story breaks in the press . . .

MONICA: Bill, no!

BILL: But it's just what you wanted . . .

MONICA: Never!

BILL: Oh, yes! Right here in this room only two days ago! You were going to be famous . . . written up in every newspaper – photographed – pointed out as a personality . . .

MONICA: I didn't mean it, Bill – honestly! I don't want anything like that . . . not now –

There is a sudden flash from the hallway. ANDY MEADE *enters, carrying a small camera and a flashlight.*

MEADE: Hold it!

MONICA: Andy . . . no . . . please . . .

But a second flash has gone off.

MEADE: Remember what old De Rochefoucauld said? Never wish too hard for anything in case it comes true! So much for the pictures . . . now for the news story of the year!

He crosses and picks up the receiver of the phone, starts to dial. The curtain falls slowly.

Mischief in the Air

(A comedy-thriller)

Characters and Original Cast

The play was first presented by J. C. Williamson Ltd. at the Theatre Royal, Sydney, in June 1944 with the following cast in order of appearance:

CLARENCE PARSONS, a radio actor	Clive Coppard
MURIEL PARSONS, his wife*	
ARNOLD VICKERY, studio supervisor	Edwin Finn
FERN SUTTON	Aileen Britton
CLAY TUTTLE	John O'Malley
LARRY CARLSON, general manager	John McCallum
CHARLES McGINNIS, a visitor	Robert Chrome
MRS. JANET VAN LEYDEN	Enid Lorimer
JOSEPH MANDELBERG, a businessman	Edward Howell

The play was produced by John Alden.

The action of the play, which is continuous, takes place in the audition room of the Rex Broadcasting studios, Sydney.

* In the original version of the play, produced in 1944, there was no character MURIEL PARSONS.

Act One

The curtain rises on a stage completely dark. Only in the left-hand corner does a chink of light suggest the closed door of a lighted room beyond. Next moment, from this room comes a piercing scream. Then a woman's voice is heard, vengeful, hard, malevolent.

WOMAN'S VOICE: Scream your head off, dear Emily – no one's going to hear you above the music. It's your requiem, my dear! Just five seconds more and then –

MAN'S VOICE *(harsh and authoritative)*: Drop that gun, sister – go on, drop it! That's better! Now . . . turn around . . .

At that moment, the stage is abruptly flooded with light. ARNOLD VICKERY, *a willowy young man in a dinner suit, stands just inside the right-hand door, his fingers still on the light switch. With an outraged manner, he walks across to the closed door and throws it open.*

VICKERY: Whatever's going on in here!

As he crosses, we see the set. It is the audition room of the Rex Broadcasting studios. No expense has been spared to make this room as theatrically luxurious as possible. There is the very latest in concealed lighting. It is bright with mirrors and flowers. The centre back wall has a television screen and beneath this a concealed loudspeaker. The whole effect is one of garish commercialism.

Four doors open into this room. The main entrance, through which VICKERY *has entered, is upstage right. This communicates with a corridor and is the only door leading directly out of the room. It has a key in the lock. Down right is a door leading to a wash room. Up left is the door from behind which the voices were heard. This is the effects room. Down left is the fourth door and this opens into the private office of the general manager,* LARRY CARLSON. *The doors are labelled in small shining chromium letters: "Washroom", "Effects", and "Mr. Carlson – Strictly Private". On the door of the main entrance are the words "Audition Room" but, as we look at the back, this inscription is only visible when the door is open.*

Between the two left-hand doors is a smart modern desk with a chair behind it. On the desk is a telephone, inter-office phone, silver box containing cigarettes, ink stand, and pens. On one end of the desk is the push-button control of the TV screen and the loud-speaker beneath it. Centre back, against the wall, is a large chest. While it does not actually harmonize with the surroundings nor does it intrude. Between the two right-hand doors is a smart glass and chromium liquor cabinet. Left and right are two armchairs, right centre a couch with a small table behind it. The time is approximately seven forty-five on a Saturday evening.

And now to return to VICKERY. *In answer to his question, two people emerge from the effects' room.* CLARENCE PARSONS *is a middle-aged balding actor with a spiteful mouth. His wife* MURIEL *is a hard-faced blonde in her early forties. Both carry radio scripts.*

PARSONS: It's all right, Vickery.

VICKERY: Is it, indeed?

PARSONS: We were just having a final run through.

VICKERY: But this is no place to be doing it!

MURIEL PARSONS *is lighting a cigarette. Now she turns.*

MURIEL: How right you are! God knows I've done some bad things in my time, but right next to infanticide I'd put this!

VICKERY: Now now, Mrs. Parsons . . .

MURIEL: What's more, if Clarry had the guts of a louse, he'd walk right into that office and tell Carlson so to his face!

VICKERY: Oh, don't be so silly! You know very well that he's having a most important conference with Mr. McGinnis in there!

As MURIEL *flicks the ash from her cigarette to the*

carpet, he utters a yelp of dismay.

And don't DO that!

He produces a hankerchief from his sleeve and, bending, flicks away the offending ash. MURIEL *shrugs. As* VICKERY *rises, her husband asks curiously . . .*

PARSONS: Trying to land the Mandelberg-McGinnis contract, eh?

VICKERY: Yes. And you're not helping the situation by screaming the place down with your rehearsals.

PARSONS *(waspishly):* He's not doing too badly at all is he?

VICKERY: Who?

PARSONS: Larry Carlson. Arrives here from London scarcely knowing a soul! In six months, he's teamed up with this American and talked himself into managing a radio station.

MURIEL: It's our food and our sunshine, Clarry. Acts like a shot of adrenalin!

She goes to flick ash again, but VICKERY *leaps forward and thrusts his hand under her cigarette.*

He's even got himself engaged to some Australian girl he met coming out on the ship . . . highbrow dame . . . she'd gone to London to study some kind of medicine.

VICKERY *is standing tapping one foot, staring with pursed lips at his wrist-watch.*

What's biting you?

VICKERY *(measured):* I really must ask you to go! In fifteen minutes, there's an audition of the Mandelberg-McGinnis beauty programme – right here in this room! *(His tone takes on a touch of awe.)* And in the presence of Mr. McGinnis himself!

MURIEL: What are we supposed to do! Salaam?

VICKERY *strides to the entrance door and throws it wide open.*

VICKERY: Please!

MURIEL *jerks her head toward her husband and saunters across to the door.*

MURIEL: Come on, Sir Laurence!

She exits with him, saying . . .

And remember, as soon as Carlson's free, you speak your mind about this Academy Award!

She thrusts the script in VICKERY*'s face as he shuts the door behind them. He pauses for a moment, surveys the room with satisfaction. His eyes fall on a bowl of flowers and he frowns. Crossing, he begins to rearrange them. The centre support slips and the blooms fall in all directions.* VICKERY *is attempting to save them when the telephone rings sharply. Flowers in hand, he turns, hesitates, dithers then, dropping the flowers, crosses to the phone.*

VICKERY: Hello! Of course this is the Rex studio! Who do you want? The manager? I'm sorry – you can't speak to him! Mr. Carlson is busy with a most important client and . . .

From waspish irritation, his manner suddenly softens to eager servility.

Why, Mr. Mandelberg! I'm so very sorry, sir . . . I didn't recognize your voice . . . Mr. Carlson isn't here at the moment. He's with your partner, Mr. McGinnis. Yes, sir . . . I'll tell Mr. Carlson the very moment he comes in! Yes, Mr. Mandelberg . . . certainly, Mr. Mandelberg . . . of course, Mr. Mandelberg . . . yes, sir . . . yes . . . yes . . . yes . . .

He hangs up, produces a handkerchief from his sleeve and mops his face.

Dear, dear, dear! What a night! If it isn't one thing to bother me, it's another! Sometimes I wonder why I ever left the ribbon counter!

He crosses and, picking up the flowers, begins to replace them in the bowl. This time he is more successful. He steps back, surveys his handiwork, and is flicking specks away when the main entrance of the audition room opens. Two people enter. FERN SUTTON *comes in with* CLAYTON TUTTLE. FERN *is about twenty-five, well but quietly dressed. Her face is perhaps too intelligent to be beautiful, but she has charm, friendliness, and a sense of humour.* CLAY *is perhaps two years older, a fast talking, quick moving young man with a keen, alert manner. He betrays his American origin in his speech and he is talking as he enters.*

CLAY: In here, Fern.

FERN *(as she enters):* You know, Clay, I'm certain I've turned up at the wrong time!

CLAY: Nuts! As Larry's fiancee, we should have laid down the red carpet for you!

FERN *is looking around the room and she smiles.*

FERN: Well, you've got practically everything else –

She stops as she sees VICKERY *hovering left.*

Oh . . . !

CLAY (*to* FERN): This is Mr. Vickery, our studio supervisor. Miss Fern Sutton.

FERN *(smiling):* How do you do?

VICKERY: How do you do, Miss Sutton. I've heard about you. You're not in radio, are you?

FERN: I'm so terribly ignorant I can't even guess what a studio supervisor does . . .

CLAY: I'll tell you in one word. Nothing!

VICKERY: Now, Mr. Tuttle . . .

CLAY *(gesturing to the chest against back wall):* What's that box doing out here? It should be in the effects room!

VICKERY: Mr. Tuttle – I am not Superman! I've only one pair of hands . . . and I've just worn myself to a shadow getting everything ready for tonight!

CLAY: Cigarettes okay?

VICKERY *(pointing to desk):* In that box!

CLAY: And the scotch?

VICKERY: I found the very brand Mr. Carlson ordered. A fine time I had getting it, too! If this Mr. McGinnis were royalty itself, I couldn't have gone to more trouble!

CLAY: Listen bud! That guy's more than royalty to this outfit! He's a sponsor . . . with a fifty grand contract balanced right on the end of his nose! And we're sticking to him tighter than a sarong!

At his vehemence, VICKERY *raises both hands in agonized remonstrance.*

VICKERY: Sssh . . . !
With reverential softness.
He's in there now . . .
He stabs a finger in the direction of the office.
CLAY: McGinnis?
VICKERY: Yes! Do you think Mr. Carlson would be very annoyed if I interrupted them?
CLAY *(pleasantly):* Oh, no. He'd just about cut your throat, that's all!
VICKERY *(plaintively):* But I've just had Mr. McGinnis's partner on the telephone . . .
CLAY *(sharply):* Mandelberg?
VICKERY: Mandelberg himself! And he wants Mr. Carlson to ring him . . . urgently! Oh dear . . . I do hope there's no trouble . . .
CLAY *(uneasily):* Could be! I don't trust that sawn-off Shylock further than I can heave a horse!
He rubs his chin worriedly.
He might want to step in right at the last moment and change the whole programme . . .
VICKERY *(aghast):* But he couldn't do that!
CLAY: Sonny-boy . . . in this game a sponsor can do anything but pay his income tax.
He pauses for a moment, obviously coming to a decision, then he snaps his fingers at VICKERY.
Listen! You couldn't find Mr. Carlson, so you couldn't give him any message! Savvy?
VICKERY *(ominously):* There'll be trouble!
CLAY: Say . . . don't you know any other word?
VICKERY: Well . . . don't say I didn't warn you . . . that's all!
With a shrug of his shoulders he exits. CLAY *turns to* FERN *who has been standing in the background, listening with quiet amusement.*
CLAY: Sorry . . . Fern.
FERN: No, I should apologize . . .
CLAY: Why?
FERN: Dropping in on my fiance out of the blue like this!

And Larry tied up in a business deal. But I'll be staying at the Midway Hotel . . .

As she speaks she picks up her handbag and gloves from the small table behind the couch. But CLAY *takes them from her.*

CLAY: You can't walk out on us like this!

FERN: Oh yes I can!

CLAY: But Larry might get sore . . . and blame me!

FERN: Larry doesn't get sore at his friends. Please, Clay, let me go. I'm sure I'm in the way here.

CLAY: Who says so?

FERN: Well . . . judging by your Mr. Vickery's attitude . . .

But CLAY *waves a hand.*

CLAY: Forget it! That guy always goes around as though his slip's showing! Now . . . sit down.

He gestures to the couch. Rather uncertainly, FERN *sits.* CLAY *brings the cigarette box from the desk and offers a cigarette to* FERN. *She takes one. During the following dialogue,* CLAY *returns box to the desk, comes down, lights* FERN*'s cigarette and his own.*

Where've you been this past month?

FERN: Up north.

CLAY: You bug-hunters certainly get around! If you haven't got your nose pushed into a microscope, you're off somewhere east of Suez!

FERN *(smiling):* Only as far as New Guinea this time. Dr. Haywood wanted some help in trying to locate the cause of scrub typhus . . .

CLAY: How did you make out?

FERN: Ask me that after I've seen the lab tests next week. But how about you . . . and Larry? *(Anxious.)* Does he still get those frightful headaches?

CLAY: He's taken to wearing glasses now. Says they help. But half the time he forgets to put them on! *(Laughs.)* You know, I get quite a kick out of Larry.

FERN: Why?

CLAY: I guess it's because he's so different. You could take his entire sense of humour – and put it under a thimble!

But that doesn't mean he's not regular.
She looks admiringly around the room.

FERN: Very regular!

CLAY: And can he handle those financiers! The way he got the Mazuma to buy into this joint was like taking candy from a baby!

FERN *(looking around):* It certainly looks prosperous!

CLAY: Don't let the facade fool you, honey! We're up to our back hair in debt over all this! That's why we've simply GOT to land this Mandelberg and McGinnis contract!

FERN: And will you?

CLAY *(grinning):* Trust old Winston Churchill in there! Once he turns on that quiet British charm, they just melt and run through his fingers!

FERN *(smiling):* You don't have to tell me, Clay . . .
She stops abruptly as CLAY *holds up a warning finger. Quickly, but quietly, he crosses to the entrance door and throws it open.*

CLAY: Come right in, Mr. Parsons.
PARSONS, *revealed, carrying a typewritten script, stands for a moment embarrassed and rather dismayed. Then he comes in, sees* FERN, *and stops.*

PARSONS: Oh! I beg your pardon, old man!

CLAY: What for?

PARSONS *(with a suspicion of a leer):* I didn't realize . . . I thought you were talking with Mr. Carlson . . .

CLAY *(nodding to office):* Chief's in conference with a sponsor.

PARSONS: Still there? Oh, never mind – I'll come back later.

CLAY: What's on your mind, bud? Anything I can do?

PARSONS *(quickly):* Oh, no, no! It's just . . . something I want to discuss with Mr. Carlson personally.

CLAY: About the programme?

PARSONS: Naturally!

CLAY *(frowning, shortly):* Listen, bud – don't worry Mr. Carlson – not tonight! If there's anything wrong, see Vickery. Because we're going to be mighty busy in here in a few minutes.

PARSONS *(shrugging):* Very well! If those in authority are completely indifferent to the reputation of this studio – why should I worry?

He exits through main entrance. As the door closes behind him, FERN *says uneasily . . .*

FERN: Clay – shouldn't you have told Larry? It might be something serious . . .

CLAY *(worried himself, but brushing it aside):* That guy's an actor! He'd dramatize his mother-in-law's funeral!

FERN: All the same, you can't afford to take chances with Joseph Mandelberg . . .

CLAY *(surprised):* What, you know the guy?

FERN *(nodding):* I've an uncle in the beauty business. He gave Mandelberg his start . . .

CLAY: No kidding? Is that so?

FERN: Yes. Six years ago – when Joseph arrived from Europe with little more than the clothes on his back. And now he's one of our most dangerous business rivals!

CLAY: You know, you can't beat some of these refugees! Give 'em a door knob and a window blind – and in six months they own a block of flats!

He pauses, then . . .

Know anything about this partner – Alex McGinnis?

FERN: I've never met him.

CLAY: Nor had we – before tonight! Guess he's the big shot who makes all the important decisions. Rumour says Mandelberg won't even change his underwear without a nod from McGinnis!

FERN *(nodding to office):* And he's in there with Larry now?

CLAY: Sure! Mandelberg is listening to the programme at home. I guess McGinnis came in here to give the studio and its personnel the once-over.

FERN: Do you think he's impressed?

CLAY *(shrugging):* Search me! The guy never talks! Last time he opened his mouth, three moths flew out!

The main door swings open and VICKERY *enters looking worried.*

VICKERY: Mr. Tuttle . . .

CLAY: Hello . . . more trouble?

VICKERY: I'm afraid so . . .

CLAY: Come on – break it gently!

VICKERY: It's Mr. Parsons . . .

CLAY: He was in here a few minutes ago. What's on his mind?

VICKERY: It's the script of that thriller they're doing tonight. He's playing up again . . .

CLAY: Why?

VICKERY: He wants some of the lines altered – right at the very end of the play where the detective arrests the woman. Parsons says they're melodramatic and completely unconvincing!

CLAY *(ominously):* Now, listen, bud . . . I wrote that script!

VICKERY *(shrugging with smug venom):* I cannot help that. I'm merely delivering a message. Parsons considers his entire part revolting!

CLAY: So what? It's just tailored to his personality!

VICKERY: Well, I'm just warning you! He means to show the ending to Mr. Carlson. And you know what will happen then?

CLAY *(sourly):* Yeah! There'll be trouble!

VICKERY *tosses his head and walks to the door.*

VICKERY: I suppose that's the famous American sense of humour!

He exits as CLAY *turns to* FERN.

CLAY: When it comes to news, that guy's like my wife! Always first with the worst!

FERN *(laughing):* Tell me, Clay . . . does this go on all the time?

CLAY: Hell, no! Sometimes . . . the studio burns down!

The door of the manager's office opens and LARRY CARLSON *enters with* ALEC McGINNIS. CARLSON *is a pleasant-faced young man in his late twenties and in manner the direct antithesis of* CLAY. *He gives an impression of extreme dependability. He speaks quietly, weighing every word.* LARRY *does not smile easily, but when he does we see evidence of the potent charm* CLAY *has spoken of.* ALEC McGINNIS *is a small, nondescript, middle-aged person who somehow tends to sink completely into the background. Yet this curiously negative personality is belied by a pair of extremely sharp, shrewd eyes that dart here and there, missing nothing. He speaks with a slight Scots accent.*

LARRY *(talking as he enters):* . . . and this is the audition room, Mr. McGinnis. We'll feed your programme through –

He sees FERN, *stops, and his face lights. He turns to* McGINNIS.

Excuse me, sir . . .

He crosses and puts out his hands.

Why, Fern . . . !

FERN *(smiling):* Hello Larry. Surprised?

LARRY: Delighted! But I didn't expect you until the end of the week!

FERN: Your telegram had me intrigued, darling. I just couldn't wait. This morning I was offered a seat on the plane . . .

LARRY *nods and turns to* McGINNIS.

LARRY: Mr. McGinnis . . . this is my fiancee, Miss Sutton. Fern this is Mr. McGinnis, our sponsor.

FERN: How do you do?

McGINNIS: How do you do, Miss Sutton.

FERN *(quickly):* Larry, if you want to talk business, I can see you later on.

LARRY: No. I'll be free in a minute . . .

He nods to office.

Wait in there.

He gives her hand a squeeze. FERN *smiles and exits into office. As she goes,* CLAY *turns to* McGINNIS.

CLAY: Has Mr. Carlson been showing you how the wheels go round?

McGINNIS: That's true.

LARRY: I've been explaining how we make the sound effects for our radio plays . . .

CLAY: There's a box of noises out here . . .

He crosses to the chest.

Everything from an elephant stampede to a teething baby with colic! I'll show you . . . these are what we call manual effects, worked by hand.

He opens the chest and produces a bulb motor-horn with a shrill, almost effeminate squeak.

A taxi in what was once Gay Paree!

He squeaks the horn, tosses it back, and produces the cowbell, jangling it.

Calling the cattle home! Radio version!

He drops the bell back, produces an alarm clock and a tambourine.

These are only a few of them . . . they do the work behind the scenes!

As he drops them back into the box and closes the lid, LARRY, *who has been hovering with the silver box from the desk, proffers it to* McGINNIS, *who takes a cigarette and observes . . .*

McGINNIS: Very interesting, Mr Tuttle. But what about when you get television?

LARRY *(lighting* McGINNIS*'s cigarette):* Oh, we'll start out in a small way at first. Talks, for instance! Something on the lines of Mrs. Van Leyden's address tonight.

McGINNIS: And would that be Janet Van Leyden, the authoress?

LARRY: Yes. D'you know her?

McGINNIS: No. But I've read a few of her travel books. Wasn't she the lady who discovered a lost valley in New Guinea a few years ago?

LARRY: That's right. She's talking on New Guinea and the native customs tonight. It's good topical stuff.

McGINNIS: She sounds very interesting.

LARRY: If you'd like to meet her, she's probably in the talks studio now.

CLAY: I could take Mr. McGinnis down before the programme starts.

LARRY *(looking at his wrist-watch):* Yes, you've got just eight minutes . . .

CLAY: Plenty of time! This way, sir.

He goes up to the main entrance with McGINNIS *following. As* CLAY *opens the door,* McGINNIS *glances down at his cigarette.*

McGINNIS *(doubtfully):* Can I smoke out there?

CLAY: I'll say! You're the sponsor!

They exit. As the door closes, LARRY *crosses to his office door and throws it open.*

LARRY: Fern . . .

FERN *comes out.*

FERN: Coast clear?

He smiles and taking her in his arms kisses her, then steps back a pace, holding her hands.

LARRY: Now, let me look at you!

FERN: Darling, it's only been a month . . .

LARRY: That's a long time when you're missing a person every day. So many times I've needed you, Fern . . . to help me straighten things out. I'm still a stranger here, you know.

FERN *(smiling):* My poor lost lamb!

LARRY: No, honestly, Fern – it IS different!

FERN: I know, darling, I know! We're a rough, uncultured babe straining at an umbilical cord twelve thousand miles long . . .

LARRY *(quietly):* Oh, no you're not. But you'd like the world to believe all that. You're building up a national fallacy . . . like the Scot's thrift, the Irishman's wit, and the American's hustle . . .

They cross to the sofa and sit.

FERN: Talking of American hustle, you and Clay seem to be an ideal combination.

LARRY: Yes! We teamed up shortly after I landed. Between us, we got together a group of business men and persuaded them to finance this studio. *(Wryly.)* NOW all we have to do is convince them it's a paying proposition!

FERN: That should be simple enough! You and Clay seem to be working very well together.

LARRY: Yes, but . . . after this week Clay may have to carry on alone.

FERN: Why?

LARRY: Doctor's orders. It's that old war wound of mine. Those damned headaches have come back. And it's starting to affect my speech . . .

FERN: Oh, Larry!

LARRY: Yes. I find myself stuttering – can't get words out. Especially when I'm excited or upset.

FERN: Then you mustn't let yourself get excited or upset!

LARRY: That's what Dr. Willis told me.

FERN: He's treating you?

LARRY: Tells me I've got to get away from business for at least a month. That's why I wired you to come down. I thought you'd arrive next week. By that time, this business deal would have gone through and . . .

FERN: Yes?

LARRY: I . . . I thought we might make it our honeymoon trip.

FERN *(smiling):* Oh, Larry . . .

LARRY: What's the matter?

FERN: Modern romance! Proposing in the middle of a business deal!

LARRY *(gently):* I know I've been some time getting round to this point Fern. But until now, I've had nothing to offer you.

FERN *(touched by his sincerity):* Oh, my dear . . .

LARRY: Now it's different! All those things we've dreamed and planned look like coming true!

FERN: You've found a good fairy?

LARRY: We've found two! Mandelberg and McGinnis! Once we get Mandelberg's name on that contract, we do a little contract signing ourselves!

FERN *(gently):* That's a promise, darling . . .

She smiles and presses his hand. Rising, she crosses to the desk, speaking as she moves.

You're sure of this contract, Larry?

LARRY: Near as dammit! Why?

FERN: This thriller going on the air tonight . . . is THAT part of the Mandelberg programme?

LARRY *(somewhat surprised at the question):* Oh, no. It's later. Just before Mrs. Van Leyden's talk . . . why?

FERN *(relieved):* Then it's all right.

LARRY: But Fern . . .

FERN: It's just that I know Joseph Mandelberg . . . and he's terribly nervous of violence in any shape or form. It goes back to something that happened when he first came to Australia . . .

LARRY: What was that?

FERN: He was so poor he took a job in a hospital – cleaner in the post-mortem room. One night a student removed a body from the p.m. table, and took its place. When Joseph came in, the lad sat up, looked at Joe, and put out his tongue. *(She chuckles.)* It took them half an hour to bring Joe back to normal!

LARRY: But what a brainless thing to do!

FERN *looks at him, smiles, and shakes her head. She crosses and takes his hands.*

I suppose my sense of humour doesn't run that way. Clay is always kidding me about not seeing jokes.

FERN: Now . . . that's where we ARE different, darling! *(She reaches up and kisses him.)* Good luck tonight, Larry!

They move apart at a sound from outside. CLAY *enters with* McGINNIS. CLAY *is looking at his watch.*

CLAY: Sorry! Guess we cut it a bit fine! We were waiting for Mrs. Van Leyden . . .

LARRY *(to* McGINNIS): Did you meet her?

McGINNIS *(shakes his head):* No! The lady wasn't there.

LARRY: Too bad! But she must be around the studio somewhere.

CLAY: If I see her on my way down I'll send her in here.

LARRY: Good!

He glances at his watch.

Now, we've just time for a drink. Care for a whisky, Mr. McGinnis?

McGINNIS *(dryly):* Ever known a Scotsman who wouldn't?

CLAY *crosses to the liquor cabinet and begins to pour drinks. He looks at* FERN, *who shakes her head.* LARRY *takes one of the chairs and pushes it upstage near the speaker above the mural.*

LARRY: If you sit here, you'll get perfect reception. *(He gestures upward.)* There's the speaker, over the mural. it's controlled from a button on this desk . . .

He moves to the desk and presses the remote control. After a few seconds, soft background music floats into the room. CLAY *comes forward with three glasses on a silver tray.* LARRY *takes a glass and hands it to* McGINNIS, *then takes one for himself.* CLAY *keeps his own glass, returning the tray to the cabinet.*

McGINNIS *(looking at* FERN): And how about the little lady?

FERN *(smiling):* Not just now.

CLAY: Well . . . here's buck teeth and bung eyes!

They drink. McGINNIS *speaks with obvious appreciation.*

McGINNIS: It's a very good taste in whisky you have, Mr. Carlson.

LARRY: Let's hope you'll say the same thing about our programme!

McGINNIS *(seriously):* Gentlemen . . . it's only fair to tell you this. The final decision about buying this programme must come from Mr. Mandelberg himself! I can't take any responsibility . . . one way or the other.

LARRY: If you're pleased, that's all we ask.

CLAY *puts down his glass and glances at his watch.*

CLAY: Uh-huh! Tempus is fugitting! I had better go down to the studio.

He crosses to the main entrance.

LARRY: Keep an eye out for Mrs. Van Leyden . . .

CLAY: Like a hawk!

He exits, leaving the door PARTLY OPEN. LARRY *gestures to the chair.*

LARRY: Now, Mr. McGinnis . . .

McGINNIS, still holding his glass, seats himself in the chair. LARRY crosses and turns up the volume, then comes around and stands before the desk. FERN, on the couch, smiles and holds up crossed fingers. The chimes of eight o'clock are heard and from the speaker comes the following announcement . . .

LOUDSPEAKER: This is Station 2RX. The time is eight o'clock and Mandelberg and McGinnis, the famous firm of beauty specialists, present . . . BEAUTY PARADE.

There is a fanfare of trumpets. Behind the next announcement, an orchestra plays softly.

LOUDSPEAKER: Beauty in music – in poetry – in colour – and beauty in women! Womanly loveliness that has swayed empires and caused thrones to totter! The beauty of the idols of stage and screen that has enslaved millions! Women! Don't envy them . . . be like them! It's no magic . . . beyond remembering the magical names . . . Mandelberg and McGinnis . . . who have chosen this number to open their programme . . .

On cue in the commercial, the half-open door is pushed wide and MRS. VAN LEYDEN enters. She looks rather surprised at the rapt attention in the room. LARRY sees her, puts a warning finger to his lips, and gestures to the couch. MRS. VAN LEYDEN nods and sits beside FERN. She is a big woman, handsome and commanding, but there is nothing masculine about her. Her power to dominate stems from her intense personality and charm. Her movements are graceful, feminine, and easy. She smiles at FERN and, sitting beside her, feels in her bag and takes out a case. Lighting a cigarette, she leans back and surveys the room, obviously seeing it for the first time. A slight clatter takes her attention. The glass has dropped from McGINNIS's fingers. LARRY moves to pick it up, saying softly . . .

LARRY: Don't worry, Mr. McGinnis. I'll get you another.

He touches McGINNIS lightly on the shoulder and crosses to the liquor cabinet. As he goes, McGINNIS slumps forward, his knees fold, and he pitches to the floor. FERN *jumps to her feet with a cry of alarm.*

FERN: Larry . . . look!

LARRY *wheels from the cabinet, sees* McGINNIS. *Horror flashes across his face. He rushes to the fallen man, but* FERN *is there before him. She bends over the body, feeling the pulse.* MRS. VAN LEYDEN *is on her feet, uncertain just what to do.*

FERN: Turn off that thing!

LARRY *crosses and switches off the remote control. He turns and looks helplessly at* MRS. VAN LEYDEN.

LARRY: I didn't see . . . what happened?

MRS. VAN LEYDEN *(shrugging):* Could be a heart attack! Saw a friend of mine collapse in the same way! Sir Edward Digby . . . in the Saguaro Forest . . .

LARRY: I'll call a doctor . . .

He reaches for the telephone as FERN *rises.*

FERN *(quietly):* It isn't a doctor you want, Larry. It's the police . . .

LARRY: Police?

FERN: I can't feel any pulse . . .

The entrance door is pushed open and CLAY *enters, rubbing his hands with excitement.*

CLAY *(as he enters):* Brother, it's a honey – a lulu . . . *(He sees their stricken faces then the body of* McGINNIS.*)* What's happened to him?

LARRY *(huskily):* We . . . we think he's dead . . .

He turns and picks up the telephone. CLAY *goggles at them.*

CLAY: Jumping catfish! . . . But how –?

FERN: We don't know. That's why Larry's ringing for the police . . .

But in one swift move, CLAY *has cleared the distance. He jerks the phone out of* LARRY*'s hand.*

CLAY: Brother are you crazy?

LARRY: But we've got to get the p-p-p—

As he stands stuttering, CLAY *gives him a resounding slap on the back.*

LARRY: Thanks! We've got to get the police in on this!

CLAY: Ring the police and they'll swarm all over this studio like ants . . . maybe even stop the programme –

LARRY: Not if we explain . . .

CLAY: Okay – we explain! And the cops ring Mandelberg – tell him his partner's flopped dead in here! Swell! Can't you see Mandelberg breaking his neck to sign that contract?

LARRY: Oh, Lord!

CLAY: Larry, whatever happens, we've got to keep this quiet until the programme's finished and Mandelberg signs!

LARRY *(on edge):* How can we keep a thing like this quiet? Suppose someone walks in here?

CLAY: Uh-huh! Vickery will scream the joint down!

Swiftly considering.

Hide it! That gives me an idea . . .

He almost runs into the effects room. MRS. VAN LEYDEN *moves forward, addressing* LARRY. FERN, *during this dialogue, has dropped on her knees beside the body, examining it for any signs of life.*

MRS. VAN LEYDEN: Seems I'm only in the way here. I'll be treading grass . . .

FERN *(rising):* Not a word outside about this . . .

MRS. VAN LEYDEN *(a fleeting smile):* My dear, people have called me some ugly names in my life . . . but never a gossip!

FERN: I am sorry!

MRS. VAN LEYDEN: Forget it. I hope everything turns out alright.

She exits. As the door closes behind her, CLAY *emerges from the effects room, wheeling a stretcher.*

FERN: Where did that come from?

CLAY: Part of our first-aid equipment . . . We keep it in there. *(Nods to effects room.)*

LARRY: But what's the idea?

CLAY: Mobile transport! Come on . . . give me a hand!

LARRY *(uneasily):* Clay, I don't like this one little bit . . .

Rather unwillingly, he helps CLAY *lift the body of* McGINNIS *onto the stretcher.*

CLAY: Now . . . where do we put him?

FERN *(pointing to effects room):* In there?

LARRY: Good Lord, no! There's a thriller going on tonight. People in and out all the time!

FERN: What about your office?

CLAY: Swell! No one ever uses that except you, Larry . . . Come on . . .

LARRY *(a last attempt):* Clay, wait . . . don't you think we'd . . .

CLAY *(interrupting):* No, I don't! Get behind this hearse!

LARRY: I say – can't we cover him with something?

CLAY: Where's that dust cloth that goes over the piano?

LARRY: In studio B . . .

CLAY: I'll get it! You stay here and keep the undertakers away . . .

He crosses to the main door, flings it open, recoils, and shuts the door quickly.

Clear the decks!

LARRY: What's wrong?

CLAY: Vickery! And coming in here!

LARRY *and* CLAY *spring for the stretcher.* FERN *pushes open the door of the office. They wheel the stretcher inside. Scarcely has* FERN *closed the door on them when the main door opens and* VICKERY *bounces in. He stops, surprised at seeing* FERN *alone.*

VICKERY: Oh . . . hello!

FERN: Hello.

VICKERY *(looking around):* Where is Mr. McGinnis?

FERN: He just left.

VICKERY: Oh dear! . . . In the middle of the audition. No trouble, I hope?

FERN *(dryly):* Oh, no! Everything's fine!

VICKERY *(confidingly):* I'm so glad, Miss Sutton. You know, he should be very pleased! Programme's going splendidly . . . absolutely running on oiled wheels!

FERN *(glancing at the office door):* Seems to be a habit around here!

VICKERY *(frowning):* I beg your pardon?

FERN: Nothing. Did you want to see Mr. Carlson?
VICKERY: Yes. Where is he?
FERN: In his office.
VICKERY: Oh . . .

He takes a step toward the office, but FERN *stops him.*

FERN *(winningly):* If I were you, Mr. Vickery, I wouldn't go in there just now.
VICKERY *(stiffly):* Miss Sutton – as studio supervisor, I have a perfect right to go where I please!
FERN: I know, Mr. Vickery. But, between ourselves, I wouldn't disturb Mr. Carlson at the moment. It might be wiser to wait until he came out.
VICKERY: Why?
FERN *(gesturing to office):* Big negotiations!
VICKERY *(with a knowing leer):* Oh . . . ! So MR. McGINNIS is in there?
FERN: Definitely!
VICKERY: Then naturally I couldn't intrude at a time like this when . . .

He stops as LARRY *comes out of the office, shutting the door quickly behind him. His face is drawn and worried, a fact that* VICKERY *does not overlook.*

Oh, there you are, Mr. Carlson!
LARRY *(snapping):* Well?
VICKERY *(surprised at his tone):* Why . . . is anything the matter?
LARRY: No!
VICKERY: But you look so upset!
LARRY: Never mind about me! Why aren't you down in the studio looking after the programme?
VICKERY *(affronted):* Well! There's no need to bite my head off, I'm sure!
LARRY *(after a slight pause – softer):* I'm sorry, Vickery. I'm just very tired . . .
VICKERY: If it comes to that, Mr. Carlson, so am I!
LARRY: What is it you want?
VICKERY: Mrs. Van Leyden asked to see you.
LARRY: Why?

VICKERY: No one ever tells me anything! She just said it was extremely urgent.

LARRY: But I can't see her now!

VICKERY: She said it would be better for all concerned if you did! I left her striding up and down the talks studio like a frenzied Cossack!

He moves to the main door and holds it open. LARRY *stands uncertain.*

FERN: You'd better go, Larry.

LARRY *(with a glance at the office):* But, Fern . . .

FERN *(quickly):* Clay and I can attend to Mr. McGinnis.

LARRY *(after a slight hesitation):* All right . . .

He exits, followed by VICKERY.

The door closes after them. FERN *stands irresolute centre stage – it should be obvious that she is worried about the death of* McGINNIS. *Suddenly she snaps her fingers.*

FERN: Dr. Haywood . . . and I can trust him!

She crosses to the desk, picks up the telephone. Waits, then . . .

Would you get me –

A knock at the door. It opens and PARSONS *puts his head inside. Quickly* FERN *says . . .*

Oh, it doesn't matter, thanks.

She replaces the receiver as PARSONS *enters, and comes round to meet him centre.*

PARSONS: I'm still looking for Mr. Carlson.

FERN: You've just missed him.

PARSONS: Confound it!

FERN: He's gone down to the talks studio with Mr. Vickery. You'll probably find him there.

PARSONS: Oh.

FERN: Mrs. Van Leyden wanted to see him rather urgently.

PARSONS *(rather bitterly):* Naturally, she couldn't be kept waiting! That's what a reputation does for you!

FERN: How do you mean?

PARSONS: A few weeks ago, I suggested to Mr. Carlson that I do a series of talks on New Guinea. I was refused – yet this novelist woman is welcomed with open arms!

FERN *(noncommittal):* Really?

PARSONS *(quickly):* Mind you, don't think I'm complaining! But I have spent five years in the islands. Mrs. Van Leyden, I believe, visited the place once!

FERN: I understood she'd written a book . . .

PARSONS *(witheringly):* My dear, any superficial observer can write a travel book! Real colour can only come from someone like myself – who knows the place and the people intimately!

FERN: I suppose so.

PARSONS: But you mustn't start me on that subject. Did Mr. Carlson say how long he would be?

FERN: No.

PARSONS: Then I'd better go and find him . . . my business is just as important as Mrs. Van Leyden's . . .

He exits. FERN *turns away as the office door opens and* CLAY *thrusts out his head.*

CLAY: Who was that?

FERN: Mr. Parsons again. He's still hunting Larry.

CLAY *emerges from office, patting his face with a handkerchief. He looks a little pallid.*

CLAY: I'm sure glad to get out of that room . . .

FERN: What's the matter?

CLAY: I've been sitting in there watching my flesh creep!

FERN: But you've seen dead men before . . .

CLAY *(sits on chair in front of desk):* Yeah, but they didn't make faces at me!

FERN *(sharply):* Clay!

Clay: I'm telling you . . . his face is all screwed up like he's got a tummy ache . . . yeah, and it's turning a queer kind of purple . . .

But FERN *is already in the office. She emerges almost immediately, her face set.*

FERN *(crisply):* Clay – we're in a mess!

CLAY: But –

FERN: It's not heart failure . . . the man's been poisoned!

CLAY: Yes, that's what . . . *(He does a sudden horrified*

double-take and jumps to his feet.) Did you say poisoned?

FERN: Yes.

CLAY: Have a heart, sister! It was bad enough before, but now . . . Are you certain?

FERN: Quite certain!

CLAY: But I don't get it . . .

FERN *(worried):* Neither do I. We've got to think . . . *(She looks around.)* It must have happened right here in this room!

CLAY: Can you tell?

FERN: By the rate of contusion, it's a quick-acting poison. Now . . . in other circumstances, we might suspect that whisky or those cigarettes . . .

CLAY *(protesting):* Now, listen . . .

FERN: I said . . . in other circumstances! Because I had cigarettes from that box . . .

CLAY: Sure you did! Just as Larry and I had a drink of that whisky!

FERN: The police will say that doesn't mean a thing. The poison might have been introduced after the whisky was poured . . .

CLAY *(in dismay):* Say, listen! Who's side are you on?

FERN: I'm only trying to sort this thing out.

CLAY: Then you're doing swell! I poured that whisky for McGinnis!

FERN: Yes . . . and Larry handed it to him . . .

CLAY: See where that gets us? Five minutes ago we were doing a stretch as accessories! Now you've got us halfway to the electric chair! That guy McGinnis was worth fifty grand to us!

FERN: So the only two people who had opportunity to kill McGinnis are the two people with the strongest motive for keeping him alive!

CLAY: Larry's going to stutter for three months when he hears about this!

FERN: Larry mustn't hear about it – not yet!

CLAY: But sooner or later . . .

FERN: Make it later! Because I've got to find out more about the poison. Tell me – do all calls from this room go through the switchboard?

CLAY: Sure!

FERN: Is there any other place I can telephone – quietly – without being overheard?

CLAY: There's a call-box in the next block.

FERN *(crisply):* Give me some change . . .

CLAY *fishes in his pocket and brings out some coins – hands them to her.*

FERN *(as she takes them):* I want Doctor Haywood's advice on all this . . . and sometimes switch-girls have very long ears!

CLAY: You're telling me! My wife was a hello-girl once – and the hush-money she collected looked like the national debt!

FERN *exits. Left alone,* CLAY *glances uneasily at the office door then around the room. His eye falls on the whisky decanter. He crosses and pours a generous tot, is about to gulp it down when he remembers. He gasps.* Poison!

Claps a hand over the glass and hurriedly puts it down. He comes down and sits on the couch, visibly shaken. At that moment, the door opens and VICKERY *enters, delighted as a young colt in a spring meadow.*

VICKERY: Hello there!

And CLAY *jumps like a startled hare.*

CLAY *(sourly):* You again!

VICKERY: Yes! Isn't it wonderful!

CLAY: What is?

VICKERY: The great news!

CLAY: I know – I know! You've got leprosy.

VICKERY: Oh, don't be silly! It's Mr. Mandelberg . . . he's here!

CLAY: Oh, is that all . . . *(Abruptly he does a double-take and leaps in horror.)* Mandelberg!

VICKERY *(smugly):* Yes! Indeed, yes! When Mr. Carlson and I were on our way down to see Mrs. Van Leyden, the commissionaire stopped us to say that Mr. Mandelberg was in the reception room!

CLAY *(groaning):* Mandelberg . . . here in the studio!

VICKERY: Flashing his diamond rings right and left!

CLAY: Great gophers – that's torn it!

VICKERY *(staring at him):* Torn what?

CLAY *(sitting):* Oh, never mind – never mind!

VICKERY: But aren't you pleased?

CLAY: Sure – sure! I'm just hysterical! What's he doing here, anyway?

VICKERY: I think he's come here specially to sign that contract . . . that's why he rang up earlier this evening!

CLAY: But he wouldn't sign if he hadn't heard the show?

VICKERY: Well . . . if Mr. Mandelberg isn't going to sign the contract, why should he ask to be shown up here to Mr. Carlson's own private office!

CLAY *(on his feet):* But he can't go in there!

VICKERY: Oh, don't be ridiculous!

With sudden fussy impatience, he walks across to the office.

And I'm sure the place must be in a dreadful state . . .

But CLAY *springs forward, grabbing him forcibly, swinging him round just as he reaches the door.*

CLAY: Just where d'you think you're going?

VICKERY *(pointing with extreme dignity):* In there . . . to tidy up.

CLAY: I'll do all the tidying up that's necessary! You run along to the studio.

VICKERY: But I've just come from there!

CLAY: Then go back!

VICKERY *(stiffly):* Mr. Tuttle, I don't mind telling you I have my suspicions that something very odd is going on here tonight!

CLAY: All right – all right! Now run along!

VICKERY: In view of the position I hold here, the very least thing you can do is to confide in me!

CLAY *(desperately):* I'll confide this much, buddy! If you're not out of this room in five minutes, you'll have no more future than a cake of ice!

VICKERY *(drawing himself up – his trump card):* Very well. I resign!

CLAY: Okay! But resign out there in the corridor!

VICKERY *turns and marches to the door – turns.*

VICKERY *(bitingly):* Sometimes I wonder if we wouldn't be better off . . . under the Communists.

CLAY *makes a leap towards him, but* VICKERY *exits and slams the door.* CLAY *stands looking wildly around the room. His eye falls on the washroom. He crosses quickly to the office, wheels out the stretcher, and pushes it into the washroom. The door closes behind as the main door opens and* LARRY *enters with* JOSEPH MANDELBERG. *He is a plump middle-aged Jew, very well-dressed, and on the fingers of his right hand a large diamond ring is conspicuous.*

LARRY: Now, Mr. Mandelberg . . . are you sure you wouldn't rather wait down in the studio?

MANDELBERG *(waving the suggestion aside):* No, no! *(He looks around, openly admiring the room.)* Very nice, very nice! Eh? Always I am thinking that the radio advertising is it a lemon, yes? But even a smart businessman can be wrong!

LARRY *(gesturing to couch):* Sit down, Mr. Mandelberg.

As MANDELBERG *seats himself,* LARRY *picks up the handbag from the couch. He takes it across to the desk.*

MANDELBERG *(noticing this):* So . . . we have the ladies present with us tonight, eh?

LARRY: This? It belongs to my fiancee, Miss Sutton.

MANDELBERG: Fern Sutton?

LARRY: Yes, I think you know her.

MANDELBERG: She's a nice lady. But I don't trust that low-life uncle of hers . . . between you and me, Mr. Carlson . . . a cut-throat!

LARRY: Oh, no . . .

MANDELBERG: Oh, yes, Mr. Carlson. Already I am smelling the rats! Why does Miss Sutton come here tonight? Now I can't have a radio programme without a business rival!

Maybe my omens was right after all!

LARRY: Omens?

MANDELBERG: You don't believe in the omens, Mr. Carlson?

LARRY: Well . . .

MANDELBERG: Listen! Tonight, just before my wireless machine breaks down – like a flash in the pan it comes to me! And now, here's the proof of the pudding, ain't it?

LARRY *(puzzled):* Proof of what?

MANDELBERG *(shrewdly):* Dumb as the fox he plays, eh? Well . . . that's good business!

LARRY *is about to speak when the washroom door opens cautiously and* CLAY *backs out. He is nervous, flushed and a trifle dishevelled.*

LARRY: Oh, Clay . . .

CLAY *gives a terrified gasp and wheels sharply, to confront* MANDELBERG *staring at him curiously. Quickly he smoothes his hair into place, straightens his tie as* LARRY *continues.*

LARRY: Mr. Mandelberg, I'd like you to meet Mr. Tuttle. He looks after the entertainment side of our business.

CLAY *(with forced heartiness):* Well . . . we're sure glad to see you here tonight, sir!

MANDELBERG *(with sudden suspicion):* Now, what's all the sudden gladness about, eh? (*To* LARRY.) You're glad – now he's glad! What's there to be glad about, I'd like to know? If it ain't the government that's robbing you, it's the charities – and if the charities don't, the unions do! And where the unions leave off, the relatives begin! You got relatives, Mr. Carlson?

LARRY: A few.

MANDELBERG: Me . . . I got 'em like the Israelites! *(He feels in his pocket and produces a cigar case.)* And if supporting my own ain't bad enough, I got to marry a woman with hundreds of them! And not one of 'em with an extra pair of pants to his name!

CLAY: You should put them to work in your factory!

MANDELBERG *(sourly):* Don't give me jokes, Mr. Entertainments Partner! The day one of those schemals does an honest day's work . . . that's the time I should drop down dead!

CLAY *(in wild alarm):* No, no . . . No!

MANDELBERG *(rising):* What's the matter with you?

CLAY *(gulping):* Nothing . . . nothing . . .

MANDELBERG *puts the cigar in his mouth, feels for matches.* CLAY *produces a box, but in his haste and nervousness he drops it. As he bends to pick it up . . .*

MANDELBERG: What for you got the shakes, Mr. Entertainments Partner? You been lighting the candle at both ends, isn't it?

LARRY *(producing a box of matches):* Oh, no! Mr. Tuttle's just a little excited! Big night for us . . . the Mandelberg programme!

CLAY *has by this time recovered the matchbox. He strikes a match simultaneously with* LARRY. *Both look at each other, blow out their matches.* MANDELBERG *is left with the unlighted cigar in his mouth. This he shoves back in his pocket.*

MANDELBERG: So . . . the shakes he gets for putting on the Mandelberg programme, eh? And for the privilege of paying for it, what should I get? St. Vitus' Dance, maybe?

LARRY: Mr. Mandelberg . . .

MANDELBERG: Don't give me no foolishness! *(To* LARRY *as* MANDELBERG *begins to walk towards the office.)* You got my contract in there?

LARRY *(blocking his way):* Well . . . you see . . .

He stops and looks helplessly at CLAY, *who points furiously in dumb show to the office and the washroom.* MANDELBERG, *watching* LARRY*'s astonished face, wheels suddenly and confronts a highly embarrassed* CLAY.

MANDELBERG: Is this the excitement you still have?

CLAY: No, I . . . *(Desperately.)* Larry . . .

MANDELBERG *(wheeling on* LARRY): What goes on here?

LARRY: I think Mr. Tuttle's just telling me he's going down to the studio.

MANDELBERG: What is he, then? A jitterbugger?

LARRY *(to* CLAY): That's all right, Clay . . . you can run along . . .

CLAY: But . . . I want to talk to you . . .

LARRY: Not now, Clay! Later!

CLAY: But listen . . . *(A last frenzied effort.)* Oddybay . . . otnay . . . officenay . . .

MANDELBERG *(sharply):* What is this? What goes on? Why don't he speak the good English like me?

CLAY *(gulping):* Mr. Mandelberg . . .

MANDELBERG *(striding up to* CLAY, *taps his chest):* You're the Entertainments Partner, eh? (CLAY *nods helplessly.*) Then go away and entertain! No one's stopping you, is it? (CLAY *shakes his head.*) You got your health and strength, ain't you? (CLAY *nods dumbly.*) Or maybe you'd like me to take my programme to some other studio where they put the entertainments in the right place?

He wheels and strides toward the main door, LARRY *after him.*

LARRY: No, no, Mr. Mandelberg . . . Clay, for heaven's sake . . . !

CLAY *(resigned to the inevitable):* Okay . . . okay . . .

He exits. MANDELBERG, *very suspicious, watches him go. Then he wheels and strides back into the room.*

MANDELBERG: Now . . .maybe we talk some business! You got my contract in that office?

LARRY: Yes. But if you'll sit down out here . . .

MANDELBERG: Mr. Carlson . . . an office is the place to do the business. Not out here.

LARRY: Well, what about the studio . . .

MANDELBERG *(advancing to him):* For the last time I am telling you. When I want the entertainments, I ask entertainments! When I do business, I do business! Tonight, I do business, not entertainments! Come on, please . . .

He walks to the office door and is about to throw it open when LARRY *interrupts desperately.*

LARRY: Wait a minute . . .

MANDELBERG *(wheeling)*: What now?

LARRY: I . . . I've just remembered! That contract isn't in my office . . .

MANDELBERG: Where is it?

LARRY: I . . . I think I left it somewhere . . . yes, that's right! I left it down in the studio . . .

MANDELBERG *crosses slowly to him, watching him shrewdly.*

MANDELBERG: You THINK you left it?

LARRY: Yes.

MANDELBERG: Now . . . don't give me that stuff, Mr. Carlson. A contract worth that much . . . you leave it lying around like it was a piece of cheese? You're too smart a fella . . . you don't get no radio station that way!

LARRY: But –

MANDELBERG: For three months you make the nuisance of yourself with this business deal! Did I come to you to buy a programme?

LARRY: No, but –

MANDELBERG: And don't give me no bluffs, young fella. Some monkey business goes on here! And what for does your entertainments partner do the nonny nonny nonny behind my back to your face?

LARRY: I told you . . .

MANDELBERG *(shrewdly)*: When I want the fairy tales, I will buy them ready printed at cut rates! Now . . . if a better price someone offers you for the programme . . . that's okay . . . I'm a businessman . . . I don't pare no cheese!

LARRY: What makes you think we've been offered more money?

MANDELBERG: Tonight I get the omen – just like that! To come along here it is important . . . eh? And what do I find? I find that your fiancial is already here to buy the programme for that schemal her uncle!

LARRY *(suddenly realizing, he turns and walks to desk):* Well . . . naturally it's a very popular programme, Mr. Mandelberg.

MANDELBERG: I knew it! Not for nothing was that mummer so polite to me in the street yesterday! But don't you do no business with him, Mr. Carlson! You'll be sorry before you're born!

LARRY: Would you be willing to make that sum free of income tax . . . that is, you pay your end?

MANDELBERG *(slowly):* So that was his terms, eh?

LARRY: Business is business, Mr. Mandelberg. I can't say more than that!

MANDELBERG *(after slight pause – shrugging):* Well, well . . . for the sheep as the goats I might as well be plucked! *(He crosses to the desk and sits in the chair.)* But I'm telling you . . . all my life I regret what I do here tonight!

LARRY: Oh, no you won't . . . *(He moves behind desk.)*

MANDELBERG: Listen! This way I figure it! Already my wife's cousin, she got the culture, so what do I do? I support an orchestra. A shareholder in some pitcher business I become, since my daughter Irma she's a great actress, she says. So what's it to me if I go bankrupt over the radio!

LARRY: You'll make five times the amount in advertising . . . *(He opens a drawer and pulls out a sheet of paper.)* Now, I'll write out a formal agreement about that income tax and . . .

During this speech, he moves the blotter on the desk, pushing it forward as he sits. The edge of the blotter catches his glass – left on the edge of the desk half filled with whisky – and tips it across into MANDELBERG*'s lap.* MANDELBERG *jumps to his feet with an angry exclamation, brushing at his trousers with a handkerchief.* LARRY *jumps to his feet.*

I'm awfully sorry, Mr. Mandelberg!

MANDELBERG: Sorry he says! Listen, young fella . . . I can

make a mess of myself for nothing! I should pay you thousands of pounds for the privilege!

LARRY has pulled open a drawer. Now he comes around holding a small hand-towel.

LARRY: Here's a towel . . . and you'll find hot water in that washroom . . .

MANDELBERG: And what about the suit? Maybe you got a pants presser on the programme, too!

He marches indignantly into the washroom. As he goes, LARRY starts toward the office door.

LARRY: Now for that contract . . .

He flings open the door, halts in amazement. At that moment, CLAY enters.

CLAY: Where's Mandelberg?

LARRY *(turning):* Never mind Mandelberg! Where's McGinnis?

CLAY: I put him in the wash –

He is interrupted by a strangled cry from the washroom. The door flies open and MANDELBERG rushes out, wringing his hands in anguish.

MANDELBERG: Oi . . . oi . . . tragedy . . . a tragedy!

LARRY: Mr. Mandelberg . . .

MANDELBERG: Don't give me no soft soap! For two pins I sue you right now! Get a lawyer . . . ja . . . get a policeman . . .

LARRY: That's no good . . .

MANDELBERG: What?

LARRY: Getting a policeman here won't bring your partner back.

MANDELBERG stares at him.

MANDELBERG: My partner?

CLAY: That guy in there . . .

LARRY: Mr. McGinnis!

MANDELBERG *(waving this aside):* McGinnis? What foolishness is this? There's some fella in there so drunk he lies down on a stretcher. But that's not my partner!

LARRY *(staggered):* Not . . . not McGinnis?

MANDELBERG: But ain't I telling you . . . that mummer's a

complete stranger to me . . . I never saw him before in my life!

LARRY *gives a gasp, drops limply into the chair staring at* MANDELBERG, *as the curtain falls.*

Act Two

When the curtain rises, no time has elapsed. The scene is the same, with LARRY *sitting staring at* MANDELBERG. CLAY *is standing near him.*

LARRY: You have never seen that man before?

MANDELBERG: Well . . . all over again do I have to explain it . . . or maybe you surprise me . . . and do something!

CLAY: But . . . what happened in there? What was the tragedy?

MANDELBERG: My diamond ring . . . my ring . . . my ring!

CLAY: Well?

MANDELBERG: Listen, Mr. Entertainments Partner . . . I am washing my hands! And my ring . . . my precious diamond ring . . . it slips off my finger and down the drainpipe!

LARRY *(with infinite relief):* Oh, your ring!

MANDELBERG: Two hundred pounds it cost me – with the sales tax extra! I should be mushugga and see it vanish with the soap-suds! Well, what are you going to do about it?

LARRY *(rising):* Don't worry, Mr. Mandelberg. We'll get your ring back.

MANDELBERG: So easy he says it? Where's the ring now, might I ask? Or maybe you got a plumber's man here in the studio?

LARRY: It's a very simple operation. It's happened before . . .

MANDELBERG: Not to me it aint!

LARRY: Now, if you'll just relax, I'll get that contract and – *(He starts for the office, but stops as* MANDELBERG *speaks quickly.)*

MANDELBERG: Not so fast, Mr. Carlson! I aint signing no contract yet!

LARRY *(turning, dismayed):* But a few minutes ago . . .

MANDELBERG: I got a right to change my mind! It's a free country aint it? Else why do we pay the income tax?

And anyway, a few minutes ago, and now, are birds of a different colour!

LARRY: Why?

MANDELBERG *(significantly):* It's the omens!

CLAY: Omens? Say, what have they got to do with it?

MANDELBERG: Everything! How do you think I make the fortune if it isn't by the stars and the omens? I'm telling you . . . tonight my radio machine she goes sick on me. Tonight I lose my diamond ring. That is two tragedies . . .

LARRY: But –

MANDELBERG *(sweeping him aside):* And where there is two there is three! Maybe it's the third tragedy for me if I sign that contract with you tonight!

CLAY: Mr. Mandelberg, you're a businessman . . .

MANDELBERG: What of it?

CLAY: You're not going to let superstition stand in the way of making the best deal of your career?

MANDELBERG: Here tonight my career aint been so good so far! For the first time I do something without a talk with my partner. It don't look so good to me. I want his advice.

LARRY: Mr. McGinnis isn't here just at the moment . . .

MANDELBERG: But you said he was!

LARRY: Well . . . you see, he was here, but . . . but . . .

CLAY *(with sudden inspiration):* He went out to make a long-distance call!

MANDELBERG: Then I wait for him. *(He sits.)* It's a nice night I got for it, anyway.

LARRY: But, you see, Mr. Mandelberg, Mr. McGinnis isn't coming back here. *(As* MANDELBERG *looks at him.)* He . . . you . . . he's going back to the sponsor's box in the studio.

MANDELBERG *(rising):* Then that's where I wait for him.

LARRY: In the meantime, I'll get my studio supervisor to tap that pipe and take out your ring. How's that?

MANDELBERG: At once would be too soon! Now, where is this box that I wait?

LARRY: Mr. Tuttle will show you.

CLAY *(eagerly)*: Sure . . . this way, sir . . .

He shepherds MANDELBERG *to the door and throws it open. But to their dismay,* MANDELBERG *halts on the threshold, turns, and comes slowly back into the room.*

MANDELBERG: Just a minute . . . just a minute . . .

LARRY: Yes?

MANDELBERG: In all the confusion, out of my mind it goes. *(He points to washroom.)* That fella in there was mighty drunk, wasn't he?

LARRY: Oh, no! We never have drunks in the Rex studio!

MANDELBERG: Then what's the matter with him?

CLAY *(quickly)*: He . . . he's very sick!

MANDELBERG: Then why don't you get the doctor to him?

CLAY: A doctor's coming up right now! That's why we put the guy in the washroom. It's . . . it's nice and quiet in there . . .

MANDELBERG: Bit unhealthy, too, aint it?

CLAY: He won't be there much longer. We're moving him to a hospital.

MANDELBERG (*to* LARRY): Bad as that, eh? What's the trouble?

LARRY *(cornered)*: Er . . . appendicitis!

CLAY *(simultaneously, helping* LARRY *out)*: Gallstones!

MANDELBERG *(looking from one to the other)*: Make up your minds, boys . . . make up your minds . . .

CLAY *(desperately)*: Well, Mr. Carlson things it's appendicitis . . . and me . . . well, I think its gallstones!

MANDELBERG: Me . . . I think it's just another bad omen! *(He turns and walks to door.)* More and more I want to talk to that partner of mine!

He walks out, hesitates, turns, and comes back. Eyeing them, he says slowly, significantly . . .

Too many things are happening here tonight . . . like the niggers in the woodpiles!

He turns and walks out, finally this time, followed by CLAY, *who spreads his hands helplessly as he exits.*

LARRY, *left alone, crosses to the desk and picks up the*

inter-office phone – speaks into it.

LARRY: Is that you, Mason? Is Mr. Vickery with you? No? When he comes back, would you give him a message? Tell him to borrow a pipe-wrench from one of the mechanics . . . yes . . . a pipe-wrench! He's to bring it up here . . . to the audition studio . . . thanks!

During this conversation, FERN *has entered. When* LARRY *hangs up, she speaks.*

FERN: Why on earth do you need a pipe-wrench?

LARRY: Mandelberg's dropped his diamond ring down the washbowl!

FERN: Oh, Larry!

LARRY: That's only part of our troubles! You know that chap who passed out here tonight . . . ?

FERN: McGinnis?

LARRY: It's not McGinnis! It's some complete stranger!

FERN: How do you know?

LARRY: Clay moved the body into the washroom. When Mandelberg went in there, we thought it was all up! But Mandelberg swears the man's a complete stranger to him!

FERN: But why should anyone want to come here masquerading as Mandelberg's partner?

LARRY *(sits in chair in front of desk):* The whole thing's utterly beyond me, Fern. I wish you'd let me call the police!

FERN: But what about the contract?

LARRY: We can kiss that goodbye! I had Mandelberg all set to sign, but now he's cooled off again. He wants to talk to his partner.

FERN: Then he believes the real McGinnis came here?

LARRY *(wearily):* It's all such a hopeless tangle. I don't know where to start . . .

FERN: I do! Is that body still in the washroom?

LARRY: Yes . . . *(As* FERN *starts for the washroom door.)* What's the idea?

FERN: I'm going through that stranger's pockets. He may have papers to identify him!

She moves to the washroom door. LARRY *is about to say something when a tap sounds at the main door.* FERN *exits and* LARRY *calls . . .*

LARRY: Come in!

The main doors open and MURIEL PARSONS *appears. She carries a script in one hand and in the other a cigarette in a long holder of curious design.*

MURIEL: Excuse me barging in, Mr. Carlson, but Clarry's been trying to nail you down all the evening . . .

LARRY: Why?

MURIEL: It's about this script we're doing tonight. Now, you've got to be fair, Mr. Carlson . . . we don't often kick about the lines we've to read! But there's a limit to everything . . .

LARRY *(frowning):* It's Mr. Tuttle's script your talking about?

MURIEL: Yes!

LARRY: I read it. It seems quite all right to me.

MURIEL: But those final lines – you had enough brute strength to wade through to the climax?

LARRY: What's wrong with the climax?

MURIEL: Speaks for itself! Listen . . .

She crosses to the desk and puts down the cigarette holder then, turning, flicks the pages of the script to the end and reads sardonically . . .

There is a long sustained burst of music that ends abruptly. Into the silence, Inspector King barks . . . Drop that gun, sister! Go on, drop it! We've got you covered from this doorway! We're going to put you right where you belong . . . behind bars!

She pauses and looks up.

LARRY: Well?

MURIEL: We can't do it, Mr. Carlson . . . After all, we are the top team in Australian radio – our reputations would never stand it! That kind of thing may be alright for the cheap cinema! But it has no place in drama!

LARRY: It's not supposed to be drama . . . It's an American crook play.

MURIEL: We've both worked our brains to the bone! We've tried it fast . . . we've tried it slow! Gielgud couldn't make that speech sound convincing!

LARRY *(sighing):* Mrs. Parsons, I'm very busy . . .

MURIEL: I know. All we want is your okay for Clarry to rewrite that ending . . .

LARRY: Certainly not!

MURIEL: But listen –

LARRY: Mrs. Parsons, you know as well as I do that the script has been passed by the sponsor! We can't alter a word without his permission.

MURIEL: But surely . . .

LARRY: If you feel so unhappy about the speech – something could possibly be cut . . . But you've left it very late.

MURIEL: I keep telling you! Clarry's been trying to see you!

LARRY: You could have spoken to Vickery . . .

MURIEL: Fat lot of help we got there! We asked him to show you this script . . .

LARRY: And why didn't he?

MURIEL: He's too busy with his own little mystery!

LARRY *(sharply):* Mystery?

MURIEL *(viperishly):* It's none of my business, perhaps, but as manager of this studio . . . I think I should enquire just what Mr. Vickery does each lunch time . . . when he goes into his private office . . . and locks the door . . .

LARRY: If I know Vickery, he sleeps!

MURIEL *(shrugging):* I'm not one to make trouble but why does he take in that curious electrical gadget that makes all those humming, buzzing noises?

LARRY: What kind of gadget?

MURIEL *(thoroughly enjoying the part):* What's more, when I asked him what it was he became positively furtive . . . and almost ran away from me!

LARRY: Very well, Mrs. Parsons, when I see Vickery, I'll mention this to him!

MURIEL *moves toward the main entrance.*

MURIEL *(quickly):* But keep my name out of it, would you?

If there's any nonsense going on here, I'd rather not be drawn into it.
At door.
Sure you won't change your mind about this?
She holds up the script.
LARRY: I'm sorry. No.
MURIEL *(bitterly):* Well, I've done my best! I only hope the critics are as tolerant!
She exits. FERN *comes from the washroom as the door closes.*
FERN: Larry . . . I couldn't help hearing . . .
LARRY: About Vickery?
FERN *(nods):* What do you think he's up to?
LARRY: If I know the Parsons, they've put two and two together and made six. *(He notices the wallet and letters she carries.)* What's that? Are they his?
Nods to washroom.
FERN: Yes . . . the stranger's wallet . . . and I found these letters.
She hands LARRY *the wallet and begins to open the letters. At the first one, she pauses, frowning.*
What was McGinnis's first name?
LARRY: Alec.
FERN: This is a tailor's bill . . . addressed to CHARLES McGinnis . . .
LARRY: Charles?
FERN *nods, goes on opening letters.*
FERN: Here's a circular from his club . . . same name! *(She puts it aside.)* An account from his wine merchants . . . *(Puts it aside and looks at the fourth letter.)* Now, this may give us something . . . *(She skims through the letter and looks up.)* Larry! This letter starts . . . "My dear brother" . . . and finishes with the signature . . . Alec McGinnis!
LARRY *(staring at her):* Then the stranger . . . this Charles . . . is Alec McGinnis's brother!
FERN: The brother of Mandelberg's partner . . . yes!
LARRY: But what the deuce was he doing here?

FERN: Open the wallet!

LARRY *does so. He extracts a slip of pasteboard. Opening it, he gives a gasp of surprise.*

LARRY: Fern . . . look at this!

She stares at the folder, reading.

FERN: Commonwealth Investigation Officer . . . Charles Edward McGinnis . . .

LARRY: It's the same man all right! There's his photograph in the corner!

He looks at her.

But what would bring a Commonwealth investigation officer here?

FERN *(quietly):* What else is in there?

LARRY *delves into the wallet again. This time he produces a number of folded papers held together with a clip. The top one is a newsprint clipping. He detaches this, unfolding it.*

LARRY: Woomera . . . Isn't that the site of the rocket range?

FERN: Yes. Up in the centre. Why?

LARRY: Here's a newspaper account of the whole project.

He passes it to her and FERN *takes it, frowning.* LARRY *unclips the next paper and unfolds it.*

Fern . . . what do you make of this?

FERN *(looking at it):* A map of the New South Wales coast . . .

LARRY: But look here! Small red circles marked "possible points of landing". Landing for whom . . . for what?

FERN: Let me see that last paper!

LARRY *unclips it and smoothes it out – a sheet of paper closely typewritten. He frowns over it.*

LARRY: It's a police description of three people . . .

FERN: Men?

LARRY *(reading):* "Victor Golovnia – Ivan Koslovski – Peter Gomotov . . . "

FERN *(frowning):* Gomotov . . . Peter Gomotov . . . ? I've heard that name somewhere before . . .

LARRY: Sure you're not thinking of Molotov?

FERN *(impatiently):* No, no!

Suddenly she snaps her fingers.

Darling, I know! Wasn't there an agent of that name mixed up in the Canadian business – when the atomic secrets were stolen?

LARRY: By Jove, yes! But all that is ancient history! And anyway, Russia's got the bomb now . . .

FERN: And so the race is to the swift! Perhaps that's the very reason she's taking an interest in other defence weapons . . . like those experiments up there at Woomera!

LARRY *(incredulous):* You mean that these men are agents . . . secret agents . . . trying to land here?

FERN: Not if national security can stop them!

LARRY: But what's all this got to do with us?

FERN *has been refolding the papers. Now she returns them to the wallet. She speaks very quietly.*

FERN: Larry . . . during the war, you were flying a Spitfire in the Battle for Britain . . .

LARRY: Yes, but –

FERN: Here in Australia, another war was going on . . . a secret, bloodless struggle . . . a fight against espionage. Every radio station was carefully monitored by the military authorities . . . to prevent enemy agents broadcasting in code . . .

LARRY: But surely all that stopped years ago!

FERN: Espionage never stops. Not while important military information can be stolen! In the next war, rocket projectiles will be linked with the atom bomb. On that range in central Australia, the best brains in the world are conducting secret experiments that may revolutionize defence!

LARRY: But Fern –

FERN: We know that at least one of these men is an enemy agent. That explains why Commonwealth security wants to keep them out of this country! But perhaps they're too late . . .

LARRY: These chaps have already landed?

FERN *(quietly):* Yes . . . and someone is already in communication with them! And what safer means than in code . . . from a radio station!

LARRY *stares at* FERN *for a long moment, then he smiles.*

LARRY: Oh no, darling, no! It's too fantastic!

FERN: Why?

LARRY: Not here in Australia!

FERN *(crisply):* Famous last words! It can't happen here!

LARRY: But why choose this station?

FERN: For two reasons, Larry! First, you're new here . . . new and comparatively unknown! Because you're new, you're more likely to be unsuspicious of this kind of dirty business! And because you're comparatively unknown . . .

LARRY *(as she pauses):* Yes?

FERN *(slowly):* If anything went wrong . . . if ever the police were brought into this . . . an unknown person is much more likely to be suspected than the established owners of other stations . . . men with solid connections built up through years . . .

She pauses and looks steadily at him.

And already these pleasant people are responsible for much of the anti-British sentiment in this country . . .

LARRY, *now more perturbed than he cares to show, attempts to brush this aside. He says with an attempt at lightness.*

LARRY: No, darling! I'm certain we're just raising ghosts to scare outselves . . .

FERN: You think so?

LARRY: We've got to be sensible about all this. After all, this whole thing is merely surmise. We've no real evidence . . .

FERN: A man is dead!

LARRY: But surely heart failure isn't a crime . . .

FERN: No. But murder is!

LARRY *(aghast):* Murder!

He grasps her shoulders.

For God's sake, Fern! What are you saying?

FERN: Charles McGinnis didn't die of heart failure, Larry . . . he was poisoned!

As he stares at her in horror.

I've been talking to Dr. Haywood on the phone, explaining the symptoms. There's not the slightest doubt about it!

LARRY *(huskily)*: But why . . . what . . . ?

FERN: We've got to face it, Larry. Someone's been using this studio to transmit information to these agents. National security got wind of it – and sent McGinnis down here to investigate. So as not to arouse suspicion, he pretended to be his brother!

LARRY: And that's why he was so interested in the studio!

FERN: Yes . . . and remember how he warned us he had nothing to do with Mandelberg buying your programme?

LARRY: Very clever . . .

FERN: But not quite clever enough! Because someone saw through McGinnis's masquerade – and stopped it in a most efficient way! Someone – right here in this studio!

An anguished LARRY *rises from the couch.*

LARRY: Now we must call in the police!

FERN: Larry – wait . . .

LARRY: What for? Until the government cancels our licence and closes us down? Even if they don't, how can we carry on in face of a treason case? Mud like that sticks a long time!

He slumps back onto the couch.

Just as everything was going so well . . . this has to happen!

FERN *takes his hands and her voice is very gentle.*

FERN: Larry . . .

LARRY: Well?

FERN: Remember how we talked of national characteristics a while ago? I think you'll find we have two outstanding traits. The first is a rooted dislike of anything that's false or underhand . . . anything that isn't – as we say – fair dinkum . . .

LARRY: I know.

FERN *(smiling):* The other is a strong sense of independence, Larry. That's the natural development of being isolated in a huge continent, thousands of miles from the heart of the world. We get it from our first pioneers, who conquered this country with nothing save their own courage and initiative . . .

LARRY: If you're suggesting we can handle this business ourselves . . .

FERN *(firmly):* That's right! We can!

LARRY: No, Fern – it's too dangerous!

FERN: You bet it is! But you're not one to side-step danger . . .

LARRY: You know I'd battle to the last ditch for this place . . .

FERN: I'm not worried about all this . . .

She waves a hand to the surroundings.

I know that if it WAS taken away, you could soon build it up again! But I'm not prepared to wait that long! You see, darling, I'm thinking of ourselves . . . our future. That's more important to me than a dozen radio stations!

LARRY *(slowly):* If only we COULD keep the police out of it . . .

FERN: Just until we've found the truth, Larry. And already we've one pointed.

LARRY: Vickery?

FERN: Yes.

LARRY: All right!

He rises.

We'll start by getting that chap up here straight away! I want to know about that electrical apparatus . . .

He starts toward the door, but FERN *restrains him gently.*

FERN: Darling, you'll get nowhere acting like the wild colonial boy! That can wait! First we must know more about McGinnis's death . . .

LARRY: How do we start?

FERN: By finding the weapon that killed him!

LARRY: Weapon? But you just said he was poisoned.

FERN *(gently):* There's more than one way of poisoning. In this case, I think it was done with a thorn or a tiny dart . . .

LARRY: How do you know?

FERN: Doctor Haywood suggested I look for marks on the exposed part of the body. On the left side of the neck, I found a tiny puncture . . .

LARRY: But there was no one near him!

FERN *(quietly):* A poison dart ejected from a blowpipe can carry fifty feet . . .

LARRY *(incredulously):* Blowpipe? Oh, no . . .

FERN: Look it up in the Brittanica . . .

LARRY: But . . . a blowpipe . . . ? Now, Fern, I've read of such things in books, but here . . . in the heart of Sydney . . .

FERN *(crisply):* I see you'll have to be convinced, my boy!

She moves to the chair, examining the covering then, pushing the chair aside, begins to scan the carpet. Suddenly she gives a sharp breath of discovery. She is about to pounce on something when, abruptly, the main entrance door opens and MRS. VAN LEYDEN *comes in.* FERN *has stretched out her hand when* MRS. VAN LEYDEN *says sharply . . .*

MRS. VAN LEYDEN: Don't touch that!

LARRY *and* FERN *look up, surprised.* MRS. VAN LEYDEN *moves to small table, puts down handbag she carries, extracts a pair of tweezers, and returns behind chair. Bending, she deftly picks up a tiny feathered dart. She holds it up and speaks without looking at* LARRY.

Would you get me an envelope, Mr. Carlson?

LARRY: What's all this?

MRS. VAN LEYDEN: The envelope first! This little devil's too dangerous to be left lying around!

There is subtle command in her tone, so that LARRY *obeys without further question. He goes to drawer and takes out an envelope. Holding it open, he lets* MRS.

VAN LEYDEN *drop the dart inside. She folds the envelope and hands it to him.*

You'd better seal that down and keep it for the police! They'll probably call it Exhibit A.

FERN: How did you know the dart was there?

MRS. VAN LEYDEN: Miss Sutton . . . it is Miss Sutton? (FERN *nods.*) I brought that dart here this afternoon with five others. A newspaper photographer wanted some publicity pictures . . .

LARRY: That's true.

MRS. VAN LEYDEN: While I was in this room earlier, the darts and the blowpipe were stolen . . . from the talks studio!

FERN: Stolen? But why didn't you report this?

MRS. VAN LEYDEN: I did! When I discovered they'd gone, I sent that studio supervisor for Mr. Carlson!

LARRY: We were going down when our sponsor arrived. That put everything else out of my head!

MRS. VAN LEYDEN: That sudden collapse began to look rather ominous. *(To* LARRY.) So when you didn't come down, I came up . . . to find Miss Sutton groping around the floor!

FERN *(comes down to couch):* Your hunch about McGinnis was right.

MRS. VAN LEYDEN *(she shakes her head):* Are you calling in the police?

FERN: Not yet.

MRS. VAN LEYDEN: I suppose you know your own business best, but . . . murder's a different proposition from natural death.

Neither LARRY *nor* FERN *answer.* MRS. VAN LEYDEN *looks from one to the other, taking in their set, worried faces. She says gently . . .*

You two seem to have got yourselves into a lot of trouble!

FERN: That's putting it midly!

MRS. VAN LEYDEN *comes down and sits in chair in front of desk. She says simply . . .*

MRS. VAN LEYDEN: I've been in tough situations myself

before now. I know just how it feels! So if there's any way I can help . . . *(She smiles.)* Sometimes, three heads are better than two.

FERN: You're right. Because we're trying to get out of this mess under our own steam . . . and it isn't easy . . .

MRS. VAN LEYDEN: Well?

FERN: Perhaps you wouldn't mind telling us something more about those weapons?

MRS. VAN LEYDEN: I brought them back with me when I returned from Dutch New Guinea – they belonged to the Bele tribe. I traded them for the tops of four jam tins . . .

LARRY: What was that blowpipe like?

MRS. VAN LEYDEN: Tube of bamboo – roughly a foot long. The end they put in their mouth was discoloured with betel juice.

LARRY: And the darts?

MRS. VAN LEYDEN: Thorns from the bushes, tipped with feathers. Small but deadly. I've seen a wild pig drop as if the beggar were poleaxed! It's the poison they use . . .

FERN: You know what it is?

MRS. VAN LEYDEN: Sap of the antiasis tree.

FERN *(on her feet):* Antiasis!

LARRY: What's that, Fern?

FERN *(quietly):* One of the deadliest of the vegetable poisons. Even in its weakened state, it can cause temporary paralysis. Once . . . during a test . . . Haywood injected a guinea-pig with pure antiasis . . . and it was dead before the syringe was withdrawn!

There is a slight pause. It is as though FERN*'s statement has brought something sinister into the room.* LARRY *is first to break the silence.*

LARRY *(to* MRS. VAN LEYDEN*):* Who knew you had those darts here this afternoon?

MRS. VAN LEYDEN: Practically everyone! I was photographed in the main studio downstairs. There were some actors there – and engineers – even some of the little typists were looking on.

LARRY: And Mr. Vickery?

MRS. VAN LEYDEN: Yes. He was there. But you couldn't get that man near the darts!

LARRY: He knew they were poisoned?

MRS. VAN LEYDEN: Everyone did! I warned them not to handle the thorns . . . and told them why!

LARRY: You see, Fern. It might be anyone in the studio!

FERN: With three exceptions, Larry: Mrs. Van Leyden, myself, and you.

MRS. VAN LEYDEN *(drily):* Can you convince the police of that?

FERN: Yes. The dart struck McGinnis in the left side of the neck. It was fired through that doorway . . . by someone standing outside in the corridor!

LARRY: Then at least we're out of it!

MRS. VAN LEYDEN *(rising):* Speak for yourself, Mr. Carlson. I was standing out there in the corridor. *(She smiles.)* But I can assure you I didn't use that blowpipe. I know too much about the habits of the Bele tribe. I wouldn't put that thing to my lips for a fortune in gold!

LARRY: What were you doing out there?

MRS. VAN LEYDEN: Powdering my nose. Mr. Vickery told me an important sponsor wanted to meet me. I thought I'd better make a good impression.

LARRY: Anyone else outside that door besides Vickery and yourself?

MRS. VAN LEYDEN: There was an actress I'd met in the studio – she came up with some papers in her hand. When she saw we were waiting to come in, she went away.

LARRY *(spreading his hands):* And there we are!

MRS. VAN LEYDEN *(she has crossed to couch, sitting):* Mr. Carlson – this is your studio and you're at liberty to run it any way you please. But I think you're making a great mistake not reporting this.

FERN: To the police?

MRS. VAN LEYDEN: Yes. Sooner or later, you're going to have to answer a lot of awkward questions.

FERN: And what about the publicity – the harm it may do this studio?

MRS. VAN LEYDEN: The public memory is very short. In three months this affair will be forgotten.

LARRY: You don't know the whole story.

MRS. VAN LEYDEN *(quietly)*: I know this, Mr. Carlson. The weapons used to cause this man's death are my property. I brought them here – I know all about their use! I'm likely to be the first person suspected!

FERN *(smiling)*: Oh, nonsense!

MRS. VAN LEYDEN: Is it?

FERN: They'd know a person like you couldn't commit murder!

MRS. VAN LEYDEN: Oh yes, I could! *(As they look at her.)* As a matter of fact . . . I have!

LARRY: Killed a man?

MRS. VAN LEYDEN: Yes.

FERN: When?

MRS. VAN LEYDEN: Some years ago . . . on my first expedition through Java. I wanted to photograph some of the ruined temples in the interior. I set out alone, except for a Balinese guide, Lenu, and ten native boys . . .

FERN: Yes?

MRS. VAN LEYDEN: On the third night out, we camped in the rain forest – a terrifying place. I was just about to turn in when Lenu came to my tent. He wanted more money. When I refused, he said he'd desert and take the rest of the boys with him.

LARRY: What did you do?

MRS. VAN LEYDEN: I refused him. Then he ran away and started calling to the other boys. Five minutes more – and I'd have been alone and helpless. I called to Lenu . . . and when he turned . . .

LARRY: Yes.

MRS. VAN LEYDEN: I shot him dead!

FERN *(turning away)*: Oh . . .

MRS. VAN LEYDEN *(suddenly harsh)*: It was his life or

mine! Self-preservation's very strong! In similar circumstances, I might do it again!

There is a rather strained pause. It is LARRY *who breaks the silence.*

LARRY *(he goes to the desk):* Very well, Mrs. Van Leyden . . . we'll do as you suggest.

MRS. VAN LEYDEN *(rising – her charm evident again):* That's very sensible of you, I think. *(She crosses to the desk and picks up the envelope containing the dart.)* And I'll keep this for the police when they arrive.

LARRY: Why not leave it here?

MRS. VAN LEYDEN: Well, I feel it's my responsibility, Mr. Carlson. *(She glances at her watch.)* I'd better be getting back to the studio . . .

She crosses and halts near the door, turns.

For all our sakes, I'm glad you've decided to call the police. Believe me, it's the wisest thing!

She smiles and exits. LARRY *reaches for the telephone.*

FERN *(sharply):* Larry, you weren't serious . . .

LARRY: We're plunging deeper into this with every step! It's proving too dangerous . . .

FERN: But it was dangerous from the start!

LARRY: No! Somewhere in this studio is a murderer with five poison darts! He killed McGinnis! He won't hesitate to kill again if –

The telephone rings sharply. Both LARRY *and* FERN *stand looking at it, almost afraid of what it may mean.*

FERN *(at length):* Go on. Answer it.

Rather nervously, LARRY *picks up the receiver.*

LARRY: Hello . . . yes, Carlson speaking . . . (Pause . . . *his face lights in sudden excitement.)* Why, yes, Mr. McGinnis!

FERN *turns and reacts.*

You liked it? Why, sir . . . splendid! That's great news . . . *(Pause, he nods his head.)* So that's what happened? We wondered why you didn't come . . . No, sir, that's quite all right. If you're willing to sign up . . . *(Pause, then . . .)* Yes, he's here. Hold the line a moment . . .

He jiggles the receiver bar.

Would you put this call through to Mr. Mandelberg . . . he's in the sponsor's box. Thank you!

He replaces the receiver.

FERN: Larry . . . ?

LARRY *(he comes from the desk, nods, his face alight):* We've done it!

FERN: The real McGinnis?

LARRY: Yes. At the last moment, he changed his mind about coming to the studio . . . some urgent business, he says. He listened to the programme at home . . .

FERN: And like it?

LARRY: He says it's one of the finest things he's heard on the air!

FERN: Oh, Larry . . . darling!

In sheer excitement, she hugs him.

You mustn't think of calling in the police until Mandelberg signs that contract!

LARRY: I'll get it out straight away . . .

He goes into his office and returns with the contract which he spreads out on the desk. Then he reaches for the inter-office phone.

Now for Mandelberg . . .

FERN: But what about his diamond ring!

LARRY *(replaces receiver):* I'd forgotten all about that! Where the devil's Vickery?

FERN: You've forgotten something else. *(She gestures to washroom.)* The stranger's in there!

LARRY: Well?

FERN: Mr. Vickery isn't going to take it quietly!

LARRY *(grimly):* It might not be such a surprise to Mr. Vickery as we think!

FERN: Darling – we can't afford to take chances – not now! We've got to move it!

LARRY: Now, Fern . . .

FERN: Couldn't we put it in your office?

LARRY: Good heavens, no! Not with Mandelberg coming in!

FERN: What about the effects room?

LARRY: It's too risky!

FERN *looks around the room. She sees the effects chest. Walking up to it, she throws it open.*

FERN: If we move the effects, there's room in here!

LARRY: No, Fern . . .

FERN *(crisply):* Larry, I don't like it any more than you! But it's this . . . or lose the contract!

LARRY *hesitates a moment, shrugs, and goes into the washroom.* FERN *leans over the effects chest, takes out the bulb motor-horn, and holds it while she pushes the other effects into a corner. She drops the motor-horn in beside them.* LARRY *comes out wheeling the stretcher. Together they lift the body of* McGINNIS *into the chest. While* LARRY *pushes the stretcher into the effects room,* FERN *closes the lid.* LARRY *comes out.*

LARRY: I feel we're going to be sorry about this!

FERN: Nonsense! Now, I'm going down to keep Mandelberg talking while you get that ring! Good luck, darling!

She smiles and exits. LARRY *gives the effects chest a doubtful glance, then crosses to the desk, takes up inter-office phone.*

LARRY: Hello . . . Peters . . . did you give Mr. Vickery my message? You did? All right . . . that's all . . .

He hangs up as CLAY *enters, looking rather drawn.*

Hello . . . is anything the matter?

CLAY *(wanly):* I'll say! I think I've gone troppo!

LARRY: Why?

CLAY *(sits on couch):* You know I was down there in the sponsor's box with Mandelberg? Well, a few minutes ago the phone rings . . . and the call's for him.

LARRY: Well?

CLAY: He talks a space, then he rings off and tells me he's going to sign that contract . . . *(A deep breath.)* Because he's just been talking with his partner, Alec McGinnis!

LARRY: That's right!

CLAY *(pointing wildly to the washroom):* But the guy's dead!

LARRY *(smiling):* That's what you think! Come here . . .

He walks to the washroom door and throws it open. CLAY *follows him, peers inside – reacts.*

CLAY: Troppo! I knew it'd catch me up . . .

LARRY *(sobering):* No, Clay. There was a body in there, but we've put it in the effects chest.

CLAY *(with infinite relief):* Great gophers – you just about scared the pants off me! Say . . . then who was the guy we put in there? *(Gestures to washroom.)*

LARRY: McGinnis!

CLAY *(wailing):* There you go again!

LARRY: No, listen Clay. We've identified that body as CHARLES McGinnis, BROTHER of Mandelberg's partner. He was a Commonwealth investigation officer . . .

CLAY *(staring):* But . . .

LARRY: Business kept Alec McGinnis at home, so brother Charles came along in his place.

CLAY: Why?

LARRY *(quietly):* Because we've every reason to believe someone in this studio has been broadcasting defence secrets to agents trying to land off our coast! Charles McGinnis came along to investigate . . . and the guilty party killed him . . . with a poison dart shot from a blowpipe!

CLAY *stares at* LARRY *for a long, long moment. Then, very deliberately, he goes to him. He taps himself on the chest and says quietly . . .*

CLAY: Me . . . I'm Margaret O'Brien . . . remember?

LARRY: Don't clown, old boy . . .

CLAY: Then I'll put it in words of one syllable. Who's crazy . . . you or me?

LARRY: Neither . . .

CLAY: Blowpipes . . . poison darts . . . for Pete's sake, Larry . . . where would anyone get things like that?

LARRY: From Mrs. Van Leyden! She brought them here . . . and they were stolen from the talks studio sometime this evening!

CLAY's *expression slowly changes from incredulity to*

horror. He runs anguished fingers through his hair.

CLAY: Oh! Brother . . . is this trouble!

LARRY: The worst kind, Clay! Because the dart was fired from outside that door during the audition . . .

CLAY: Say! I was outside that door!

LARRY: During the audition?

CLAY: No . . . just as it began . . .

LARRY: Anyone else out there with you?

CLAY *(considering):* Vickery . . . Oh, and Mrs. Van Leyden. She was doing a re-paint job on the old pan.

LARRY: So she told us. Clay . . . what about Vickery?

CLAY: He was just – Larry!

He stops and stares at LARRY.

But you surely don't suspect . . . ? Oh, no, no . . . not dear old Trouble!

LARRY: Don't let Vickery's manner fool you, Clay! It might all be a very clever piece of acting.

He eyes CLAY *for a moment then.*

When you've been around the studio, have you noticed Vickery with a kind of box?

CLAY: Come to think of it . . . I have!

LARRY: People say it makes curious humming, buzzing noises . . .

CLAY: What people?

LARRY *(reluctantly):* Well . . . Mrs. Parsons . . .

CLAY: That dame? She lies like a rug! No, Larry . . . you're right off the rails. I'd say that Old Trouble was just about the last possible person . . .

LARRY *(interrupting quietly):* Perhaps that's why he was chosen!

The main entrance door opens and VICKERY *enters. His manner is an odd mixture of nervousness and defiance.* LARRY *turns on him.*

Well! You certainly took your time!

VICKERY *(waspish):* And why not, Mr. Carlson? My time is my own . . . now!

LARRY: Since when?

VICKERY: Oh? Didn't Mr. Tuttle tell you? I've resigned!

CLAY *(sourly):* Horsefeathers!

LARRY: Now what's all this?

VICKERY: Frankly, Mr. Carlson, I don't think I'm appreciated in this place! Heaven knows I don't ask for praise, but I do object to being spoken to like a lackey!

LARRY: Who did that?

VICKERY: You . . . and Mr. Tuttle!

Disgusted, CLAY *rises and walks upstage.* LARRY *speaks soothingly.*

LARRY: Now, look here, Vickery. Surely you've been long enough in radio to know you mustn't take what people say too seriously. This has been a wearing night for us all . . . and sometimes, tempers get a little frayed . . .

VICKERY: I've considered all that!

LARRY: If Mr. Tuttle and I have been a little short with you, we're both sorry. There now, we can't say any more than that, can we?

VICKERY: Well . . . it's not only that, Mr. Carlson.

LARRY: Oh?

VICKERY *(waspish):* I've been giving this matter a great deal of thought. It seems to me that there's no future in this place.

CLAY *(stung):* No future!

LARRY: Now, Vickery . . . do you realize that, in a few minutes, we're signing one of the biggest contracts ever given to radio?

VICKERY: Mandelberg?

LARRY: Yes. But there's been a slight accident. While Mr. Mandelberg was washing his hands, his diamond ring fell into the drainpipe of the washbowl. Naturally, he's rather anxious about it.

VICKERY *(shrugging):* Naturally!

LARRY: And since Mr. Tuttle and myself will both be busy on this contract, I was wondering . . . as a personal favour . . . if you'd mind getting it out.

VICKERY *(staring at him):* Good heavens, Mr. Carlson! I'm not a plumber!

LARRY *(patiently):* It isn't a job for a plumber. Just a

matter of unscrewing a nut at the bottom of the pipe . . .

CLAY: Two minutes work!

VICKERY: Then let one of the engineers do it!

Behind VICKERY*'s back,* CLAY *clenches both fists. But patient* LARRY *draws a deep breath and tries again.*

LARRY: We don't want to do that, Vickery . . .

VICKERY: And why not?

LARRY: This happens to be a diamond ring worth two hundred pounds. We'd like someone . . . well . . . responsible to do it.

VICKERY *(thawing):* Oh . . .

LARRY: Once that ring is found and returned to Mr. Mandelberg, naturally I'll see that you get the credit for the job!

VICKERY *hesitates, then . . .*

VICKERY: I'm weak, of course . . . just weak! *(He reaches inside his coat and extracts a pipe-wrench.)* But since I've gone to the trouble to bring this thing up . . .

LARRY: Thank you, Vickery.

VICKERY *takes off his coat and lays it on the couch. Very carefully, he places it in position, folds it over, folds the sleeves, brushes a speck of dust from it, and gives it an affectionate little pat. Then he rolls up one sleeve and, carrying the pipe-wrench in the manner of a flag, turns . . .*

VICKERY: Now then!

He exits into the washroom. LARRY *picks up the coat.*

CLAY: What's the idea?

LARRY: I don't like doing this, but I think we're justified . . .

He feels through the pockets and finds a folded piece of paper. Tossing the coat carelessly on the couch, he opens the paper.

I wonder what this is!

CLAY *(coming down to him):* Probably advice to the lovelorn!

LARRY *has unfolded the paper. His eyes suddenly*

dilate and he swallows excitedly.

LARRY: L-l-l- . . .

CLAY *slaps his back.*

Look at this! *(He reads.)* "Here are final details on big draft Magyar line. Remember to start scarlet flare at inlet marked on chart. Chart also gives plan, but if a storm, use no flares. Suggest you use bell instead . . . "

CLAY: Well – here . . . lemme see that!

LARRY: Read it yourself!

CLAY *takes the paper and sits on the couch, ruthlessly crushing* VICKERY*'s coat under his weight.*

CLAY: "Big draft Magyar line . . . start scarlet flare at inlet . . . chart also gives plan . . . " *(He looks up.)* Well, tar and feather me! What d'you make of this?

LARRY *(grimly):* I'd say it's obvious! Three enemy agents are trying to land off our coast . . . possibly by submarine . . .

CLAY: And here's Vickery's instructions in black and white! *(He peruses the paper again.)* Magyar line . . . Ever heard of it?

LARRY: No.

CLAY: Not that it means a red cent! It's probably a code-word to cover the real name!

LARRY: Give me that!

CLAY: What are you figuring to do?

LARRY: He's not getting away with this! No wonder Commonwealth investigation suspected the place. Here's absolute proof that Mrs. Parsons was right!

CLAY: So help me – so help me! It looks like it!

He moves upstage as VICKERY *emerges triumphantly from the washroom, holding the ring which he is wiping on his sleeve.*

VICKERY: Here you are!

LARRY *(grimly):* Hand it over!

VICKERY *hands him the ring. Without a word more,* LARRY *thrusts it into his pocket.*

VICKERY: Well? Is that all you have to say?

LARRY *(quietly):* No, Mr. Vickery! We've got quite a lot to say to you! What's in that box you've been using downstairs?

VICKERY *(starting):* That's my business!

LARRY: It also happens to be ours, Mr. Vickery! You can't do that sort of thing in this studio!

VICKERY: So that's it! Someone's been spying!

CLAY: Listen, bud! You got in first!

VICKERY *(wheeling on him):* I don't know what you . . .

He stops as his eyes fall on his crumpled coat. He points dramatically.

Who did that?

LARRY: I did!

VICKERY *moves to couch and snatching up his coat, turns in fury.*

VICKERY: Now, Mr. Carlson, if there's one thing I detest, it's people touching my clothes!

CLAY: You bet!

VICKERY *(to* CLAY): Now what do you mean? (*To* LARRY.) What is all this?

LARRY *(opening the paper and holding it out):* Is this yours?

VICKERY *takes one look at the paper, then makes a vicious grab, snatching the paper from* LARRY*'s hand.*

VICKERY *(panting):* How dare you!

LARRY: Hand that back!

VICKERY: I'll do no such thing! You stole it out of my pocket! You've no right to touch my private possessions!

LARRY: Vickery, I'm warning you! We've read what's on that paper! We know just what you're doing!

VICKERY: It's an outrage!

CLAY: There's another name for it, too!

VICKERY *(wheeling on him):* Mind your own business!

LARRY: When we find one of our men doing a thing like this, it is our business! Vickery, you ought to be ashamed of yourself!

VICKERY: So you might think! But let me tell you this! It takes all sorts to make a world!

LARRY: Not your sort!

VICKERY *(shrilly):* My sort! And what about you? You're the one to be ashamed! I come up here to do you a favour! The moment I turn my back, you rifle my pockets! On top of that, you insult me right and left! This is the last straw . . . I'm leaving!

He turns and, quivering with anger, starts for the door when LARRY*'s voice stops him.*

LARRY: If you take one step outside this studio, we'll have you arrested!

VICKERY: You wouldn't dare!

LARRY: Try it and see!

VICKERY *(pale with anger):* You can't bluff me! I'd simply deny the whole thing! And what a couple of fools you'd look then! All right – go ahead and have me arrested . . . if you dare!

He exits, slamming the door behind him. There is a silence.

LARRY: Well . . . are you satisfied?

CLAY: If ever I saw Mata Hari wearing trousers, it just went out that door.

LARRY: The paper's gone, too.

CLAY: Without that, we haven't enough evidence to cover a mustard seed!

LARRY: There's that box of Vickery's! We've got to get hold of that!

CLAY: Leave it to me!

LARRY: If you're going down to the studio, you'd better give this to Mandelberg . . . *(Hands* CLAY *the ring.)*

CLAY: Sure! And after this, he'd better wear it through his nose!

He exits. LARRY *stands still for a moment, pressing his hands to his head. Then he rubs his eyes and, feeling in his breast pocket, pulls out a pair of spectacles which he puts on. He crosses to the couch, sits, and holds his head in his hands.* FERN *enters through main door. She sees* LARRY *and her face shadows.*

FERN: Larry . . .

LARRY *(looking up):* Oh, hello . . . where's Mandelberg?

FERN: I left him talking to Clay. But darling, those glasses . . .

LARRY: I just put them on. My head's splitting.

FERN *sits beside him.*

FERN: Can I do anything?

LARRY *(putting out his hand to take hers):* No . . .

FERN: Darling, you're not well . . .

LARRY: It's just nerves . . .

FERN: Why don't you go down to the chemist and get a draught?

LARRY: I can't be away from the studio – not with Mandelberg coming up here to sign that contract!

FERN: Clay can look after him. Or Mr. Vickery . . .

LARRY: Vickery! Why, he's our man!

FERN: You're sure?

LARRY: He was here a few minutes ago. Do you know what we found in his pocket?

FERN: The blowpipe?

LARRY: Something just as incriminating! A paper . . . containing detailed instructions for signalling a landing party!

FERN: Larry!

LARRY: Everything written down . . . orders to put scarlet flares at certain points marked on a chart!

FERN: Good heavens! Have you got the paper?

LARRY: No. He snatched it out of my hand!

FERN: But what did he say about it?

LARRY *(slowly):* Not quite what I expected . . . I thought he'd either be scared . . . or attempt to bluff the whole thing out! But Vickery seemed more embarrassed than frightened. I can't make it out, Fern.

FERN: Where is he now?

LARRY: I told him not to leave the studio. That's all I COULD do. Without that paper, we've no evidence at all . . . unless we find the blowpipe . . .

FERN: Larry, I've been thinking . . .

LARRY: Well?

FERN: The actual pipe need not have been used at all. It

might have been stolen just to put us off the scent.

LARRY: But –

FERN: Any kind of tube could propel that tiny dart.

LARRY: Then it's looking for a needle in a haystack, Fern. The more I think of it, the more my head aches!

He presses his hands to his head. FERN *watches him anxiously for a moment.*

FERN: Darling, I do wish you'd get that draught! If Mandelberg comes up here, I won't let him leave till you come back.

LARRY: Yes, but . . .

FERN: You won't be more than five minutes. Please, Larry . . .

LARRY: All right! It's hopeless trying to carry on like this. I can't even see straight.

FERN: Run along, darling.

LARRY *presses her hand and exits.* FERN *goes across to the desk, looks over it, and sees the contract. She smiles, then checks pens, ink, etc. She sees the blotter missing.*

Blotter!

She looks toward LARRY*'s office, nods, and exits inside. As she goes, the door opens and* PARSONS *enters rather uneasily. He comes inside and stares around the room for a moment. Then his eyes go to the desk. He crosses and picks up a long cigarette holder from the ashtray. He is halfway across the room when* FERN *comes out, holding a roll blotter.*

FERN *(surprised):* Why, hello, Mr. Parsons.

PARSONS *(turning):* Oh . . . hello.

FERN: Don't tell me you're still looking for Mr. Carlson?

PARSONS: Oh, no. I came up here to get my wife's cigarette holder. She left it here a while ago.

FERN: Oh . . . ? Do you mind if I see it? It's rather unusual . . .

PARSONS *(quickly):* Look here, would some other time do? I'm on the air in a few minutes.

FERN: Of course! Your play.

PARSONS: Such as it is! I still think it's very foolish not to change that last scene, but then my opinion doesn't count! Now, you'll excuse me, won't you?

He exits rather hurriedly. FERN *makes a move as though to stop him, but he has gone. She turns and looks at the ashtray on the desk. She stands thoughtful for a few seconds then walks to the chest. Standing with her back to the door, she opens the lid and looks down.*

FERN: If you could tell me one thing . . .

As she speaks, the door opens noiselessly and MANDELBERG *enters. He stands looking at her, his shrewd little eyes narrowed.*

MANDELBERG *(sharply):* What goes on here!

FERN *gives a gasp of surprise and drops the lid, wheeling.*

FERN: Mr. Mandelberg!

MANDELBERG: What have we in there?

FERN: Nothing. Nothing at all!

MANDELBERG: So . . . you are holding soft conversations with a nothing? Come now, Miss Fern, you don't pull no wool out of my eyes that way! Some monkey business goes on here tonight!

FERN: Nonsense!

MANDELBERG: Such nonsense that smells like a herring! Tonight, I ring up here on the telephone – my partner is with Mr. Carlson they say. Then when I come in, my partner they tell me is ringing up on the long distances. Now my partner calls me up and, by Gollus, he aint been near this studio at all he tells me! Now what goes on, Miss Fern?

FERN: Mr. Carlson will explain!

MANDELBERG: No, Miss Fern. You will explain! What have you got in that box?

FERN: A few effects for the plays . . .

MANDELBERG: Now now, please! Am I a schemal? Do I believe you are talking with the effects for company? For the last time . . . what you got in that box?

FERN *(desperately):* You really want to know?

MANDELBERG: For why do I waste the breath?

FERN: All right! You asked for it!

She turns and throws open the lid. MANDELBERG *looks in – recoils.*

MANDELBERG *(pointing to washroom):* That's the mummer that was in the washroom . . .

FERN: Yes.

MANDELBERG: And for why do they put him in with the effects?

FERN: He's dead.

MANDELBERG: Dead? But they told me he was only sick?

FERN: He was dead when you saw him in the washroom.

MANDELBERG: Oh, by Gollus! The . . . the appendicitis or the gallstones?

FERN *(closing the lid):* Neither!

MANDELBERG *(slowly):* What do you mean?

FERN: That man didn't die a natural death, Mr. Mandelberg. He was murdered!

MANDELBERG *(goggle-eyed):* Murdered? Murdered! Oh, by Golly, let me out of here!

FERN *(standing in his way):* No . . . wait!

MANDELBERG: Let me pass . . .

FERN *(pointing to desk):* Not until you sign that contract!

MANDELBERG: Stop talking through the hats, please! I don't sign no contract with murderers!

FERN: Mr. Carlson had nothing to do with this!

MANDELBERG: That is for the police to say!

FERN: The police know nothing about this . . .

MANDELBERG: What? What? You got a murder here and you are not telling the police? What's the reason?

FERN: You are!

MANDELBERG *(jumping):* In Rachel's name, what's it to do with me?

FERN: Everything! You're in this mess just as much as we are, Mr. Mandelberg!

MANDELBERG: Oi . . . oi . . . what is she saying! Never before in my life have I seen that mummer!

FERN: Listen! That man came here tonight masquerading as

your partner! When he was killed, believing him to be Alec McGinnis, Mr. Carlson hid the body!

MANDELBERG: Why?

FERN: He was afraid you wouldn't sign the contract! And that contract means everything in the world to him!

MANDELBERG: About all that I wouldn't know . . .

FERN *(hotly):* You're right – you wouldn't know! It's nothing to you that Larry's gone almost grey with worry trying to keep this man's death a secret! Because once it was made public, the police would be all over this studio – ruining your programme! That programme which is the finest thing your partner has heard!

MANDELBERG: Maybe so, Miss Fern, but . . .

FERN: Anyone else would have given up – let the programme slide! But not Larry! With everything against him, he battled on! And that's what you call resource, Mr. Mandelberg – resource, courage, and initiative!

MANDELBERG: Maybe this fella of yours is a smart businessman! I take off the hats to him for that, yes. But, being mixed up in murders . . . that aint so good . . .

FERN: You won't be mixed up in it!

MANDELBERG: No, by Gollus, because I'm getting out of this place like you wink an eye . . .

He turns and strides for the door.

FERN *(desperately):* Mr. Mandelberg . . . wait!

So urgent is her tone that MANDELBERG *stops and turns slowly.*

MANDELBERG: Well?

FERN: Where would you be now if my uncle had said that to you six years ago?

MANDELBERG: What's this?

FERN *(quietly):* Have you forgotten how you came to Uncle John begging for a start? Where would you be now if he'd refused?

MANDELBERG: By Gollus, Miss Fern . . .

FERN: I'm asking you to give Larry Carlson his chance just

as you were given yours!

MANDELBERG *(watching her):* So . . . it's the return favour you want, eh?

FERN, *feeling she is persuading him, walks quickly to the desk, dips the pen in the ink pot, and holds out the pen toward him.*

FERN: This is no favour, Mr. Mandelberg! It's a watertight business deal! You're putting your money into a gilt-edged proposition! Larry Carlson!

There is a long pause. Then MANDELBERG *shrugs and, walking across, takes the pen from* FERN*'s hand and, sitting at the desk, takes up the contract.*

MANDELBERG *(grumbling):* That fella of yours got his head screwed on the right way after all!

FERN *(smiling):* You bet he has! That's why he's marrying me!

MANDELBERG *(looking up from contract):* When?

FERN: Practically as soon as you sign that contract!

MANDELBERG: So . . . so . . . so . . . Now it's the fairy godmother I am, too, aint it!

He dips the pen in the ink. With a flourish he signs the contract. He blots and folds it, then presses it into FERN*'s hand.*

That's a mighty expensive match I make for you two, but no one shall ever say that Jo Mandelberg had a stone in his heart . . .

FERN: Joseph, you're a darling!

She kisses him on the top of the head.

MANDELBERG *(irritably):* Oi . . . oi! Keep your affections for that other fella!

FERN: I mean to . . . but first I must show him this!

She starts across the room with the contract. She has her hand on the door when MANDELBERG *calls.*

MANDELBERG: Oi . . . wait . . . please!

FERN *turns.* MANDELBERG *rises to his feet and moves to the chest. He stabs a finger at it.*

What about him?

FERN: Oh . . . he's all right!

MANDELBERG: Maybe he is. But . . . what about me? I don't stay here with no dead fellas . . .

FERN: Why not?

MANDELBERG: Now, Miss Fern . . . no foolishness, please! Once before that happen . . . it aint so good! I am still getting the nightmares!

FERN: That's just silly! You know a dead man can't hurt you!

MANDELBERG: Sure I know it . . . but does he know it!

FERN *(laughing):* Don't be a coward! You stay right here till I get back!

MANDELBERG *(as she exits):* Oi . . . wait . . . please . . .

But FERN *has gone.* MANDELBERG *stands looking uneasily around the room. Then, nerving himself with an effort, he crosses to the chest and very gingerly lifts the lid, peering inside. He gives a convulsive shudder.*

Just like the other one he looks . . . only more so! I've got to get out of here . . .

He closes the lid and turns, walking quickly to the door. But, as he puts his hand on the knob, the motor-horn within the chest gives a gasping, wheezing groaning honk! MANDELBERG *jumps as though stung and, wheeling, surveys the room. His eyes rest on the chest. He says slowly, suspiciously . . .*

Something it goes on here behind my face, by Gollus . . .

He crosses the stage slowly, still staring at the trunk. Braving himself, he puts out one hand to touch the lid when the cowbell inside jangles abruptly. MANDELBERG *backs downstage with a gasp. Now he is beyond the desk when suddenly the lid of the chest moves . . . It opens slowly, perhaps six inches. From inside, a white hand appears, clutching spasmodically at the empty air as* MANDELBERG *screams.*

Mr. Carlson! Oi . . . Mr. Carlson . . . he comes to the life . . . he comes to the life . . . Mr. Carlson . . . help . . . help . . .

He rushes from the room screaming as the curtain falls quickly.

Act Three

When the curtain rises, the scene is the same. No time has elapsed. The hand is still protruding from the lid of the chest. Then the lid is pushed up and slowly, painfully, CHARLES McGINNIS *rises to his feet. It is obvious from his pallid face and feeble manner that he is a very sick man. He sways unsteadily in the chest, then with a great effort steps out and moves weakly to a chair. Supporting himself with one hand, he passes the other over his face, then shakes his head in an effort to recall his surroundings. At that moment, the main entrance door bursts open and* LARRY *and* CLAY *rush in. They stand in the doorway, chained in astonishment at the sight of the resuscitated* McGINNIS.

CLAY: Great balls of fire! It's a ghost!

LARRY: McGinnis! We thought –

McGINNIS *turns painfully toward them, then abruptly his legs sag and, as* LARRY *and* CLAY *leap forward, he drops limply into their arms.*

CLAY: What's the pay-off?

LARRY: Don't know! Help me . . .

Together they support the sagging figure of McGINNIS *to the couch and lay him down.* FERN *enters quickly.*

FERN: Larry . . . ?

LARRY *(looking up):* Seems your first diagnosis wasn't so good, Fern!

FERN: Let me see . . .

She bends over the body, feeling the pulse, then she places her ear to the heart. As she straightens.

We've got to get this man to hospital! Bring out that stretcher, Clay . . .

LARRY: It's in the effects room . . .

CLAY *exits, leaving the door open.* LARRY *turns to* FERN.

Then he wasn't dead?

FERN: No. But his pulse was feeble enough to have fooled

an experienced medical man.

LARRY: But you're a doctor?

FERN: Darling, I'm a bacteriologist. There's a difference! And this is my first experience of vaso-motor paralysis!

LARRY: Whatever's that?

FERN: Vegetable poisons – antiasis among them – paralyzes the respiratory centres. Heart, lungs, and pulse.

During this dialogue, CLAY *has returned wheeling the stretcher.*

LARRY: But you said this antiasis was deadly!

FERN: In full strength, yes! But in its weakened state, it can cause temporary coma . . . like this! *(Nods to body.)*

LARRY: But listen –

FERN: Larry, don't you understand? How long since Mrs. Van Leyden brought those darts back from New Guinea?

LARRY: Some months.

CLAY: I got it! The dope was deadly when it was first put on, but since then . . .

FERN: Action of time and exposure to air weakened the poison! But the murderer wasn't to know this! He believed the weapons still deadly!

CLAY: Then it's not too late to save this guy?

FERN: No. They'll inject with picrotoxin. But there's no time to waste!

CLAY *wheels the stretcher to the couch and they lift* McGINNIS *onto it.* CLAY *wheels the stretcher to the door.*

CLAY: I'll bring up the elevator . . .

He exits, pushing the stretcher. LARRY *turns to* FERN.

LARRY: If this isn't murder, there's no reason why I can't call in the police.

FERN *(smiling):* When you get down to hospital, they'll bring the police to you!

LARRY: All the better! I want to ask them to arrest Vickery as quietly as possible. Now, what about an ambulance?

FERN: I'll ring through to Westlake . . . they know me there.

CLAY *(offstage):* Larry . . .

LARRY *(calling):* Coming . . . !

He smiles at FERN *and exits.* FERN, *at desk, picks up the telephone.*

FERN: Would you get me Landseer doubleone-doubleone, please?

Receiver in hand, she waits, straightening the objects on the desk, then . . .

Hello, Westlake? Casualty room, please. *(Pause.)* Hello . . . is that you, Mike? Fern Sutton here. Listen, can you get an ambulance around to the Rex studios at once? Is Dr. Roberts on duty? It's just his cup of tea – severe vaso-motor paralysis! Thanks, Mike . . . Oh, I'll be round there one of these days . . . Goodbye, Mike.

She hangs up as LARRY *enters, carrying a polished wood box, some two feet long by one foot wide. It is obviously heavy and is locked with a padlock.* FERN *stares at it.*

Whatever's that?

LARRY *(grimly):* Clever Mr. Vickery's box of tricks?

He sets the box down on the desk.

FERN: Where did you find it?

LARRY: In the cloakroom. We put McGinnis in there – had to move a few things to make room for the stretcher. And tucked away in a corner, we found this . .

He walks around and opens a drawer of the desk, taking out a screwdriver.

Vickery must have hidden it in case we searched his office.

FERN: Is Clay with McGinnis?

LARRY: No. He's with Mandelberg. Poor chap's had a nasty shock. Clay had to give him brandy!

Screwdriver in hand, he approaches the box and begins to force the padlock.

FERN: Whatever is it, Larry?

LARRY *(grimly):* Shortwave set – you bet your boots! Now, if I can only force this damn padlock . . .

FERN: Wouldn't it be better to leave it for the police?

LARRY: If it's a transmitter, I want to know first . . . *(There is a click.)* That's got it! Now, stand back, Fern . . .

FERN *retreats nervously across the stage.* LARRY *runs his screwdriver around the crack in the lid.*

No concealed wires, anyway . . .

FERN: Darling, be careful!

LARRY: Trust me! *(He draws a deep breath and grasps the lid.)* Now then . . . !

With a swift movement he whips back the lid. A smart electric sewing machine is revealed. A piece of paper is jammed in the flywheel.

FERN *(laughing from sheer relief):* Oh, Larry . . . !

LARRY *(staring at it in amazement):* Why . . . it . . . it looks like a . . . a sewing machine!

FERN: No wonder it hummed and buzzed! Poor Mr. Vickery!

But LARRY *has taken the folded paper from the flywheel. He opens it and crosses to* FERN.

LARRY: Poor Vickery nothing! Here's the paper we found in his pocket. Read that!

He hands it to her. FERN *takes it, glances through the wording, and turns away, shaking with laughter. It is a few seconds before she can speak.*

FERN: Oh, Larry . . . Larry . . .

LARRY *(irritably):* Well, what's so funny about it!

FERN: Darling, put the lid back on that machine and take it back to Mr. Vickery's office. You owe that poor man a profound apology . . .

LARRY: Apology! But you read those instructions?

FERN: Clearly!

LARRY: And . . . they make sense to you?

FERN *(nodding):* I took a dressmaking course myself once!

LARRY: D-d-d-d . . . (FERN *slaps his back.*) Dressmaking!

FERN *(smiling):* It's all here. Instructions for making some kind of costume. *(She glances at paper.)* Start scarlet flare at inlet means to insert a piece of scarlet material! Sailor and storm are types of collars . . . just as bell refers to a certain kind of sleeve . . .

LARRY: But . . . but what's all this about the . . . the Magyar line?

FERN: Magyar is a type of blouse. The line refers to the cut . . . and the chart mentioned is merely the stock dressmaking chart with the design!

LARRY: So that's what Vickery was doing? Dressmaking!

FERN: I'm afraid so.

LARRY: No wonder he was so hostile! But why this camouflaged cover? Why couldn't he explain?

FERN: He was probably a little shy about it. Well, darling . . . so much for your chief suspect!

The inter-office phone buzzes suddenly. LARRY *crosses and answers it.*

LARRY: Hello? Yes, Clay . . . thanks. I'll be right down.

He hangs up and turns to FERN.

The ambulance is here.

FERN: You'd better run along.

LARRY *(coming to her):* Dash it all, Fern, I don't like leaving you here alone . . .

FERN: Why?

LARRY: That enemy agent's still in these studios. And if it isn't Vickery, God knows who it might be!

FERN: But why should this man want to harm me?

LARRY *(seriously):* He might think you're getting too inquisitive. No, I mean it, darling! This isn't a research laboratory – you can't put a potential murderer under a microscope!

FERN: I'm quite capable of taking care of myself. Clay will be within screaming distance!

LARRY: This room's so isolated – it isn't part of the main studios. And if you go acting like a policeman, you may get treated like one! They didn't hesitate to shut McGinnis's mouth!

FERN: That's true.

LARRY: And you won't go nosing round the studio as soon as my back's turned?

FERN: All right. I'll stay here in this room.

LARRY: And when I'm gone, you'd better turn that key in the lock . . . *(Nods to entrance door.)*

FERN *(laughing):* Oh, no! I might lose the key.

LARRY: I always carry a duplicate. *(He takes her in his arms.)* It's for your own good, darling. Now that I've got the contract, I don't want anything to happen to the girl!

He kisses her fondly.

Bye-bye, Fern . . .

He moves to the door. FERN *turns and sees the machine.*

FERN: Oh, Larry . . . *(As he turns.)* Would you like me to speak to Mr. Vickery about this? *(Nods to machine.)*

LARRY *(grinning):* Yes . . . would you?

FERN: I'd better. It's a situation that's going to need a lot of tact!

LARRY: All right. But remember – he comes up here! I'll tell him myself. Bye-bye . . .

FERN *(smiling):* Good luck, Larry . . .

FERN *crosses to machine and closes to machine and closes the lid. She looks around the room and at that moment the inter-office phone rings. She crosses to it and answers.*

Hello . . . yes, Clay . . . he just left . . . few seconds ago. Clay, tell me, has your play gone on the air yet? It's started? Then how long before Mr. Parsons is through? I see . . . Clay, could you come up here – I want to talk to you . . .

She hangs up and, crossing to the chest, closes the lid. At that moment a knock sounds at the door. It opens and VICKERY *enters. He has calmed down considerably, but his manner is still angry and defiant. He walks into the room. Then his eyes fall on the box on the desk and he stops dead.*

FERN *(gently):* Yes, Mr. Vickery. I'm afraid there's an apology due to you.

VICKERY *(stiffly):* Oh, really!

FERN: And an explanation. Mr. Carlson has asked me to make both on his behalf.

VICKERY: I'm afraid this has gone too far for apologies, Miss Sutton!

FERN: I'm sorry you think that because . . . the police may not be so kind . . .

VICKERY: Police?

FERN: Sit down, Mr. Vickery . . . *(She gestures to a chair.)*

VICKERY: Thank you. I prefer to stand!

FERN *(sitting):* As you wish. I mentioned the police because, very shortly, they're going to be all over this studio. *(She is watching him.)* You see, tonight there's been an attempt at murder!

VICKERY *(aghast):* Good heavens!

FERN: The attempt was made on the life of a national security officer who came down here because he believed some person in this studio has been broadcasting information to enemy agents in this country . . .

VICKERY *stares at her horrified. His legs give way under him and he sinks down into the chair.*

So you see any attempt at concealment must naturally appear suspicious. That was the reason for Mr. Carlson's behaviour toward you earlier in the evening.

VICKERY *(on his feet – horrified):* My gracious! He thought that I . . . I . . .

FERN *(quickly):* We were all equally under suspicion, Mr. Vickery. But let's forget about that! Somewhere in this studio is a potential killer! You can help us lay hands on that person!

VICKERY: Oh, no . . . no!

FERN: Why not?

VICKERY: I'm not a policeman!

FERN *(quietly):* Perhaps not. But if, between us, we could bring this agent out into the light, it would be quite a feather in your cap, don't you think?

VICKERY: Well . . .

FERN: Certain people might be quite surprised – they'd have to acknowledge how wrong they'd been about you . . .

VICKERY: That's true enough!

FERN: Then you will help me?

There is a slight pause. Then VICKERY *steps forward.*

VICKERY: Yes, Miss Sutton, but . . . it isn't that I mind, but I can't go running into any danger. I . . . I'm not an independent part . . . I have to support my mother . . .

FERN *(gently):* Yes?

VICKERY: She . . . she's crippled with arthritis . . . can't move her hands . . . That's why sometimes I have to do things for her that . . . that other people might not understand.

He pauses, embarrassed at this confession.

FERN *(very gently):* Why didn't you explain this to Mr. Carlson?

VICKERY: And be laughed at?

FERN *(quietly):* Mr. Carlson isn't the type to laugh at decency. Nor is Mr. Tuttle. But I'd like to explain, if you don't mind.

VICKERY: Miss Sutton, I . . .

FERN *(smiling):* Leave it to me.

She nods to the box.

Now, I suggest you take that downstairs again . . . out of sight – out of mind, you know! And then come back . . .

VICKERY *picks up the box and begins to exit. He is halfway across when* CLAY *enters. He sees* VICKERY *with the box and grins sheepishly.*

CLAY: Larry told me about that. Guess you think we both stink?

VICKERY *(stiffly):* Oh, I'm not one to bear malice, Mr. Tuttle.

CLAY *claps him on the back.*

CLAY: Attaboy! Everyone makes mistakes . . .

As VICKERY *exits with the box he turns to* FERN, *says disgustedly . . .*

Maybe next time Mrs. Parsons will keep her dainty trap shut! That dame knows more about other people's business than Dorothy Dix! So . . . we're right back where we started!

FERN: Not quite! Clay, tell me something. Does everything that is broadcast go before a censor?

CLAY: Sure!
FERN: Even the plays?
CLAY: You betcha!
FERN: And the Parsons would know that?
CLAY: Yeah! But what's on your mind?
FERN: Just what do we know about Mrs. Parsons?
CLAY: Actress least likely to win academy award!
FERN: No . . . seriously, Clay. I'm trying to find out why she's so insistent on changing those last lines in your script.
CLAY: Shakespeare couldn't satisfy that dame – artistically, I mean!
FERN *(working it out):* But if she interpolated words of her own . . . who would know?
CLAY: Everyone – including the producer, the sounds effects boy, and . . . *(He stops.)* Say . . . what's on your mind?
FERN: Someone's been doing it, Clay!
CLAY *(staring at her):* And you think that Mrs. Parsons . . . ? Hell, no! What would she know about blowpipes?
FERN: Her husband told me he'd spent five years in New Guinea . . .
CLAY: Now I come to think of it . . . she was pussyfooting outside that door when the audition started . . .
He starts for the entrance.
That settles it!
FERN: Where are you going?
CLAY: To cut their show off the air –
FERN *(sharply):* No, no – wait! We've made one bad slip with Vickery! This time we MUST be sure! If only I could get a closer look at that cigarette holder she carried . . .
CLAY: Mrs. Parsons?
FERN *(nodding):* You see, Clay – I believe Mrs. Van Leyden's blowpipe was stolen as a bluff! The real weapon is some kind of tube . . . disguised as a simple object one could use without arousing suspicion.
CLAY *(slowly):* Like a cigarette holder . . .

FERN: Now . . . if we could only get our hands on that . . . even for a few minutes . . .

CLAY: It's practically there!

FERN: But be careful!

CLAY: It's a push-over! They're both too busy kissing the mike . . .

He throws open the door and in walks VICKERY.

Say, what is this? Musical chairs?

He exits. FERN *nods to* VICKERY.

FERN: Would you close the door? – and come over here and sit down.

VICKERY *does so.*

VICKERY *(nervously):* Well?

FERN: Mr. Vickery, I believe you were out in that corridor just before the audition began tonight?

VICKERY *(nodding):* With Mrs. Van Leyden.

FERN: And you'd just come up from the talks studio?

VICKERY: That's right. Mr. Tuttle told me Mrs. Van Leyden was wanted in this room. I brought her up . . .

FERN: Did you notice anyone else outside the door?

VICKERY: Mrs. Parsons was there!

FERN: What was she doing.

VICKERY: She wasn't DOING anything. She was waiting to catch Mr. Carlson to complain about the script.

FERN: Did you speak to her?

VICKERY: No. I was talking with Mrs. Van Leyden. She was smoking and I pointed out that smoking was forbidden in the corridors. She crushed out her cigarette on the floor saying, "That's the waste of a good Club Castle . . . " Then I remember she began doing up her lips . . .

FERN *(slightly impatient):* Yes, yes. But I'm more interested in Mrs. Parsons. SHE was smoking, too, wasn't she?

VICKERY: Certainly not!

FERN *(slightly taken back):* Not a cigarette in a long holder?

VICKERY: I've just told you, Miss Sutton. Smoking outside is forbidden! When Mrs. Parsons heard the audition start, she walked away . . .

FERN *measures him with a worried stare.*

FERN: When the audition started? You're sure of that?

VICKERY: Positive. I was watching her all the time!

FERN: I see . . . all the same, I'd like to get a closer look at that holder . . .

VICKERY *(complacently):* Then you shall!

He feels in his pocket and produces the identical holder. FERN *blinks as he holds it out.*

FERN: Where did you get it?

VICKERY: I found it in the rehearsal room a few minutes ago. That woman's ALWAYS leaving it lying around . . .

FERN *takes it and examines it closely as* VICKERY *goes on.*

You'll see! Presently, she'll come raging in here saying someone's stolen it! Just as if we haven't trouble enough!

FERN, *dismayed by this casual refuting of her theory, hands back the holder. During the next conversation, the door of the audition room opens slowly.*

FERN: But Mrs. Parsons was outside in the corridor? And she did have this holder?

VICKERY: But she went away after a few minutes. I waited with Mrs. Van Leyden. Since the audition had started, she was nervous about going in. But Mr. Tuttle appeared and nodded to her to enter.

FERN: Leaving you out there alone?

VICKERY: Only for a moment. Then Mr. Tuttle came . . . He sent me to the musicians' studio with that clarinet . . .

FERN: Clarinet?

VICKERY *(twiddling his fingers):* Thing you blow through! He'd found it lying around somewhere. We walked to the end of the corridor, then he went on to the main studio.

FERN *(quietly):* I see. Thanks, Mr. Vickery — that's all.

VICKERY *(rising):* Have I helped you, Miss Sutton?

FERN: I'm afraid not . . .

She walks with him to the entrance door, talking as she goes.

You've completely ruined a very promising theory that I . . .

She stops suddenly, seeing the door half-open.

Mr. Vickery! Didn't you close this door?

VICKERY *(staring at it):* Of course I did! I . . . Oh, Miss Sutton – what's going on here?

FERN: Nothing you need be afraid of. Would you tell Mr. Tuttle to come here? He's somewhere in the studio.

VICKERY *(nervously):* Yes . . . yes, of course!

He goes out, closing the door behind him. FERN *stands motionless for a few seconds, her face thoughtful, worried. Then she gives an uneasy little shrug of her shoulders, as though dismissing an unpleasant idea. Crossing to the desk, she picks up her handbag and returns to the couch. She sits then, feeling in her bag, produces a compact. Opening it, she holds the mirror up and twists her head to the light. Then suddenly she stiffens. In the mirror she sees what is taking place behind her . . . the door of the audition room opening slowly and the fingers of a hand appearing round the edge. She leaps to her feet.*

FERN: Who's there?

The door swings wide. MANDELBERG *stands in the entrance, eyeing her curiously.* FERN *gives a sigh of relief.*

Oh, it's you!

MANDELBERG *closes the door and comes downstage.*

MANDELBERG: What's the matter?

FERN: Coming in like that, so quietly, you startled me . . .

MANDELBERG: So I am not the only one getting the shocks tonight, eh? *(He looks around.)* And where is Mr. Carlson?

FERN: He's gone to the hospital.

MANDELBERG: Why?

FERN *(nodding to chest):* We had a very sick man on our hands.

MANDELBERG: Miss Fern . . . tonight I do for you the favour. Now you do one for me. What is going on here?

FERN *(sitting):* It's a long story, Mr. Mandelberg. We all believed that man was dead. But it was a coma, caused by poison.

MANDELBERG *(shrewdly):* Someone tries to commit the murder on him?

FERN: Yes.

MANDELBERG: Who?

FERN: That's what I'm trying to find out!

MANDELBERG: So now you're a policeman lady, too?

FERN *(shaking her head):* I'm a scientist.

MANDELBERG: All that I know. But that aint finding out a murderer.

FERN: I think it is.

MANDELBERG: What do you mean?

FERN: When we want to discover the particular type of germ causing a disease, we isolate the types of bacteria present in the body. We identify these types. If one remains unclassified, that is the suspect germ . . .

MANDELBERG: Above the belt all this talk goes . . .

FERN: Here we have a studio filled with people. I'm trying to classify them . . . until I find the person causing all this trouble.

MANDELBERG: And what if he finds you first?

FERN *(quietly):* That's a risk the bacteriologist takes every day!

MANDELBERG *(shaking his head):* Not one little bit do I like all this. Now, you put on your hat and come home . . .

FERN *(shaking her head):* Sorry . . .

MANDELBERG *(seriously):* Miss Fern, you take my advice. Don't you be no fly in the ointment – not tonight.

FERN: Why?

MANDELBERG: It's the omens!

FERN *(a worried smile):* Oh! . . .

MANDELBERG: It's no smiling matter, this one . . .

He feels in his inside pocket, producing a small paper-covered book which he thumbs through. Finding a page, he looks up.

Listen to this, Miss Fern. A mixed week, it says. Do not take people at face value. Watch out for unseen enemies. On the fifteenth, avoid taking chances of personal danger – especially after eight p.m. *(He looks up.)* That is now!

FERN *(smiling):* Do you honestly believe in that nonsense?

MANDELBERG *(stuffing the book in his pocket):* Nonsense, she says!

FERN: Isn't it?

MANDELBERG: Nothing is nonsense that makes for me the fortune!

FERN: Can you name me one time when that kind of advice helped you?

MANDELBERG *(meaningfully):* And what about the Breath of Passion?

FERN: Whatever's that?

He takes from his vest pocket a small lipstick in a gold case.

MANDELBERG: This is that! Breath of Passion lipstick! Fifty thousand of these we put on the market last week – ahead of your uncle! We sweep the market . . . and all because the stars are saying it is time to make the deal! You mean to say you aint heard of this?

FERN: I've been away . . .

MANDELBERG: Young girls cry for it! Wives rob their husbands! Here – you take it, Miss Fern – you try it sometime!

He puts the lipstick on the desk.

FERN: Thanks. I will. But you still haven't convinced me about the stars.

MANDELBERG: Maybe something else convince you – in a way you don't like! Nor me, neither!

FERN: I'll be quite all right. Larry is bringing the police here.

MANDELBERG: When?

FERN: As soon as he gets back from the hospital –

The inter-office phone buzzes sharply. FERN *crosses and picks up the receiver.*

Hello . . . yes, he's here. Yes, very well – thank you.

She hangs up and turns to MANDELBERG.

Your car is down below. They've been ringing all over the studio for you. Goodbye, Mr. Mandelberg . . . *(She puts out her hand.)*

MANDELBERG *(taking it):* Maybe I ought to wait here . . .

FERN: No, please! You've helped us enough tonight. And I'll never to able to thank you as long as I live!

MANDELBERG *(he walks to the door and turns):* That's just what I'm worried about!

He stands looking at her for a second, then he shrugs and exits, closing the door. FERN, *leaning against the desk, stands for a few seconds, then she picks up the lipstick, examining it idly. She takes the top off the case and is about to raise it to her lips when she stops, struck by a thought. She takes the lipstick away, turning it slowly over in her fingers.*

FERN *(slowly):* Very clever . . . ! No wonder we never guessed!

She stands stock still, working it out in her mind. Then she looks around the room and crosses to the cocktail cabinet, taking from the ashtray a half-smoked cigarette. She examines the brand and nods to herself. Suddenly she stiffens and turns, facing the door, thrusting the cigarette end behind her.

FERN *(looking at door):* Come in!

There is no reply. Still holding the cigarette end behind her, FERN *advances to the door and throws it open. There is no one there. She closes it again, walks quickly to the desk, opens a drawer, and takes out an envelope. Dropping the cigarette end inside, she seals it down, all the time watching the door. She has barely returned the envelope to the desk drawer when the door is flung open.* FERN *wheels sharply as* VICKERY *enters.*

Where's Mr. Tuttle?

VICKERY: He's busy in the play studio . . .

FERN: Oh . . .

VICKERY: Is there anything I can do, Miss Sutton?

FERN: No . . . *(She stops, then says quietly.)* Yes, Mr.

Vickery. Just how brave are you?

VICKERY *(blinking):* I . . . I don't know.

FERN *(going to him):* Remember I told you there's an enemy agent loose in this studio? I know the name of that person. But I need to find one more piece of evidence . . .

VICKERY: Good heavens! But what do I do?

FERN: That person has made one mistake! They may come up here to cover it! Whatever happens, you must keep that person talking till I come back! Can you do this for me?

VICKERY *(after a moment's hesitation – gulping):* I . . . I'll try!

FERN *(she presses his arm and smiles):* Good man! I knew you wouldn't let me down!

She exits quickly, closing the door behind her. Left alone, VICKERY *gives a little shiver and looks apprehensively around the room. He crosses to the effects room door and peers inside, then does the same with the door of the office. Returning to the centre stage, he sees the effects chest and, crossing, lifts the lid and peers inside. A slight noise at the main entrance attracts his attention. He wheels . . . to see the door opening slowly.* VICKERY *gulps and croaks.*

VICKERY: Who . . . who's there . . . ?

There is no answer, but a hand slips through the partly open door, feeling for the light switch. Even as VICKERY *stares in horror, every light in the room goes off. From a completely black stage comes* VICKERY*'s horrified voice.*

Who did that? Who put out – ?

The words are suddenly choked on his lips. There is a brief struggle, then silence. Somewhere a door closes softly. After a few seconds the room is flooded with light again. FERN *stands at the door, her hand on the switch. She stares around the empty room.*

FERN: Mr. Vickery? *(She comes in.)* Mr. Vickery . . . !

She waits, then shrugs, a motion dismissing VICKERY

for cowardice. She looks around the room, her glance stopping at the small table behind the couch.

It was here all the time!

She crosses and picks up the handbag left by MRS. VAN LEYDEN *in the second act. Bringing it centre stage, she opens the bag and begins to rifle through it as . . . the effects room is flung open.* MRS. VAN LEYDEN *is revealed.* FERN *has not heard the door open.* MRS. VAN LEYDEN *speaks quietly.*

MRS. VAN LEYDEN: Is that my handbag?

FERN *wheels with a sharp breath of surprise, dropping the bag on the floor.* MRS. VAN LEYDEN *comes forward and picks it up.*

It seems I came just in time.

FERN *(fighting to recover her poise):* What do you mean?

MRS. VAN LEYDEN: Do you usually go through other people's handbags? That's what you were doing, wasn't it?

FERN: I suppose it must look rather odd . . .

MRS. VAN LEYDEN: How else did you think it would look? Just what were you after? Money?

FERN: No.

MRS. VAN LEYDEN: Well?

FERN *(quietly):* I was looking for your lipstick.

A sudden tightness contracts MRS. VAN LEYDEN'S *body. Her tone is soft, dangerous.*

MRS. VAN LEYDEN: What possible interest could you find in my lipstick, Miss Sutton?

FERN: I wanted to use it.

MRS. VAN LEYDEN: Use it? But haven't you one of your own?

FERN: I must have mislaid it somewhere. Stupid of me!

MRS. VAN LEYDEN *looks at her, uncertain. Then, with something of her old charm, she feels in the bag and takes out a lipstick.*

MRS. VAN LEYDEN: It's share and share alike these times I suppose. Here you are.

FERN *(taking the lipstick):* It's very good of you. Some

people might have been very annoyed . . .

MRS. VAN LEYDEN *(a warning):* People who peer and pry into the affairs of others never annoy me, Miss Sutton. I can usually handle them without a fuss . . . .

FERN: Yes. I should imagine you could!

She has opened the lipstick and rubbed a little on the back of her hand.

Oh . . . ?

MRS. VAN LEYDEN: What's the matter?

FERN: It isn't indelible?

MRS. VAN LEYDEN *(rather shortly):* No.

FERN *(smiling):* Oh, well . . . beggars can't be choosers! But I was hoping you'd let me use your own lipstick.

MRS. VAN LEYDEN: That is my own lipstick . . .

FERN *(she shrugs, as a good natured person not prepared to argue):* Oh . . . all right!

MRS. VAN LEYDEN *watches her closely as she crosses to one of the mirrors on the wall and proceeds to make up her lips.*

MRS. VAN LEYDEN: Miss Sutton . . .

FERN: Yes?

MRS. VAN LEYDEN: You doubt my word?

FERN: Oh, no! Obviously, I've made a mistake! Though I could have sworn you used an indelible lipstick . . .

MRS. VAN LEYDEN: Why?

FERN *(still busy at mirror):* Just before you came into this room, when the audition was on, Mr. Tuttle and Mr. Vickery noticed you making up your lips outside that door . . .

MRS. VAN LEYDEN: Anything wrong in that?

FERN *(turning):* Not wrong, Mrs. Van Leyden. Just puzzling . . .

MRS. VAN LEYDEN: I don't understand . . .

FERN *(quietly):* Nor do I, Mrs. Van Leyden! Because, when you came into this room a few seconds later, you lit one of your own cigarettes – a Club Castle! The half-smoked butt I found in that ashtray . . . WITHOUT A TRACE OF LIPSTICK ON THE END!

MRS. VAN LEYDEN *(after a slight pause):* You are a very observant young woman, Miss Sutton. Why should you take the trouble to examine the cigarette end so closely?

FERN: I think Mr. Tuttle and Mr. Vickery were both wrong . . .

MRS. VAN LEYDEN: They're reliable witnesses!

FERN *(smiling):* Men? Reliable where make-up is concerned? I don't think you were making up your lips at all.

MRS. VAN LEYDEN: My dear . . . they saw me!

FERN *(quietly):* Or perhaps they saw you using a small blowpipe . . . disguised as a lipstick!

A pause. MRS. VAN LEYDEN *stares at her. Very calmly she speaks.*

MRS. VAN LEYDEN: You realize what you're saying?

FERN: Quite!

MRS. VAN LEYDEN: You accuse me of trying to murder this man — a complete stranger to me! My dear child . . . think back! If I were guilty, am I likely to bring suspicion on myself by reporting the loss of those darts?

FERN: It put us off the scent for quite a while.

MRS. VAN LEYDEN: But I wanted the police brought here!

FERN: Not at first! You thought you'd fooled us with your talk of heart failure! Then when you discovered I knew something about poisons, you were afraid I might find out too much! So you wanted matters taken out of our hands!

MRS. VAN LEYDEN *(slowly):* You'll have to think out a much better story than that to keep your Mr. Carlson out of prison . . .

FERN: Prison? Larry?

MRS. VAN LEYDEN: My dear, it was plain to me from the beginning! Why else should you want to hide that body?

FERN: But Larry had no motive! He believed McGinnis was an important sponsor!

MRS. VAN LEYDEN: Stop lying! Carlson wanted to stop the government from finding out what was going on here! They would have closed this station — ruined him!

He tried to kill McGinnis because he was a national security off –

Abruptly she stops. There is a pause. FERN *says quietly . . .*

FERN: Go on, Mrs. Van Leyden. *(As she does not speak.)* We didn't know McGinnis was a government officer until we searched his clothes. But you knew from the start! Because you are the person McGinnis came here to arrest! The person selling defence secrets –

Abruptly the inter-office phone rings. Without taking her eyes from FERN, MRS. VAN LEYDEN *reaches out a hand and takes up the receiver. Calmly she speaks.*

MRS. VAN LEYDEN: Hello? Yes, speaking. Very well – at once.

She replaces the receiver.

At any other time, Miss Sutton, I should enjoy listening to your fairy tales. But I am on the air . . .

FERN: With another message for Moscow? You're not getting away with it this time!

She runs to the entrance door, but MRS. VAN LEYDEN *is there first. The woman turns the key and puts it in her pocket. As she turns,* FERN *puts out her hand.*

Give me that key!

MRS. VAN LEYDEN *moves into the room. She stands without moving.*

MRS. VAN LEYDEN: Come here, Miss Sutton . . .

FERN *hesitates.* MRS. VAN LEYDEN *has not taken her eyes from her. There is a clash of wills and* FERN *is first to capitulate. Against her will she moves slowly to where* MRS. VAN LEYDEN *stands.*

Miss Sutton . . . you are a very intelligent young person. Surely you must realize that if I am stopped from doing certain work tonight, someone else will merely take over. We are a very efficient organization. *(Slight pause.)* We can also be extremely . . . generous . . .

FERN: You surprise me.

MRS. VAN LEYDEN: To save the face of an agent in an

embarrassing situation, we have been known to pay as much as . . . a thousand pounds . . .

FERN *(pleasantly):* A little bribery?

MRS. VAN LEYDEN: My dear, why ever should I want to bribe you? You're quite helpless. This studio is isolated . . . and completely sound-proof. The one entrance door is securely locked. If I cared to be melodramatic, I could kill with the utmost ease –

The inter-office phone buzzes again. FERN *makes a quick movement and reaches the desk. She is about to stretch her hand to the instrument when* MRS. VAN LEYDEN *whips out a tiny automatic.*

Keep away from that!

FERN *freezes, and speaks slowly.*

FERN: So it is melodrama?

MRS. VAN LEYDEN: Wasn't it Oscar Wilde who said that life follows art? And life can be a very precious thing . . .

FERN *(slowly):* You wouldn't dare . . .

MRS. VAN LEYDEN: Remember that native guide?

FERN: This isn't the jungle!

Over her next line, the telephone stops.

Any moment the police will be in this room!

MRS. VAN LEYDEN: Through a locked door?

FERN *(desperately):* Larry has a duplicate key!

MRS. VAN LEYDEN: And that's why you're playing for time! *(She nods to the effects room.)* You've got to be kept quiet, my dear . . .

FERN *(backing in terror):* What are you going to do?

MRS. VAN LEYDEN *(with her free hand she takes an envelope from her pocket):* Antiasis is very quietening . . .

FERN: Not if I scream –

MRS. VAN LEYDEN *(interrupting):* You'll never be heard! *She reaches forward still holding the envelope and presses the remote control button on the desk. As* FERN *backs to the effects room door, music from the speaker on the wall swells into the room.* FERN, *realizing the futility of screaming against the noise, has backed to the door. She is feeling for the door knob when the music stops abruptly. Into the silence, like the staccato rattle of a machine gun, a man's voice barks.*

LOUDSPEAKER: DROP THAT GUN, SISTER! GO ON – DROP IT! NOW, TURN ROUND!

On the first word, MRS. VAN LEYDEN *starts. She is not fooled so much as completely taken off her guard by this sudden sharp command sounding in what she knows is a sealed room. She half turns her head for an instant, but it is enough for* FERN, *who leaps forward, knocking the gun from her hand.* FERN *leaps on the gun and picks it up as a burst of music follows the words from the loudspeaker. Then, as* MRS. VAN LEYDEN *turns and looks up at the speaker on the wall, the following comes over . . .*

And so concludes "MURDER IS EASY", a radio drama written by Clayton Tuttle and starring Clarence Parsons in the role of Inspector King –

FERN, *atuomatic in hand, reaches out and switches off the speaker. At that moment, the door handle of the entrance door is rattled.*

LARRY *(offstage):* FERN . . . !

FERN *(calling, her eyes on* MRS. VAN LEYDEN): You'll have to unlock it, Larry. I'm busy!

A key turns in the lock. The door is flung open. LARRY *and* CLAY *enter quickly, taking in the tableau at a glance.*

LARRY: Fern!

FERN: There's your agent, Larry! But be careful, she's got the dart!

CLAY *takes the automatic from* FERN *and, crossing to* MRS. VAN LEYDEN, *digs her in the ribs with the weapon.*

CLAY: Okay! Get going, please, Honourable Madam Poison Ivy!

MRS. VAN LEYDEN *walks to the door. All her old poise and charm have suddenly returned. At the door, she turns to* CLAY.

MRS. VAN LEYDEN: We don't really need the automatic, Mr. Tuttle. It isn't loaded!

She exits, followed by a rather startled CLAY. LARRY *takes* FERN *in his arms, but they both wheel as a muffled groan sounds from the chest.*

LARRY: Whatever's that?

FERN: Look!

She points to the lid of the chest which rises slowly. VICKERY *raises himself upright – a very dishevelled* VICKERY, *with a gag handkerchief round his neck. He is pale and trembling with rage. He sees* LARRY *and* FERN *and folds his arms, drawing himself up in outraged dignity.*

LARRY: Vickery!

VICKERY *(he steps out and with a voice quivering with passion):* Mr. Carlson! This time I really mean it! I RESIGN!

The curtain falls.

Appendix: Works by Max Afford

NOVELS

Blood on His Hands (London: Hutchinson, 1936)
(New York: Appleton Century, 1936)
Death's Mannikins (London: Hutchinson, 1936)
(New York: Appleton Century, 1936)
The Dead Are Blind (London: Hutchinson, 1939)
(New York: Appleton Century, 1939)
Owl of Darkness (Sydney: *A.B.C. Weekly* and Angus & Robertson, 1948)

(All four were republished in White Circle Crime Club editions by William Collins, London, 1949.)

STAGE PLAYS

Honeymoon Hotel	(Musical comedy – book and lyrics by Max Afford) Produced Adelaide, 1934
Pas De Six	(operetta – book and lyrics by Max Afford) A.B.C. production, 1936 Won A.B.C. competition, 1936
Lady in Danger	Produced in Sydney, 1941 and 1944; Broadway, New York, 1945; and televised by the A.B.C., 1959 Included in the American Burns Mantle "Best Plays of 1944–45"
Sleep No More	Produced Sydney, 1943
Mischief in the Air	Produced Sydney, 1944
Colonel Light the Founder	(later rewritten as "Awake My Love") Produced Adelaide, 1936; Won South Australian Centenary Competition, 1936
Awake My Love	Produced Sydney, 1947 (also broadcast in radio form)
Dark Enchantment	Produced Sydney, 1949; Toured English provincial theatres, 1950

Appendix

FILMS

Smithy Story treatment on Kingsford Smith for the 1944 Columbia-Cinesound production
Cobb and Co. 1948 Charles Chauvel production

RADIO

Hour and half-hour plays written 1932–36

Avalanche
The Crime with 200,000 Witnesses
The House of Fear
Blackmail
The Sin Flood
The House to Let
Sacrifice at Dawn
Four Frightened People
The Flail of God
The Pantomime Cat
War to End War
Cat Creeps at Night
Wax Museum
Old Christmas Shades
Terror by Night
The Working Class
Two Men in a Shell Hole
Lord Ingleby Dies
An Experiment in Acoustics.

Hour and half-hour plays written under contract to A.B.C. 1936–41

Merry-Go-Round (won A.B.C. competition 1936)
Woman Called Ruth
Quest
The Legend of the Moonlight
Revenge with Music
The Fantastic Case of the Four Specialists (won prize on Polish radio 1938)

Works by Max Afford

All Passions Spent
Die for a Lady
Silver from Satin
I am Albert Jones
Oh, Whistle When You're Happy
For Fear of Little Men
The Golden Age
Five White Fingers
A Cat Across Their Path
Heroisms All Around Us
The Queer Affair at Kettering
Murder in Miniature
Mr. Allchurch Comes to Stay

Serials for A.B.C. 1936–41

The Tomb of Sir William Marle
The Labours of Hercules
Mr. Morte Takes a Holiday
Eighty-nine Men
Fly By Night

Children's serials for A.B.C. 1936–41

Five Miles Down
The Adventures of Chump and Co.
The Return of Chump and Co.

Blackburn radio serials – written for A.B.C. before 1950

The Mysterious Mr. Lynch
Grey Face
It Walks by Night
The Blackburns Take Over
Owl of Darkness

Serials written for commercial stations 1941–49

First Light Frazer (624 episodes, 2GB)

Digger Hale's Daughters (416 episodes, 2GB)
Casanova (an adaptation, 2UE)
Danger Unlimited (624 episodes, 2UE)
Hagen's Circus (800 episodes, 2UE)

Hour plays written under contract to A.B.C. 1950–54

Consulting Room
Awake My Love (adapted from his stage play)
Out of This Nettle
Lazy in the Sun

Serials written under contract to A.B.C. 1951–54

Double Demon
Murders Not for Middle Age
Silver Ridge (which he also produced)
Stranger Come in (400 episodes, which he also produced)

His serials and plays were sold to New Zealand, South Africa, B.B.C. (London), C.B.S. (Canada), and Egypt. They were translated into Polish for Polski Radio, Warsaw, and into Afrikaans for South African Radio.